NATIONAL INSTITUTE SOCIAL SERVICES LIBRARY
NO. 49

THE PRACTICE OF SOCIAL WORK WITH GROUPS

National Institute Social Services Library

THE PRACTICE
OF SOCIAL WORK
WITH GROUPS
A Systematic Approach

Ken Heap

*Norwegian Lutheran School of Social Work
(Diakonhjemmet), Oslo, Norway*

London
GEORGE ALLEN & UNWIN
Boston   Sydney

George Allen & Unwin (Publishers) Ltd,
40 Museum Street, London WC1A 1LU, UK

George Allen & Unwin (Publishers) Ltd,
Park Lane, Hemel Hempstead, Herts HP2 4TE, UK

Allen & Unwin, Inc.,
Fifty Cross Street, Winchester, Mass 01890, USA

George Allen & Unwin Australia Pty Ltd,
8 Napier Street, North Sydney, NSW 2060, Australia

First published in 1985

British Library Cataloguing in Publication Data

Heap, Ken
  The practice of social work with groups.
—(National Institute social services
library; no. 49)
1. Social group work
I. Title   II. Series
361.4   HV45
ISBN 0-04-362059-0
ISBN 0-04-362060-4 Pbk

Library of Congress Cataloging in Publication Data

Heap, Ken, 1929-
  The practice of social work with groups.
(National Institute social services library; no. 49)
Bibliography : p.
Includes index.
1. Social group work.   2. Group relations training.
I. Title.   II. Series.
HV45.H4184 1984   361.4   84-9185
ISBN 0-04-362059-0 (alk. paper)
ISBN 0-04-362060-4 (pbk. : alk. paper)

Set in 10 on 11 point Times by
Mathematical Composition Setters Ltd.
Ivy Street, Salisbury, Wiltshire, UK
and printed in Great Britain by
Billing and Sons Ltd,
London and Worcester

CONTENTS

PREFACE

———◆———

There is a continuing increase in the use of group methods in social and health services. Whether we talk of 'clients', 'patients', or simply 'members' we have for over forty years witnessed growing awareness of the gains of forming small groups of people who are in some way burdened or threatened. The self-help and mutual help arising from such groups is today mobilized in prevention, clarification, or solution of a very extensive range of social, emotional and health problems. Many professions are involved in this important development. Recognition of the value of group methods may be seen in social work, nursing, residential work, psychotherapy, school services, milieu treatment, youth work and community organization among other fields.

Much suggests that this increased use of group methods will accelerate further during the coming decades. Large sections of the general public, hitherto well functioning and only sporadically and rarely the subject of helping services, will be placed at serious and possibly chronic disadvantage. Several conditions will compel such a development. The change in the population structure, particularly with regard to the increase in the members of elderly and aged; the protracted economic crisis, bringing millions into unemployment and insecurity; the staggering tempo of cultural diffusion and change; the breakdown of neighbourhood; the disaffection of vast numbers of Western youth – these are only some of the factors whose impact will cause increased demands upon community services.

The urgent problems to which these changes give rise are collective and interactional in character, so that both preventive and remedial effort should as far as possible also be at the collective and inter-actional level. Group work will therefore have an increasingly important role to play and its literature must function as an accessible and well suited tool, facilitating improvement and adaptation of the method in its new and demanding applications.

It is not difficult to write introductory material on group work principles, built as they are on well established folk traditions recognizing both the comfort and the power of being together with others 'in the same boat'. But formulating specific ways of understanding group behaviour and the actual methods of working in groups with troubled people proves, in contrast, to be extremely difficult. The difficulties have their roots in the nature of group work.

Good group work is conscious, rather complicated and

capable of producing observable effect. But good group work is also sensitive and strongly influenced by values which are both beautiful and elusive of definition. These two sets of qualities are not readily compatible, so that much group work literature – high though the general standard is – fails to reconcile them and emphasizes one at the expense of the other. The pragmatic disappears in the mist of sensitivity. Or the sensitive is sacrificed in the pursuit of the systematic. This is a serious problem, since these aspects of group work method are interdependent and of equal importance.

This volume is an attempt to formulate a systematic and learnable approach to group work practice which – far from sacrificing sensitivity – builds precisely upon awareness and insight into group members' needs and feelings. Good group work is here viewed as conscious and thoughtful response to what is happening in the group. This requires understanding of group behaviour and it requires the clearest possible framework for defining the tasks of the worker. To this end I have proposed two major systems. One of these displays an overview of the process of group work and of the worker's tasks throughout the process; the other suggests a systematic approach to understanding what is happening in the group. A number of recurrent situations and functions of workers leading groups – such as offering service, leading the first meeting, planning joint leadership – are also expressed as small models or as systematized overviews. As much as possible of the practice principles considered in this volume is concentrated into such summaries, as well as being discussed and exemplified.

This approach to group work method has been developed through many years of practice, teaching and consultation in Scandinavia and the United Kingdom. The actual formulation and disposition of the material is based on a sequence of annual seminars entitled 'Sense and System in Social Work with Groups' which I have held since 1979 at the National Institute for Social Work in London.

It is intended that the approach described here should be relevant and useful to colleagues and students in all areas of social work. Similarly, it should provide a basis also for colleagues in other helping professions who use group work in the social and health fields. I have chosen to avoid discussion of different group ideologies and schools. I have, instead, tried to construct a system which embraces the central features of group work method common to all its applications, without reference to its relationship to complementary and competing doctrines as would have been appropriate in a more theoretical book. I permit myself, in this context, a kind of happy pragmatism. Thus the reader seeking clarification of theory bases will be disappointed.

The reader in search of a more readily learnable approach to practice will, I hope, find much here that is useful.

The overviews and systems I propose have been developed mainly on the basis of my own practice. They are, nevertheless, also informed by the theory of group dynamics and group work as well as by the inspiration drawn from the extensive and excellent practice literature particularly characteristic of social work publication. This enables me to draw attention to a great deal of the literature in this field, so that the book may to some extent also function as a selective literature review and as a reference to further study and to other sources of practical guidance.

I have written this book in fits and starts over a number of years, using whichever hand was empty at the time and trying not to make too much mess with the midnight oil. It has been an enjoyable process. That it has necessarily been protracted has in fact been an advantage, since my use of this material in teaching and consultation has produced illustration, confirmation and criticism over a period enabling me to revise and improve it in the light of the responses of many practising colleagues and students. This has also enriched my sources of examples and strengthened my belief that the approach I propose has relevance and utility for all of us who work with groups, in whatever contexts.

It is then, a privilege to be able to express my thanks to the colleagues in Norway, Denmark, Sweden and the United Kingdom whose professional commitment and whose generous and critical co-operation have contributed so much to the shape and content of this book. Regrettably, I have had less contact with American and Canadian colleagues, but these also – through correspondence and through meetings at the occasional conference – have given me much encouragement.

Finally, thanks to the ones who have done the really hard work: Irene Masdal and Rønnaug Refsaas, two incredibly patient ladies, have written and rewritten and have followed the arrows, deciphered the alterations, peered under the Scotch tape, decoded my handwriting, skilfully stroked their IBMs – and produced a typescript. It remains only to hope that reading and using it will be a helpful and interesting experience for colleagues using group work or preparing to do so.

KEN HEAP
Oslo,
Spring 1984

PART ONE

———◆———

INTRODUCTION

Chapter 1

GROUP MEMBERSHIP IN DAILY LIFE

WE BELONG TO MANY GROUPS

We have all spent a great part of our lives in group situations of various kinds. Membership of groups has given us security. It has in large measure formed us and has changed us, and it continues to do so throughout life. Group participation has made a great deal of our learning both possible and more efficient. Opinions and values which are important to us have often been clarified and strengthened through their examination in groups, while others have been modified or abandoned because of group influence. The realization of many of our ideas presupposes group support and mobilization. Many pleasures are intensified by their being experienced collectively. As both social and physical beings we are in fact dependent upon membership of groups for the satisfaction of our most basic needs such as shelter, production, defence, learning, protest, emotional warmth and – not least – assurance of our own worth.

Among the many groups which have importance for us are the families into which we are born and the new ones which we later establish as adults. There are the groups we have played and learned with as children, in the streets, at kindergarten and at school. Our peer groups during puberty have had particular importance for us all. There are so many groups with whom we have worked, trained, fought or studied. We have our neighbourhood groups. There are other groups where we manifest ourselves politically and others where we co-operate with colleagues in furthering the skills or the conditions of our profession. There are many different groups where we seek cultural or spiritual stimulation and others where we let ourselves go and unfold impulses otherwise denied expression. From one person to another these can vary from Bible discussion to a sing-along at the pub, from the mud of the football field to the subtleties of playing in a Renaissance quartet. Different strokes, as they say, for different folks.

MUTUAL INDEPENDENCE OF INDIVIDUAL AND GROUP

All of these groups give us something in return for our participation and they also influence us. As individuals we in our turn contribute qualities to our groups and influence their development, their purpose and their style. Without members, groups cannot exist. Without groups, many important needs of individuals would remain unmet. This mutual dependence and influence of the individual and the group is a pervading and decisive feature of the human condition.

At times we find this oppressive and restrictive. Indeed, members' compliance with the demands of their groups may even have quite destructive consequences. This is true in street gangs, in the drug milieu and in certain religious and political sects. But even in quite ordinary and benign group situations we may often protest against the restrictions on autonomy as too high a price for the gains of membership. We then withdraw, or attempt to change the group or make new affiliations. The ambivalence inherent in group membership is a factor as important to those who will understand groups as is the necessity for group membership.[1] But, however we deal with this, the mutual dependence between ourselves as individuals and our many groups remains insistently present as the major theme of social life and organisation.

In our daily lives we become sharply aware of the advantages and value of group membership when we need help and support from others. We have surely all experienced how comforting and helpful it is to be with others 'in the same boat' during some episode of anguish or difficulty. We have all at some time experienced a rebirth of self-esteem when, during a depressed and unsuccessful period, we have met a friend who values us and is clearly pleased by the encounter. We have all experienced how clarifying it can be to discuss a problem or a pending decision with others for whom we have affection or respect. Similarly, we have all experienced that crises seem less threatening and more manageable when we share them with others, or at least are given an opportunity to talk about them. Many have also experienced situations where self-control, purpose, or courage have been regained because of the presence of others, making possible a better response to a frightening and disorienting situation. (Perhaps the physical presence of others has not even been necessary. The internalized influence of one's reference group's[2] standards can suffice to provide this kind of reinforcement.) Yet others have experienced individual powerlessness in a vulnerable situation, subsequently to find that protest or demand for change has had greater impact because of the solidarity of others in similar situations or of like mind.

These very common life experiences compel to our attention the potential inherent in group situations for problem-solving, clarification of decisions, the lending of support, the alleviation of isolation, the development and maintenance of purposive forms of behaviour and the effective representation of viewpoints and demands. We note, however, that these are also major aims of much effort in the fields of social work and health service. So we may say that observation of the strengths and possibilities of everyday group life has given social and health workers both a realistic and a logical basis for a development of group methods in their fields which has become very extensive indeed. This development has taken place during the major part of the present century, although the past twenty years have reflected a particular intensification of the move towards increased use of group methods.

In the following, I shall try to say something useful about the nature and uses of group processes as they are seen in modern social work.

Group work consists of understanding and responding to these processes, though with different aims and in different ways, depending upon the setting and its functions and depending upon the aims and needs of the group members concerned. This book describes ways of evaluating those needs and ways of both planning for and responding to them. While the examples have, of course, the limitations of my own experience and communications, I have good reason to believe that the principles and guidelines presented may readily be applied elsewhere, where they might give rise in different settings to different though appropriate ways of using, leading and responding to the group.

NOTES: CHAPTER 1

1　The notion of 'group ambivalence' refers to the opposing tendencies to integration and differentiation which continually give life and tension to groups. We continually engage in collective experience and effort, but are simultaneously very concerned to assert our individuality and separateness. In Heap (1977b) I have tried to select and order those areas of group theory which are most useful to group workers. Integration and differentiation holds an important place here.

2　In Heap (1977b) I have defined this rather slippery term 'reference group' thus: 'Certain periods of life and certain situations find us more ready, at least temporarily, to suspend the assertion of our individual identity in return for the advantages of high conformity to a particular group or groups. We then appraise the appropriateness of our behaviour in relation to the standards of such so-called reference groups' (pp. 67–75).

Chapter 2

_____•_____

HOW CAN GROUPS 'HELP'?
SOME POSSIBILITIES, PRINCIPLES AND PROBLEMS

I would like first to mention some features of helping relationships in general and then to consider, at somewhat greater length, group work as a possible source of help.

CAN WE 'HELP' OTHERS AT ALL?

We could probably provide illumination for a number of major cities with the energy used daily in 'giving a bit of advice', in saying 'If she were my daughter, I would jolly well ... etc.' and in propounding 'The best thing you can do right now is ... '. The giving of wise counsel and moral advice is a time-honoured and cherished human occupation. And hardly any of it helps! Few questions give us a warmer glow than 'What would you do if you were me?', but our sagely nodded reply is largely a waste of breath.

How can we possibly 'advise' when we meet such questions as these? 'Should I leave him, do you think? He's been giving me hell for twenty years.' 'Ought we move to Stavanger, where there's oil money to be earned, instead of hanging on here at the farm?' 'It wouldn't be right, would it nurse, to have him put in a home? He can't help the way he is?' And so on.

The answers to these questions are inextricably interwoven with and entirely dependent upon the wishes, values, relationships, dreams, history and – not least – resources of the person asking the question. And we may only answer the question on the basis of our own subjective relationship and associations to the problem raised and in the light of our own values, life experiences and resources. It is highly unlikely, therefore, that our wise counsel harmonizes with the needs and possibilities of the counselled. At best, it is therefore rejected. But it may also be acted upon. It may then work out badly, whereupon we are held responsible and blamed. We are then no longer in a position to aid further the person in distress. It may, by chance, work out moderately well, in which case – instead of meeting the expected gratitude – often encounter coolness or hostility, alternative products of the dependency and feelings of inferiority which our superior judgement has induced. (Oscar Wilde said it very well, in referring to his long feud with the painter Rex Whistler – 'I don't know why he hates me so much. After all, 'I've never tried to help him.')

This is, of course, yet more difficult in the many situations encountered in the social and health services where the persons to be "helped" have not sought this themselves, but have in some way been coerced into the client or patient role. We meet this frequently in child care, in probation and aftercare, with alcohol problems and in mental health services, among others. The difficulties of 'helping' are thus compounded by the further problems of ambivalence, aggression and dependence which usually follow in the wake of compulsory measures.

Whether voluntary or compulsory, however, a major problem seems to be that we confuse the notion of help with that of advice. While we may only very rarely advise in useful and relevant ways, we have in fact numerous ways of helping others who are in distress, conflict and need. It is, for instance, 'help' to provide necessary material aid: for many clients, money, a job, a place to live, medical attention are sufficient and relevant 'help'. It is 'help' to give information about facilities, provisions and rights. It is 'help' to encourage the consideration of alternative solutions to problems and to reflect about the consequences of different choices. It is 'help' to listen closely to another person as he struggles to define and clarify a problem and to share the work of a clarification with him. It is 'help' to show both respect for the other's struggle with his difficulties and acknowledgement of his other achievements and successful coping. It is 'help' to show acceptance and understanding of the feelings experienced by the other, no matter how strange or strong they may be. It is 'help' to offer a warm but non-possessive relationship as a support in a time of trouble. It is, above all, 'help' to recognize and assert others' ability and right to solve their own problems in accordance with their own values, resources, wishes and cultural traditions. The term 'help to self-help' is a cliché which in fact encompasses all of these aspects of help, and whose simplicity conceals a vision of a complex interaction and an extremely demanding relationship.

THE HELPING RELATIONSHIP

It has long since been established that successful helping presupposes a relationship characterized by respect, equality, acceptance, non-manipulation and empathy. These, however, are qualities which are as easy to list as they are difficult to realize. The helper's subjective views, cultural and class traditions, prejudices and own unresolved problems and conflicts distort his perceptions of the client's needs. They may cause him to favour 'solutions' which harmonize with his own lifestyle, rather than with the realities of the client's situation and with the validity of the client's perhaps very different view of the world. Here are some common examples.

EXAMPLE 1

(a) The detached youth worker reaching out to drop-out gangs in a rough urban setting is more or less at ease, more or less able to hear and understand what they are saying, more or less able to avoid moralism and manipulation, depending upon his own lifestyle, the degree of his comfort with deviation, and the rigidity or flexibility of his own cultural identification and attachments.

(b) The social worker discussing the alternatives of home care or institutional placement of an aged and frail parent with the adult children will try to help the family on the basis of their resources, relationship, wishes and possibilities. But the question 'what is right?' thrusts itself forward and her own views, personal attitudes, relationship to her own parents and her cultural norms inevitably colour her perceptions.

(c) The social worker who counsels couples struggling with marital tension and considering separation or divorce as a solution functions perhaps quite differently in periods when her own family life is harmonious and gratifying than she does when she herself is experiencing marital dissatisfaction or crisis. In such periods she may come perilously near to 'taking sides' and manipulating others to fulfil or buttress her own solutions and decisions.

The struggle to avoid these distortions of help, to define appropriate helping relationships and to develop skills in establishing such relationships has been a central feature of practice and literature in professional social work throughout our century. Emphasis has been on illuminating and developing skill in one-to-one relationships or in work with families. Among the wealth of literature which could be referred to here, attention should be drawn to Richmond (1917), Hamilton (1940), Ferard and Hunnybun (1962), Irvine (1964, 1979), Foren and Bailey (1968), Salzberger-Wittenberg (1970), Hollis (1972), Bratt (1963), Keith-Lucas (1974) and Killèn-Heap (1982). This could have been a very long list. The preoccupation with the helping relationship which it reflects is an indication of how seriously the helping professions have worked with the challenge of finding ways of helping

which build upon the client's or patient's own resources, own definition of the problem, own cultural norms and own work with the
problem.

THE GROUP AS A MEANS OF HELP

While one important strand of work in the human services has been
directed towards understanding and developing helping skills in one-
to-one relationships or in work with families, an alternative or
supplementary mode of providing help has been developed in group
work.

Already in the first years of our century, the activation of collective
effort among disadvantaged groups in the general population was to
be seen in the growth of the urban settlements, labour organization,
adult education, and organized youth work through such bodies as the
YM/WCAs, scouting, and so on. In North America this developed
early into a profession of group work with a well articulated philosphy
– though for a time a less well articulated methodology (discussed in
Heap, 1982). Here in Europe, however, a slower and more pragmatic
development occurred. It was not until the 1940s that practitioners in
the fields of social work and mental health began to any extent to use
group methods. This was not an outgrowth of a democratic educational
philosophy seeking a means of expression as in North America. It
was, rather, a result of the discovery by practitioners in the social and
health fields that group methods were a useful addition to traditional
ways of offering help and that they facilitated the prevention and
solution of certain particularly stubborn social and clinical problems.
Perhaps most important, group methods seemed to offer practical
means of making greater use of clients' (or patients') own resources,
of solving problems in ways which increased rather than decreased
self-esteem, and which to a greater extent achieved solutions or
decisions determined by and relevant for the clients themselves. Group
methods were thus seen to ameliorate some of the problems of giving
and receiving help which were encountered at the one-to-one level.

USE OF THE GROUP PROCESS

What is it about group membership and the use of groups which so
often increases the quality and the relevance of help?

This question brings us back to the observations made earlier about
the strong tendency for human beings in distress both to seek and
to give each other support. The basic idea of group work is that members may help both themselves and each other by exchanging ideas,
suggestions and solutions, by sharing feelings and information by

comparing attitudes and experiences and by developing relationships with each other.

This being so, it becomes not only logical but also an important statement of principle to emphasize the primacy of the group process as the main resource in group work. Of course, the group worker has important functions. But unless we recognize and stimulate the resources and possibilities inherent in the group situation itself we have difficulty in explaining the point of forming groups of clients or patients at all.

Over the years, this basic idea has been expressed in many different ways. In the literature of group work we meet such formulations as 'the group is a mutual aid system' (Shulman, 1979), 'the work of the group is the main dynamic of treatment' (Schwartz, 1971) and 'the group is not merely the context of treatment, it is also the means of treatment' (Vinter, 1974). Yet earlier, Konopka (1963) defined the aim of social work with groups as 'enhancing the individual's social functioning through purposeful group experiences'. Many such formulations assert the common recognition of 'use of the group' or 'use of the group process' as the dominant characteristic and the main resource in this method of working.

SOME CONSEQUENCES AND PROBLEMS OF THE PRIMACY OF THE GROUP AS RESOURCE

It would be naive to suppose that any chance constellation of clients will produce a group situation which is viable as a means of treatment and growth. It would be equally unrealistic to assume that groups' resources will flourish and direct themselves purposefully without leadership of some kind and without that leadership having found ways of facilitating the group process without also invading and dominating it. Thus the need to clarify the conditions for viable group composition and development and for purposive sharing of responsibility between the group and the worker are prerequisites for realising the principle under discussion.

Use of the group process presupposes that exchanges and relationships between members will occur. But they will not do so unless the members experience some wish for such exchanges, unless they are in some way drawn to each other and unless they have some vision – no matter how unclear – of possible gains from participation in the life and work of the group. This is in the first place a question of planned composition, of members' motivation and of the worker's understanding of members' needs. We shall return to these questions in later chapters.

However, even when the conditions for active interaction between (a)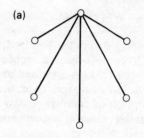

(b)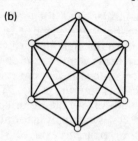

Figure 1

members are in fact present, we see in practice a marked tendency for quite another pattern to assert itself. Rather than rich exchange between members being facilitated and supplemented by the worker (Figure 1(b)), we tend to see a pattern of directive instruction by an active worker who establishes and maintains a focal role, members being correspondingly inactive and interacting more with the worker than with each other (Figure 1(a)).

EXAMPLE 2

(*a*) The health visitor and social worker jointly leading discussion groups on child care in a well-baby clinic find themselves answering questions.

(*b*) The social worker in a geriatric day centre ends up lecturing to a group of old people who were intended to compare their experiences of living alone and to share their solutions to common problems.

(*c*) The worker who has formed a group of withdrawn, unemployed young adults with drinking problems conveys his own tentative insight to the group instead of helping the members work towards their own.

This common tendency limits the gains of much group work and treatment, and involves serious loss of its most valuable resources, namely the clients'.

WHY DOES THIS HAPPEN?

The problem is partly cultural in origin. Both our clients and we are socialized to a conception of helper-helped relationships characterized by subjugate supplication to authoritative expertise. The traditional role of the one being helped is to lay problems before the expert helper and passively to receive a solution; the role of the helper is wisely to consider and then to provide a solution. We all learn this as schoolchildren and it is progressively reinforced with every visit we make throughout our lives to doctor, lawyer, housebuilder – indeed, all those whose vocational expertise leads us to consult them. It would be strange if this did not strongly influence the role expectations of clients entering groups. To those already burdened with experiences of inadequacy, failure or confusion, the assumption of familiar passive roles is not only natural but is rather attractive, since it also offers the apparent gain of relief from responsibility for unmanageable problems.

The client's problem becomes the worker's. Furthermore, if it proves too difficult also for him to 'solve', then this is evidence for its intransigence. This may give the client a temporary relief from feelings of inadequacy – but he still has the problem.

The group worker often compounds this difficulty. He too has experienced similar models of helper–helped relationships throughout his life and has also learned that 'good' help means 'active' and 'much' help. While the helping professions have developed less obstructive and more activating helping methods in one-to-one or family situations, it proves more difficult in groups to free oneself from familiar images of how experts behave, and the members' passive expectancy often meets a reciprocal activity and directive expertise from the worker. This is perhaps also because of the connotations of teaching situations which group leadership suggests. Sometimes, too, it reflects the worker's anxious attempt to maintain some control over an unpredictable and complex situation. Perhaps – occasionally – it reflects exploitation of the power satisfactions always offered by the leadership of client groups.

However, with experience and self-critical appraisal, particularly if supervision is also available, most workers are able to achieve an increase in their use of the group process. It becomes possible to decrease one's own investment in the authority, language and aloofness of middle-class professionalism, and to register, respect and engage oneself in mobilizing the resources which even the most unsuccessful and defeated clients bring to the group. This transition from emphasis on 'use of self' to 'use of the group' provides the most common difficulty for practitioners first using group methods. It seems, usually, to be capable of solution even though it is a major shift in orientation for most professionals.

It must, of course, also be said that most groups will initially need guidance and leadership from the worker. The group has been established at his initiative and it is reasonable that he become the focus of members' attention and expectations during the newness and uncertainty of the group's formation. However, both the situational and emotional determinants of this initial dependence change and it is intended that the worker move out of the focal position as quickly or as gradually as is possible from group to group.

Members' resources and potential for development are important variables here. It would be absurd to suppose that all groups are capable of a high level of purposive and autonomous functioning, but all may increase their level. Wilson and Ryland (1949) were early writers on this theme. They showed how the worker's degree of active investment in leadership functions is inversely proportional to the social and mental health of the group members. Thus, for example, the worker leading a group of withdrawn chronic psychiatric patients will inevitably adapt a more directive style of leadership than a colleague working with highly motivated and well functioning couples discussing common problems of family life. In both cases, however, the principle applies that the worker progressively shifts leadership into the group in harmony with members' increasing ability to contribute to and gain from the group. Whatever the starting point and whatever the limitations and possibilities of different groups, the maximum possible mobilization of the group process is the guiding principle.

Locating and adjusting the delicate balance between 'use of oneself' and 'use of the group process' is a continuing task for the group worker in whatever setting he may find himself. In another context, I have described this process as 'abrogating the role of Central Person' (Heap, 1968) and I regard it as a precondition for maximally using the resources inherent in the group situation.

NOT ALL GROUPS 'WORK'

Not just any old group is capable of giving support and warmth, and of facilitating growth and the solution of problems. It depends greatly upon how it is formed, composed and led. We need only examine our own life experiences. We have surely all experienced membership of groups where the only positive experience has been the relief of withdrawing. We have been in groups where we have felt quite foreign, acutely ill at ease, or disoriented. We may have experienced strong conflicts, which gave no hope of constructive resolution, or which derived from insoluble dispute about the aims of membership. This brings us to the nuclear questions and challenges of all group methods.

THE BIG QUESTION

How far can we ensure that group situations in fact facilitate members' relating to and helping each other? What are the conditions for the presence and activation of group resources and do they vary from one group to another? Do we know anything about group formation, group bond, group size, which can help us to increase the viability of client groups? In what ways can group workers contribute to the group process, both during formation and afterwards? Do group workers have different functions at different stages of group life and can we recognize such stages? Can we reconcile the primacy of group process with the extent of the planning decisions and the nature of the interventions which seem necessary to ensure an optimally well functioning group?

Simply by asking these questions we engage in a kind of reflection and evaluation which in itself excludes the authoritarian and traditional leadership style which I have described as a problem. At the same time, such questions confront us with an idea which is fundamental to all purposive help with social and emotional problems, namely the notion of differentiated diagnosis and treatment. That is to say that it must be recognized that there is no one 'correct' way of composing groups and of conducting groupwork, just as there is no one 'correct' way of giving social help or therapy at the individual level. Just as each individual is different so is each group, and they must be approached differentially. *The art of group work is that of contributing in different ways to the life and work of different groups on the basis of differentiated understanding of their problems, needs, resources and ways of behaving and coping.* Further, an approach based on differential diagnosis reduces the likelihood of the worker assuming either the directive 'expert' role or its currently fashionable alternative in group therapy of omniscient and watchful passivity. Neither of these alternatives is suited to the aim of maximizing clients' awareness of their own resources and their confidence in being able to use them for the tasks of growth and problem-solving.

The worker's role may nevertheless be decisive and considerable skill is involved in finding a balance between the extremes of too much and too little intervention in the life of the group. The worker contributes to the group process and his tasks include planning, initiating, suggesting, informing, interpreting, confronting, supporting and facilitating. But at all times the basic principle is that of containment, in the sense that the worker should never be more than necessarily active and that the group itself must as far as possible be the main source of help, the 'means of treatment'.

A SUGGESTED MODEL

In an attempt to make group work process both more understandable and more learnable I have earlier (Heap, 1979) constructed a simple model. The model attempts to display progressively the central features of the group process, giving these primacy, at the same time as the group worker's function in facilitating that process is shown as involving specific tasks at different stages. In brief, the group process is shown as commencing with a particular type of group composition, characterized by close similarity of psycho-social *needs* and *problems* on the part of the members. In social work and related fields such problems will usually subject members to *stress*. In groups which are composed in this way, where *size* of the group is appropriately determined, and where the group has sufficient *time* available for its objectives, interaction will occur. That interaction will lead to *discovery of commonality* and thus to a degree of *mutual identification*. The resulting *group bond* or *'we-feeling'* is the source of members' ability to give each other *support*, to exert *mutual control*, to facilitate *recognition* of both hidden feelings and strengths, to alleviate feelings of isolation and deviance by *generalisation* and to enable more successful self-representation through *collective power*. These qualities are the resources of the group. To 'use group process' is another way of saying that we seek to generate and mobilize these qualities in groups.

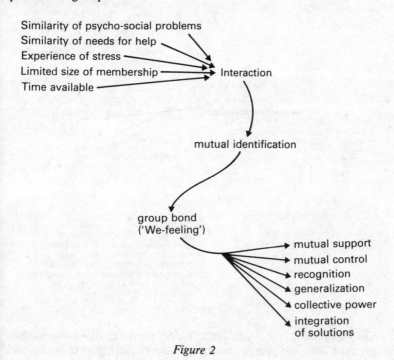

Figure 2

Figure 2 represents a model of the 'use of process' in diagrammatical form. This depicts the development of the group process as a resource. The worker, whose function is to facilitate the group process, has a number of tasks to perform. Different tasks are emphasized at different stages of the group process, so that if we add the worker's role to the development of group process we get the model shown in Figure 3.

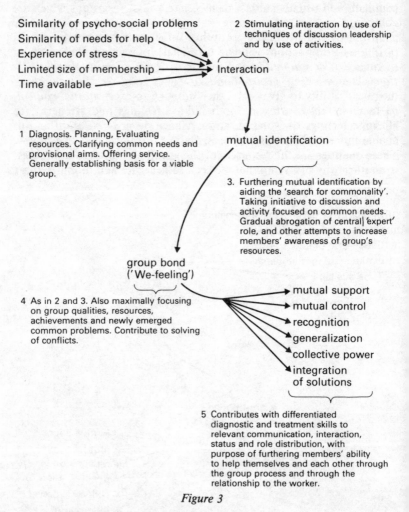

Figure 3

The foregoing is to be regarded as a brief reminder of basic principles in group work. The present book is, however, intended to go beyond introductory statements and I assume that the reader is familiar with the ideas in the preceding pages. The particular overview I have sketched here will be unknown to those who have not read my own introduction to the field (Heap, 1979) but I hope that it is sufficiently clear in itself to provide a framework for both experienced colleagues and the student reader who may associate to it and use it at different levels. The more ambiguous terms and more complex functions included in the model will be clarified in later chapters.

My main purposes have been to stress the primacy of the group as main means of treatment and the worker's complementary role as facilitator of group process. I have also pointed up some difficulties encountered in realising that principle.

I wish now to develop these ideas further and to explicate a systematic approach to group work practice. I shall do so by focusing on separate stages of the worker's tasks in facilitating process. It will be convenient to deal in turn with the worker's tasks during group formation, with the content of the first meeting or meetings, with active contribution during the working phase of the group and with termination. Experience suggests that these four stages lend themselves to separate discussion and that each raises its special questions, possibilities and challenges to the practitioner. Two special subjects, namely co-leadership and the use of non-verbal activities, might have been dealt with independently of these phases. They have actuality throughout the whole group work process, but I choose also to discuss them in the section on the working phase since we are in practice most aware of them during that phase.

PART TWO

THE STAGES OF GROUP WORK

Chapter 3

•

GROUP FORMATION AND PLANNING

WHAT PLANNING DEMANDS OF THE WORKER

Before the group comes into being the worker has functions which are so vital that they may quite finally determine the value to members of their participation in the future group. These functions may be described as diagnosis — in the sense of achieving understanding of resources and needs — and planning. ('Diagnosis' is not too happy a term for 'understanding and insight in relation to group members' experiences and needs'. It is often misunderstood, but I will stick with it until something less ambiguous and equally brief is introduced. I return to the term in Chapter 5.)

This preparatory work is careful, reflective and systematic. It requires professional knowledge of the members' common problems and as much information as is obtainable concerning the potential group members. (Of course, the availability of such information varies greatly from one situation to another.) It requires the ability to see contexts and connections between wide societal circumstances, cultural influences, group processes, the dynamics of family life and the configurations of individual clients' traits, ways of coping and specific problems. It requires understanding and a preparedness to be wrong and to continue to learn about the particular problem which brings members to a group. It requires the ability both systematically and sensitively to project reasoning and evaluative thinking into an as yet non-existent group situation. It requires empathy.

This list of exacting requirements is not intended as an immodest detailing of group workers' personal qualities and virtues. I intend it as a statement of the factors which in practice thrust themselves compellingly forward where group workers choose to invest in preparatory efforts aimed at ensuring clients as promising a group situation as possible.

PLANNING? – OR MAGIC AND GAMES?

There is, however, a choice — or an illusion of choice. Some colleagues in group-oriented agencies of various kinds — not least in hospital psychiatry – invest little in preparatory work at all. Even the decisive question of composition may be left to chance. Aims may not be clarified; the possibilities and limits of expectations and the working agreement may not be thought to need exploration. This reliance on the inherent magical qualities of groups is a serious current problem in the mental health field and in social work. My emphasis on planning and extensive prior reflection is meant to provide a more defensible and hopeful alternative.

I have used the term 'magical' advisedly and wish to comment it a little further. I mean quite seriously that some misuse of groups seem to involve the invocation of magic.

From man's earliest history we have seen his strong tendency to ascribe magical powers to circular formations: Stonehenge, the ring-shaped burial mounds of long-dead Vikings, the cyclical element dominating both Brahmin and Buddhist theology, optimistic bridegrooms still putting rings on fingers 'till death do us part' despite overwhelming evidence for more cautious prognosis, Coleridge's 'Weave a circle round him thrice' and much more throughout the ages.

Similarly, therapists, educators and social workers, burdened by high expectations of healing and change in a disintegrating society, find their limited successes confusing and painful to bear, and return to the magic of the circle. Some reassurance, some illusion of increased potency in the tasks of treatment and societal change seems to be derived from the mere act of gathering clients in a circle. Some magical curative powers enter the picture by virtue of there being a group whether or not its composition is reasoned, its aims and manner of working clear, and the respective roles of members and leader understood. Sometimes we see the kind of excessive direction I have already described as one unhappy attempt to weld individual treatment traditions with group processes. We see, too, another kind of focal role, where the therapist remains 'one-up' in omniscient silence, observing the futile and embarrassed flappings of the group members trying to find what the hell it is all about.

LOGIC AND SENSE

There are alternatives to such non-productive games. With increased understanding we depend less upon magic and group ritual. We become more able to work with groups in ways which accord with their individuality, their potential and their needs. There is logic and there is sense in the traditions of group work and treatment. The adjustment of content and style of helping to members' differing needs is a cardinal consequence of differentiated diagnostic thinking, which is a basic principal in all social work.

The worker is committed to sensitive use of responsible judgement. There is an assumption that he is present in order to contribute in appropriate, respectful and differentiated ways. Leading groups is a learnable skill, which the worker has taken the trouble to acquire. Far from being magical and inaccessible, major features of group work method are capable of systematization and conceptualization. They may be readily understood, though of course less readily reflected in practice skill.

The preparatory stage, so decisive for the outcome of group work and treatment, certainly lends itself to such an approach and I strongly advocate it. For some years now I have been using the following model.

A MODEL FOR PLANNING

Preparation and planning for group work projects falls into six related but discrete areas of consideration. The questions 'Who? Where to? Why do it this way? How many? How does one offer? How will it be?' embrace evaluations and decisions which are necessary in the planning of every group of clients.

'Who?' refers to composition. 'Where to?' refers to aims of the group. 'Why?' refers to justification of the choice of method. 'How many?' refers to group size. 'How does one offer?' refers to the areas of motivation and contract. 'How will it be?' refers to informed speculation about the atmosphere, possibilities and problems of the first meeting of the group. Answers must be found to all six of these questions during planning.

I shall discuss these components of the planning process each in its turn, though in practice several of them are carried out concurrently. Their high degree of interdependence provides a situation where growing clarification of each one of these evaluations increases the worker's understanding of the others and his ability to make decisions about them. (It is rather like changing a car wheel, tightening each nut a little at a time.)

'WHO?' THE QUESTION OF COMPOSITION

Development of group bond – the feeling of sharing and fellowship – is the most decisive group process for all treatment and growth in groups. Without it, groups' resources simply do not become available.

Clearly, however, group bond may only develop in conditions where a particular composition or a particular shared experience makes mutual identification possible. The most far-reaching evaluations and decisions made by group practitioners are therefore those

which influence or determine the composition of groups under
planning.

Natural Groups

Workers may not always be able to decide this, of course. Some group
work consists of co-operation with 'natural groups' or groups formed
by some transient chance commonality. Such groups already exist and
function in their milieu and the worker may only be of assistance
within the confines and possibilities of the group's existing
composition.

Residential group work is a field in which this situation provides the
rule rather than the exception. Here a very wide spectrum of clients
is represented – the institutionalized elderly, children in care or in-
patient therapy, the mentally ill, imprisoned offenders, and many
others. Payne (1978) discusses clearly the general issues and principles
of residential group work. One application of this method currently
being quite intensively developed is growth-oriented group work with
institutionalized mentally defective patients (Breslin and Sturton,
1978; Laterza 1979). One of the most creative case studies of Scandinavian group work documents a politically oriented project with
just such a natural group (Røren, 1976). Similarly, much group
work in medical settings has no choice but to accept a given ward
population as the context of help and to work with the resources present and with the existing potential for group bond without further
evaluation of alternative composition. Of many examples in the
literature I recommend Euster (1979). Her use of crisis theory in group
work with mastectomy patients involved work with the whole population of women with breast cancer who were in-patients at her hospital
at any one time. However, hospital group work could equally well be
exemplified from the areas of renal disease (Glass and Hickerson,
1976; Roy, et al., 1982), cardiac failure (Goldner and Kyle 1979;
Hackett, 1972), multiple sclerosis (Welch and Stevens, 1979; Eisenstein, 1959), geriatrics (Kartman, 1979; Harris, 1979; Friis and Müller,
1979; Burnside, 1971, 1981), or childhood cancer (Knapp and Hansen,
1973; Ross, 1979).

Other fields which involve work with already existent groups are
neighbourhood group work (Goetschius, 1969; Haberman, 1977;
Thomas, 1978, Joseph and Conrad, 1980) and unattached youth work,
not least in the milieu of drug abuse. An early, but still useful, source
on this area is Spergel (1966). Goetschius and Tash (1967), Marchant
and Smith (1977) and Marchant et al. (1972) are the best British
studies. From Sweden, Borgelin (1972) has described unattached work
with groups of very young glue sniffers in condemned property.
Weisman (1978) has a particularly clear exposition of the possibilities

and problems of group work with hard-drug users in a typical big city park. Lie (1981), in describing work with young drifters in Norwegian cities, has made an important contribution to conceptualizing method in work with contemporary natural groups.

Formed Groups

Most commonly, however, group work and treatment are carried out in formed groups where the worker has the opportunity during planning of determining or influencing composition. What are the criteria for a well composed group in these contexts?

It is necessary that members become involved in and identify with each other. But it is also necessary that difference and diversity should be present so that exchange, comparison, alternatives and stimuli may be present in the group's work. This ideal balance between similarity and dissimilarity is called 'The Law of Optimal Distance' by Redl (1953), though that doesn't help us very much. Practice strongly suggests that the most decisive area in which similarity is required is in the nature of the problems and needs which are to be brought to the group. Common needs make mutual identification probable and also, therefore, consensus on goals and ways of working. In itself the recognition of common need demands skill. It is not enough to offer group service to a given number of people who appear to suffer the 'same problem', since their subjective experience of the common problem and their resources for dealing with it may make quite different aims and ways of working appropriate. The worker should attempt to provide a group setting in which the areas of felt need are as alike as possible.

One might, for example, wish to offer group support to 'single mothers'. But who are they? Are they poor, rejected, frightened teenagers with one unwanted baby? Are they somewhat older women with several children at school, recently widowed or deserted? Are they articulate and politically aware young women who by choice remain unmarried and find it meaningful but difficult to establish an alternative to the conventional family constellation? The 'problems' are not the same and the kind of help which is needed is different in each case. Identification of common needs among single mothers as the basic criterion for composing a group is well illustrated in the type of evaluation reported by Wayne (1979). In a program of child abuse prevention, with cognisance of common aetiology in child abuse and neglect, she offered membership of an activity-based social group to 'single mothers in their 20s ... who were not retarded, psychotic or drug addicted ... who might well have alcohol problems ... whose social functioning was impaired ... who had no known employment, friends, interests or stable relationships ... whose children were known by the visiting nurses to be poorly fed, generally unclean and already in infancy spanked in frustration and anger'. Clearly such highly specified selection will produce a group whose members are compatible and where commonly acceptable aims and means of using the group experience are likely to appear.[1]

Compatibility as a criterion for successful composition of problem-solving groups has long been recognized by group workers. Practitioners' impressions of this are well supported by one of the few scientific inquiries into group composition (Shalinsky, 1969). Compatibility must not, however, involve excessive investment in harmony and consensus since disagreement and diversity are necessary conditions for a group's ability to produce change and growth.

The Importance of Difference
It is important during planning to consider areas of dissimilarity. It is probably as impossible as it is undesirable to compose a group which is totally homogeneous. But in what areas is dissimilarity acceptable – or even desirable?

It seems that we have difficulty in sustaining protracted and close contact with others with whom we experience little commonality. This being so, demographic differences – of social class, educational and cultural background, age, articulateness – should not be great in groups which are expected to last over a long period or which are intended mainly to meet social needs and to invite personal relationships of some duration. Many groups, however, are formed in order to solve a circumscribed social problem, to clarify attitudes to some painful situation, to cope with a shared crisis or to take decisions. Where this is so, group life is shorter, members are under pressure from the common problem – which is sharply in the focus of their concern – and it seems that dissimilarity of demographic characteristics is in comparison of little importance to the members. When planning such groups, therefore, a much greater degree of heterogeneity is acceptable outside the one factor of common problems and needs which has brought the group into existence. Indeed, such differences seem often to enrich the work of the group. For example, Taylor (1980), describing short-term work with divorce clients, advocates wide demographic heterogeneity but argues for the importance of homogeneity in the one factor of members' positions in the divorce process.

Taylor's view reminds one of the kind of evaluation advocated by Bertcher and Maple (1977), although it is not entirely consistent with their model. These authors have made a serious attempt to increase systematization in group composition and I will attempt to summarize their proposals. It will be seen that the principles on which their method of 'creating' groups is based do not differ greatly from my own, whilst some of their more particular proposals are interesting new formulations and increase precision in the difficult area of group composition. They distinguish between 'descriptive' and 'behavioural' attributes. They propose that groups are more likely to be 'effective' when they are homogeneous with regard to descriptive attributes and heterogeneous with regard to behavioural traits. (An 'effective' group in this sense is one where members are interactive, responsive and – again – compatible.) Similarity of descriptive attributes sets the stage for interaction and the development of compatibility. Difference in behavioural attributes makes it likely that each individual will have something useful to contribute so that interaction is responsive.

Bertcher and Maple further refine the concept of heterogeneity. They are concerned with what they call 'balance' in the areas of dissimilarity. In achieving balanced composition, the worker must first judge which behavioural attributes are critical – of the many forms of behaviour which are manifested by the potential members. A few such attributes will usually be identified without much difficulty, the guiding criterion being their relevance to the group's objectives. Once such attributes have been chosen, the intention is that the members selected should represent an even distribution along a linear continuum of the attributes concerned. Such a continuum is of the 'much–moderate–little' variety, so that the extremes of the attributes should either not be represented or should be represented evenly and that the representation of the attribute concerned, viewed totally, should balance. A brief illustration of this could be useful at this point.

EXAMPLE 3

A descriptive criterion of a group under planning – and thus a homogeneous feature – could be a grave illness either in the members or their immediate families. The author is currently involved in planning group work with parents of children suffering cancerous diseases. This shared condition is expected to facilitate interaction and compatibility between the parents. However, in order to provide a helpful situation in the group, a situation should be provided in which members are stimulated to exchange experiences and practices and to compare their thoughts and solutions. We will probably conclude that critical behavioural attributes should include 'discussing illness with child', 'responding to siblings' questions', or 'being protective towards patient'. Such traits should be represented heterogeneously and should 'balance'. This means that if overprotective parents are included, overcompensated parents should also be present and there should be a middle group of optimally coping parents, who are in touch with the child's anxiety and pain, in contact with their own despair and hope, and sensitive at most times to the signalled needs both of the patient and their other children. In such a situation, members may be expected to be 'responsive' to each other and thus to be supportive, accepting of feelings and optimally able to clarify the many issues and decisions which arise.[2]

Little Data – General Aims
In some planning situations, of course, there is simply insufficient data to facilitate identification of common need, beyond selection of a problem area, far from engaging in the refined evaluations suggested by Bertcher and Maple. In such cases, the possible aims of the group are necessarily limited to clarifications and solutions at a more general or superficial level. This does not at all mean that they are valueless, but it does imply an important restriction with consequences for our contract with the potential members. The less specific the criteria for composition, the less specific the content of the group's work. The greater role played by chance in determining areas of homogeneity or heterogeneity, the more general must be the aims of and contract for the group be. Thus, for example, groups of couples having some defined common problem in their relationships (Showalter and Jones, 1980; Ochetti and Ochetti, 1981), or their parental functioning (Walker, 1978; Barnett, *et al.* 1980), or their sexual life (Lopiccolo and Miller, 1975; Adelson and Peress, 1979), or the divorce transition (Stephenson, *et al.*, 1981) may be planned as offering more specific, personal and incisive qualities than chance-composed groups of, say, young couples responding to an open offer of discussion groups on 'marriage and parenthood', (Miller, 1975; Bornstein, 1980).

WHERE TO? THE QUESTION OF AIMS

Concurrent with and informed by the evaluation of composition, the planning process considers possible appropriate aims for the group-to-be. I have already remarked how often this overridingly important evaluation is neglected and the confusion which follows. If we do not know where we are going, we do not know how to get there and we do not know when we have arrived. But the more we are able to establish realistic and relevant aims for our different groups, the better are we able to:

give potential members an honest and clear basis for accepting or rejecting the offer of membership;

aid the group in finding relevant content and style;

evaluate content, structure and interaction in the group as more or less gainful;

recognize the group's need for guidance or other intervention from the worker;

give potential members a basis for alternative or supplementary suggestions regarding aims for the group;

evaluate the group's readiness for termination;

evaluate retrospectively (and thereby learn from) the completed project.

Six Aims of Group Work

As an aid in making this kind of evaluation, I have earlier proposed one way of differentiating between aims (Heap, 1977b). The needs for help, which one may observe in different settings and which determine composition, suggest particular aims as most relevant. These may be described as:

alleviating isolation;

promoting social learning and maturation;

preparing for an approaching crisis or other life change;

solving or clarifying problems at the personal/familial level;

solving or clarifying problems in the members' environment;

achieving insight.

I shall give brief examples of two of these aims to indicate the kind of connections and contexts involved in this stage of planning.

The withdrawn, resigned single mothers quoted earlier as described by Wayne (1979) were markedly isolated, both physically and emotionally. Knowing that isolation contributes both to parental depression and to risk to children, group work was planned which primarily aimed at alleviating isolation. This aim had implications for the organization, content and duration of the group. The group was seen as having protracted, indeterminate duration which could allow relationships of some closeness to develop. It could thus provide, during a crucial phase of family life, an alternative to excessive inter-dependence between members of two-person families. Content was to be neither verbal nor confrontive, both because of the members' lack of verbal facility and because of the dangers of increasing further their feelings of inadequacy and guilt. Activities were expected to provide a focus for members, with the purposes of enabling them to maintain interpersonal distance until they felt safer, of providing an opportunity for mastery and thus improved self-esteem, and simply of enriching their life experiences. A pleasant, non-threatening and supportive atmosphere was hoped for. Comparable profiles and content emerge in the planning of other groups whose major aim is alleviating isolation. These are most commonly met in services for the elderly, in provisions for physically handicapped, in psychiatric aftercare and in work with single-parent families.

A very different group profile could emerge from the planning of a group aimed at helping members prepare for an approaching crisis or change. The clients may be awaiting prison discharge, anticipating an adoptive child, preparing for a traumatic operation, or approaching retirement.

Common to such groups is a content including the provision of information about the new situation, the expression and exploration of feelings aroused by the change and usually some decision-making. Such groups are of rather short duration. They provide support and clarification throughout the period of change and are cognisant of the emphasis placed in crisis theory on immediate, intensive and time-limited 'worry work' and 'grief work'. Such anticipatory crisis group work most frequently uses focused discussion as the vehicle for treatment. Further, it is consistent with crisis treatment principles that the worker accepts a fairly high degree of responsibility for structuring the work of the group.[3]

It will be seen that the aims of anticipatory crisis groups give rise to a different content and style from those which are appropriate in groups aimed at alleviating isolation. Similarly, our other categories of aims give rise to each their characteristic group profile.

Social learning groups are found in clubs, day centres and residential agencies. They are of long life and involve using the group as a mini-society in which social skills of sharing, resolving conflict, inhibiting impulse and taking decisions and responsibility may be practised. Miller (1964), exploring innovation in the borstal system, referred to this kind of group work as 'growth to freedom'. Significantly, the best Norwegian book on club work with youth is called *A Place to Be – A Place to Learn In* (Frønes, 1979).

Problem-solving at the personal-familial level tends in contrast to be circumscribed both by contract and time. It is mostly based on problem-focused discussion, deals with actual crisis as well as situational or chronic problems, involves clarification of feelings, attitudes and wishes and has an end product such as a decision or some change in family relationships or in ways of coping with a problem.

Problem-solving *groups oriented on externally-derived difficulties* involve recognition of the need for collective activity and the organization and execution of some kind of outward manifestation of need, protest or proposal for change. Such groups vary very widely in their duration and may even develop into large formal organisations.

Finally, *insight-developing groups* utilize more profound discussion and/or self-confrontive exercises and often work at a level involving the articulation of pre-conscious material, thus representing the overlapping area between group work and psychotherapy.

Aims May Change

While the practical consequences of these evaluations for the group's immediate future are clear, it is nevertheless important that the worker's initial conception of group aims is not regarded as certain and immutable. It is provisional and to some extent speculative. From the first encounter with the potential members – whether individually at intake or at the first group meeting – the worker will receive impulses from the clients which confirm or weaken the conception of aims which he has already reached. He must be open to modify and supplement his ideas in the light of notions and needs emanating from the group. With experience and increased skill, however, it becomes less likely that disparity will include factors of major importance. The beginning stage of group work is usually characterized more by refinement of diagnostic understanding than by fundamental change, though the possibility of serious misinterpretation or omission must always be in the worker's mind at this stage.

The consideration of aims at the planning stage will sometimes suggest to the worker another aspect of possible subsequent change. The completion of work towards one set of aims may open up new questions or needs for the group and thus suggest new aims and a new way of working. For example, isolated and chronically ill clients may at first enter a group aimed at alleviating isolation. With the development of security and supportive relationships they may in time wish to use the group in order to confront painful feelings and problems. Or a group which has been formed to work on the problems of parenting severely handicapped children may wish later to form an action group or a supportive organization for similarly situated parents. If such possible developments are envisaged, the worker should either prepare to discuss this early in the life of the group or, alternatively, propose an open-ended working agreement with the group which facilitates such a transition should it be wished.

WHY DO IT THIS WAY? THE QUESTION OF RESOURCES

Client groups may be established because the worker wishes to gain experience in groups. They may be established because they have become an expected feature of the image of a progressive agency. They may be established because the director says so. None of these reasons, alone, is good enough.

At an early part of the planning stage the worker must critically appraise his selection of group work as the method of choice. It should be possible to locate resources in the projected group which are believed to be of particular relevance for the clients concerned. It should seem likely to him that these resources are greater or at least equal to the gains which each member could be expected to achieve by more familiar means of help. The demands and tensions which group members may so often be expected to experience must be counterbalanced by likely gain. Where this is not so, I suggest that the ethically proper decision is to abandon the planning of the group and to go back to the drawing-board. But what are the indications for group work as method of choice?

Indications for Use of Group Methods
Anderson (1979) proposes that clients may gain from group service if they lack social competence at the level necessary to meet their felt needs, if they experience powerlessness, alienation and hopelessness, if they are victimised, if they do not feel understood in their current human relations or if they are inadequate or feel inadequate in the face of the wish to change systems of which they are a part.

These are useful general guidelines, but in practice the worker must evaluate at a more narrowly focused level. The model of the group work process earlier summarized specifies and differentiates between different aspects of group resources. These concepts are used at this point. In confirming group method as an apt choice the worker must be able to conclude that the resources of support or control, recognition or generalisation, or of collective power are likely to be present. Further, he must conclude that they are germane to the needs and aims of the clients concerned. This evaluation must be concrete and specific.

Could Group Support Help?
Consider young single mothers, heroically ensuring the mini-family's survival, yet encountering only concealed moral disapprobation or criticism of their imprudence. It is reasonable to assume that they may grow in both stature and performance as a result of group support reflected in collective rejection of discriminatory attitudes (Kolodny and Reilly, 1972) and in acknowledgement of shared achievement. Such support relates to central areas of their needs, is a probable result of group formation and therefore argues for offering group service.

This idea of recognition of achievement as group support was clearly expressed by a member of an alcoholics' group with whom I worked some years ago. He had been a revolving-door patient in individual therapy for years before entering the group. On one occasion, this client said that in individual therapy he clearly saw himself as a man helplessly doomed to go on monumental benders two or three times a year. In the group, however, he saw himself as a man who was able to resist very strong temptation for four or five or even six months at a time.

There are other aspects of group support. Anxious and puzzled parents of learning-disabled children (Gitterman, 1979) who in their confusion and despair blame both the children and the school system and who resent and envy more successful pupils may be expected to gain from that important feature of group support which may be termed 'borrowing ego-strength'. By this I refer to the gains from group membership reflected in improved perception of reality, in identification of the need for decision or change, and in the mobilization of both appropriate feelings and increased rationality. In individual psychological terms these are 'ego-functions'. It is a result of membership of a well functioning group that mutual support tends to reinforce precisely these important functions.

Another aspect of support is what I term 'enrichment of identity'. Throughout life, we are all confirmed in our sense of having value by the company and the responses of others who welcome and accept us. Our identity is linked to and enriched by belonging to a number of such fellowships. Our picture of who we are, of being a person, has important group components. Some clients, however, are so socially impoverished that their sense of identity and worth – already at risk because of chronic social or health problems – is further undermined by loneliness, whether caused by withdrawal, rejection or enforced isolation. Frail and withdrawn elderly people (Saul, 1982), handicapped and homebound teenagers (Kolodny, 1976), chronically ill and disabled adults (Parry, 1980; Philipp, 1981) and single parents living in poverty (Wayne and Avery, 1980; Breton, 1979) are examples of populations whose isolation and threatened integrity has been alleviated by group work, where the rationale behind the offer of group service has included the aspect of support which I have called enrichment of identity.

Might Group Control Develop?

The choice of group methods is well indicated in work in clubs or residential agencies with youth at risk or with others whose behaviour is impulsive, immature or antisocial. Mutual control is usually present in such peer groups. Criticism, limits and encouragement from peers have much more impact than admonitions and reactions from professionals who are 'outsiders' or from adults in authority. There is a strong tendency, also among the immature, to behave in ways which gain the approval of groups on which one is dependent or where one wishes to be accepted. This could be called 'socialization through identification'. Such group control is perhaps the most valuable single resource in social learning and growth. It may in group work contexts be mobilized in the development of more mature, responsible and mutually considerate ways of behaving (see Frønes, 1979; Ericsson and Johansson, 1980). However, our traditional and authoritarian attitudes towards organizing institutions have negated its potential value and blinded us to a long history of convincing documentation of its utility (Aichhorn, 1939; Jones, 1959: Konopka, 1970; Larsen and Mitchell, 1980).

In the past few years, however, we have seen a greater willingness to recognize the advantages of democratization of institutions and other collective agencies. This is largely due to the creative use made of group control both in therapeutic communities and in self-help groups and communes established by people struggling with common problems of drug dependence.

The probable development of group control argues for choosing group methods not only in growth-oriented endeavours but also in certain more problem-oriented treatment ventures. This is particularly the case where denial defences and flight from change are common. This applies, for example, to counselling alcoholics (Ogren *et al.*, 1979; Levinson, 1979) and to the treatment of certain types of sexual offence or aberration (Freese, 1972). Where such groups have achieved a stage of development where problems are confronted instead of denied, they are unlikely to acquiesce in members' defences and tend to use normative control to hold each other in a treatment position. It is as if the group members say, 'Save it! We've all gone through a stage of trying to solve this problem by pretending that it doesn't exist. That doesn't work. Come on, now, you're wasting time and opportunity.' This is one reason why continuing open groups rather than time-limited closed groups are often encountered in these areas of treatment. The issue of 'open or closed' group, when not governed by practical factors, is usually determined in connection with the present planning question of 'Why do it this way?' The desirability of an established norm of problem-confrontation, maintained by group control, will often argue for the choice of an 'open' group, though depth and intensity of work seems sometimes to be sacrificed by this choice.[4]

Are Problems Denied or Repressed?

What about the resource of recognition in the context of planning? In considering service to clients in certain situations, it is often reasonable to believe that strong and repressed feelings are present and that expressing and working through these feelings is a necessary step in solving the problem or, at least, in finding some better ways of living with it. Some of the feelings engendered by burdensome life situations are culturally unacceptable – natural and inevitable though they may be. Examples of this include the parents of severely defective, terminally ill or seriously handicapped children (Mandelbaum, 1970; Robinson and Robinson, 1976; West *et. al.*, 1979), spouses of severely damaged stroke patients (Beaulieu and Karpinski, 1981) and the recently widowed (Toth and Toth, 1980; Witkin, 1979), all of whom are profoundly influenced, conflicted and restricted by family members' handicap or death.

In such situations the group work resource which I have termed 'recognition' is particularly valuable, since forbidden feelings may become both legitimized and liberated by witnessing others give expression to them.

EXAMPLE 4

Some of the author's own group work has been with the wives of incurably sick elderly men living at home. The conflict between relief and guilt at the patient's hospitalization or death, and the bitterness and intense ambivalence about the devastation of their own lives during the long years of nursing have been seen to be buried under layers of socially demanded attitudes of unambivalent sacrifice, limitless compassion and idealization. Such approved and conventional attitudes have characterized several of these groups up to a point where one member has given expression to negative feelings or to fantasies about release from her situation – 'His death will be a release for both him and me ...'. Such painful but honest statements seem to have brought relief to these groups, since other members have then been able to recognize in themselves and to permit themselves similar feelings or fantasies.[5]

The possibility of such recognition occurring in relation to concealed or denied feelings and wishes will often be a factor underlying group work as method of choice.

Might Generalisation Occur?
Similarly, the hope that the resource of generalization will develop will encourage the worker to choose a group method in helping clients in certain other life situations.

This is particularly relevant where other problems are exacerbated by the additional burden of experiencing either real or imagined deviance. Joining a group where others also experience the ostensibly deviant condition gives relief from the feeling of being singled out by a malign fate, of being doomed to painful difference. Such normalisation increases self-esteem, thus improving members' ability to work on their problems. In addition, of course, relationships are developed which further combat the isolating and humiliating effects of deviance. Among numerous cases in point are examples of group work with transsexual clients (Wicks, 1977), with parents of autistic children illogically bearing burdens of shame and guilt (Samit *et al.*, 1980), with sufferers from isolating and debilitating diseases such as emphysema (Bennet, 1979), or with children of alcoholic parents (Hawley and Brown, 1981).

Impotence Versus Power

The relevance of collective power as a potential resource is readily seen at the planning stage. Where aims include representation of views, protest, or suggestions through collective action or organization, and where clients' life situations are characterized by political poverty, the use of group work as a means of effective self-representation strongly suggests itself.

An overview of this conception of group resources as differentiated characteristics of groups may be useful at this stage:

Resources .... *which involve*

→ being realistic
→ facing need for change
→ thinking rationally
→ experiencing appropriate feelings

Group support
→ lending ego-strength
→ awarding recognition/acknowledgement of achievement
→ enriching identity

Group control
→ socialization through identification
→ impulse control
→ problem-confrontation

Recognition ————→ achieving expression of hitherto concealed or denied feelings and/or wishes

Generalization ————→ relief from self-image as deviant

Collective power ————→ aggregation of individual resources, freeing from political impotence

Integration of solutions ————→ (characteristic of *all* group work, that solutions and decisions achieved through collective work are well integrated and more capable of being acted upon)

The probable presence of one or more of these resources gives the worker valuable support for the appropriateness of group work as the method of choice. Additionally, systematic reflection around this question increases the worker's awareness of potential resources and their connection with group needs and aims. In turn, this increases his ability later to help the group in finding useful ways of working, in clarifying attitudes and priorities and in solving problems. He is not merely 'oriented' towards use of group process, but already sees that certain aspects of group process have specific relevance for a particular group under planning.[6]

HOW MANY? THE QUESTION OF GROUP SIZE

We know from our own daily life how differently we function in groups of different size. Professionally, we have also learned a great deal from both practical experience and research about the impact of the number of members on such diverse group qualities as security, comfort, degree of active participation, status distribution, probability of self-disclosure, identification with the group, and other factors.

I will not again detail this important aspect of planning. I have elsewhere (Heap, 1977b) reviewed the most important research findings in this area. In other publications (Heap, 1979) I have given examples from practice of a variety of decisions about group size taken with regard to different kinds of groups.

In the present context, I will limit myself to a recapitulation of the main questions to be raised. Again, the overriding principle is that of differentiated evaluation, relating what we know about size to the needs and characteristics of the members and to the purposes and tasks of the group.

It is very useful to know that groups of four or five members are experienced as most secure and comfortable, that groups of up to seven members are increasingly well suited to task-centred discussion, that groups of increasing size over seven are progressively characterized by elitism and impoverished interaction, that the optimal size for groups of parental or marital couples is four pairs, and so on. Such guidelines are readily learnable, but in group work practice they must be supplemented by more differentiated and specific consideration of the characteristics of the particular clients concerned and the aims with which they form the group. Are they more or less anxious than the 'normal' population envisaged in the guidelines? More or less burdened with failure or guilt? More or less accustomed to coping with group situations? More or less likely to go under in a larger or more demanding group? Do the aims of the group require intimacy and security? Efficiency and broad representation of opinion? Resources and numbers facilitating organized action?

Such questions are raised by the worker when planning has reached this advanced stage. They lead to one of the few tangible decisions he may make, and the results of those decisions may be far-reaching.

In some situations, of course, the worker is not free to determine size. This is true of work with natural groups or other constellations already in existence. Where this is the case, it is nevertheless most valuable that the worker consider the possibilities afforded and the limits imposed by the group's given size. In this way he ensures that the aims and intended content of the group are not in conflict with factors governed by size. In doing so, he sometimes also identifies possible problems to be approached once the group has been formed. Uneven distribution of activity and influence in medium-to-large groups is the most common example of this.

EXAMPLE 5

In a hospital ward treating serious renal disorders, there were observed recurrent patterns of family tensions and problems associated with the disease, with dialysis or with transplantation. Because of this commonality and the relatively long period of hospitalisation, it was decided to approach these problems through an open discussion group led jointly by the social worker and a medical colleague. However, the ward contained sixteen patients within this spectrum of clinical and familial patterns. (Group size was thus predetermined).

While the workers believed that they would normally be able to cope with so large a group, they were aware that two or three very anxious patients dominated daily ward life by their compensatory over-activity, almost continually talking and frequently interrupting. They were also aware that the size of the group would conduce to the continuation of this behaviour. It was decided during planning that during the first meeting the group would be invited to agree 'rules and procedures' about sharing time, encouraging the quiet ones, not interrupting, etc., 'since everyone here has much to share with the others'.[7]

HOW DOES ONE OFFER GROUP SERVICE?
THE QUESTIONS OF CONTRACT AND MOTIVATION

The offer of group service is not a simple routine procedure. It may and should be included in the planning phase, since its possibilities may be discovered and its difficulties and pitfalls identified prior to their actually being encountered.

The offer of service involves motivation, contract negotiation and commencement of relationship. By this stage of planning, the worker has made as good an assessment of the group's needs and resources as is possible with the information and impressions available. On that basis he has a provisional vision of useful aims for the group and of ways of working which should serve those aims. The main purpose of the offer of service is to convey this set of ideas to the potential members in such a way that they make an informed choice of acceptance or refusal. A number of difficulties are commonly encountered here.

Some Difficulties
One problem involves communication. The ideas to be conveyed have been worked out in a professional frame of reference, often jointly with colleagues, consultant or supervisor. Thoughts have been developed, exchanged and formulated in the barbarous semantics of clinical or administrative jargon. They are not necessarily unclear for the workers involved in planning because of this, but they are couched in terms which are woefully at variance with the general public's customary usage of words.

If the worker truly wishes that clients shall have free and clear choices about joining, he will translate his conception of perceived aims and proposed content into ordinary daily language and rehearse it. I often quite literally rehearse this, both in my own groups and in those where I am supervisor or consultant. Role play of the offer of service with colleagues or students seems, in common with the real-life situation it simulates, to confront the worker time and again with the demand for clearer explanation. 'Yes, but what will we actually do?' and 'But what are we supposed to get out of it?' It is a most useful exercise, not least because the possibilities exist that our heavy reliance on jargon sometimes in fact conceals lack of clarity and that our team discussions use esoteric language as a protective device rather than for the precision which technical language is intended to provide.

The question of our own ambivalence arises here, however. Do we genuinely wish the client to enjoy 'free and clear choice'? It is probably true that we have by this stage of planning a considerable investment in the idea of the group. We have worked many hours in planning. The interest and expectations of our colleagues are also a source of pressure. It follows that our personal wish to see the group come into being can then defeat our acknowledgement of the client's right to choice and to an informed basis for that choice. We may be tempted to describe the group both cryptically and attractively and attempt strongly to influence the client's decision. We sell instead of offer, persuade instead of motivate. What are the differences?

One difference lies in honesty about intended purpose and content. Unless this is stated in some true and comprehensible manner, the worker has no ethically acceptable sanction for guiding discussion into areas of personal difficulty and pain and he may justifiably be criticized for seducing clients into treatment. The offer of attractive activity, for example, is often made without reference to its purpose, so that an apparently recreational goal may conceal what has been called 'therapy by stealth'. Another important difference between persuasion and motivation lies in our reaction to clients' resistance. How we deal with this has important implications both for their ultimate decision and for the quality of their subsequent relationship with the worker. Common initial responses to the offer of group service are anxiety, puzzlement and scepticism − 'I'm not very good at talking with other people', 'My trouble is too private', 'How can we be of help to each other when we can't manage our own affairs?' 'I can't see much good coming out of it'. The worker's wish to recruit for the group and perhaps his well-motivated and valid belief that the client concerned will benefit from membership readily cause him to argue *against* this anxiety and scepticism. He attempts to reduce it by reason, logic and explanation − or, at times, to ignore it. These responses are not fruitful.

It is necessary that the worker prepare himself to meet these common reactions in some better though perhaps more difficult way. Such reactions are to be regarded as meaningful and legitimate statements by clients, to be experienced empathetically and reacted to on that basis. Thus, instead of attempting to argue scepticism and anxiety away, the worker accepts it. He recognizes the client's right to refuse, avoids getting up-tight about this and shows his understanding of it. Indeed, he may go further and actively help inarticulate and anxious clients more clearly to express doubts which they are unable to verbalize. Responding to underlying feelings rather than explaining or defending around purported obstacles or concrete questions about details is one important way of helping clients express such doubt and anxiety. Consider the following exchange, taped from a student's 'offer of service'/intake interview.

EXAMPLE 6

Client: Would the group be on Tuesday, you say? At 8.30?
Student: Yes. That's right.
Client: Well, I'm afraid I can't come then. The kids are just in bed then and there are no baby-sitters in our street, and even if there were I just can't afford them.

Student: That's no problem. We can provide a baby-sitter from the clinic here. It's part of our service.

Client: Even so, it's such a long way to travel and besides the buses don't run very often at night. And it's over the waste ground at night to get to the bus-stop – and all sorts of things go on there.

Student: Well, that's all right too. We have some volunteers who make up a transport service. You can be picked up by one of them.

Client: It's not only that though, is it? I'm just no good in company. I'd feel so daft talking about things with a lot of strangers. And there's a lot of posh people who come to the clinic; I know, I've seen them.

Student: Oh! I don't think you have to see that as a problem. We see here that people soon get at ease with each other. It doesn't seem to make any difference what kind of background they have. And I'm quite certain that you have a lot to gain from coming.

The student here is answering accurately on concrete details, he is helpfully removing obstacles from the client's path and he is encouraging her. He is also being insensitive, obtuse and manipulative. The client is probably feeling increasingly powerless and scared and less and less hopeful about being understood. By now, the student worker should have shown her that he has picked up her anxiety and that he is well able to understand it; that while he truthfully believes that she could gain from membership, he equally well understands that she hesitates to commit herself to something so foreign and threatening. He must make it easier for her to say no.

This approach no doubt keeps some clients out of group treatment. That is their privilege and choice. But it also contributes, perhaps paradoxically, to enabling other clients to opt for membership. The experience of being listened to, understood and accepted, and of contact with a non-possessive, non-manipulative helper, is both rare and encouraging and seems to represent a motivating factor even for very anxious clients. In addition, the presence of these qualities in the initial contact contributes to establishing and defining the relationship between the worker and the members, giving as it were samples of the attitudes and values which will shape the worker's role in the group. The basis for choice is thus extended.

It Will Be the Members' Group
Another feature of the offer of service has bearing on both contract and motivation. In presenting the idea of the group, the worker will

indicate an impression of his own intended function. This will probably deviate from the authoritative, expert role anticipated by the intended members. It will therefore also be necessary for him to articulate his hope that the members will be active, responsible and maximally in charge of the process. While this sometimes both confuses clients and raises their anxiety, it also provides an opportunity for the worker to make explicit his belief that the intended members have something both to give and to receive from each other. Considering the sometimes chronic burdens of failure and disapprobation which our clients bear, such an indication of belief in their ability to give and to use life experiences creatively is in itself highly supportive of self-esteem and thus also motivates them to participate. It is the difference between 'We'll see if we can be of help to you' and 'You have all been through such a lot, and have in different ways managed so much, that you must have a very great deal to give each other.' Again, to sum up. The recurring themes and challenges of the offer-of-service situation are:

the extension of real choice;
demand for clarification of aims and intended content in concrete terms;
motivation versus persuasion;
samples of the worker's attitudes and values, of recognition of the clients' strengths and resources, and of recognition of the clients' rights and autonomy;
indication of anticipated active roles for members;
worker responds to the feelings underlying clients' resistance or ambivalence about joining.

In conclusion, I wish to stress that all of these possibilities and problems involved with the offer of service may be anticipated. Much can be foreseen and prepared for which otherwise becomes lost opportunity or unexpected difficulty. We do not have to wait for these difficult interviews before we reflect on their possibilities and problems, and – as indicated earlier – it is useful to role-play them beforehand.

It is of course not always the case that an offer of group service takes place by means of individual interview. Members are sometimes invited by letter or simply by a poster put up in a well-baby clinic, a shopping mall or in the factory canteen (Fritz, 1982; Coplon and Apgar, 1982). This is particularly true of preventive group ventures, where general social issues or the common recurring problems of family life are discussed.[8] Even in these less individualized offers of service, however, the guiding principles I have indicated obtain. It is possible also to formulate letters and posters in ways which give clear indications of aims and style of working, which show respect for members' ways of dealing with their own lives and which acknowledge the experiences and resources which members bring to the group.

HOW WILL IT BE? 'TUNING IN' TO THE GROUP

The final step in planning is the accumulation and concentration of all foregoing thoughts and impressions in preparation for the first meeting with the group. So much that has been abstract is about to become reality; so much that has been speculation in the world of ideas and theory is about to be materialized in a group of troubled people. The ideas so interestingly garnered are now to be challenged as to both their utility and validity. This is where the worker puts up his 'Engaged' sign and sits and thinks about it all. And tries to feel.

Some years ago this would have been called 'the diagnostic stage' but, as we later shall see, that is an unhappy and misleading designation. It would be more correct to describe this activity as anticipatory diagnosis, but I will not be responsible for introducing further multisyllabic artefacts. William Schwartz (1971) simply and aptly uses the term 'tuning in to the group'. I think this is a good term. Tuning in has several aims. It is intended to ensure maximum utilization of all foregoing thought, fact-gathering and contacts. It is intended to heighten clarity about the initial tasks of the group and about what is hoped to be achieved in the first meeting or meetings. It provides a situation and a time in which the worker requires of himself informed and imaginative speculation about the situation he is soon to meet. He reviews his knowledge of the problems and needs represented and consciously strives for insight – for empathetic understanding of how *these* people with *their* backgrounds, resources, experiences and limitations are likely to experience both their common problem and the group situation in which *they* are to work. He tunes in to the group so that he is maximally oriented towards helping them on their terms and at their speed to find their solutions. He gears himself towards registering and understanding the myriad exchanges and shifts, resistances and assertions, alliances and conflicts, ambiguities and insights which will make up the life of the group, which is soon to begin.

What Do We Ask Ourselves?

On the basis of all the information, knowledge, experience and impressions so far the worker must ask himself what needs, hopes, tensions, defences, attitudes and fears may be expected to characterize the group. He must ask himself how he expects members to react to the strangeness and demands of the first meeting. Should he anticipate silence and anxiety? Watchful circumspection? Openness? Anger? Superficial and defended socialising? Purposive goal-directed activity? Passive self-abnegation? He must evaluate the degree of clarity, consensus and apparent finality with which group aims and organization have been discussed during intake. How much remains unsaid, unclear, unexplored from the intake stage and how much emphasis should be placed therefore on collective contractual affirmation or change? Always some, of course, but many clients first feel strong enough to differ from or supplement the worker when they are supported by others. This is most useful and he must prepare for alternative ideas emanating from the group, while still planning as well as possible on the basis of impressions so far gained. He must think in terms of probabilities, while remaining open to find his speculation invalid or incomplete.

Proposal of Contract
The worker knows and intends that aims, ways of working and mutual expectations – that is to say the 'contract' or 'working agreement' – will be taken up in the first meeting of virtually all groups. He will prepare a way of presenting his own conception of these, which also facilitates and encourages members in either identifying with them as their own aims and wishes or in supplementing or modifying them. The worker does not 'decide' the aims. He proposes them as negotiable material. During tuning in he may quite literally prepare a statement about this. It might be said that that is the only contribution which the worker may with certainty plan beforehand, since all other contributions are a response to relatively unpredictable group processes. This, too, may be rehearsed and improved by role play.

Anticipated Atmosphere
Tuning in to the anticipated atmosphere of the group – eager, excited, depressed, angry, subjugate or anxious – is also of value to the worker in examining his own response to such feelings. He should use this opportunity for self-critical appraisal of his own probable functioning when exposed to such affects or attitudes. He thus prepares himself for the self-discipline and self-awareness which are always a feature of the professional helping relationship. For example, anticipating passivity may make him aware of his own anxiety about silent groups. This should help him to reflect about his own ways of dealing with anxiety and to ensure that these do not interfere with his leadership of the group.

Short-Term Goals

The worker's anticipation of the group's probable atmosphere quite often also has value in aiding him in identifying short-term goals. I am thinking here of situations where members' emotions, attitudes or habitual role behaviour may inhibit them in engaging in the long-term work of the group. Where the worker is aware of this it may help him to see short-term goals, which are preconditions for the fulfilment of the groups' long-term aims.

For example I have experienced a recurrent process in treatment groups of prison inmates where members' suspicion and their resentment of manipulation have been barriers to their engagement in treatment. The ventilation, acceptance and working through of these highly rational problems has therefore been a short-term goal whose attainment was a prerequisite for the members' engagement in the groups and their long-term goals. Similarly, task-oriented group work in the treatment of teenage delinquents (Larsen and Mitchell, 1980) sees the definition and acceptance of mutual responsibility, of specific, concrete, and attainable aims, and of a confrontive style of interaction as a necessary short-term goal. All readers who have worked with this rationalizing, projecting and provocative clientéle will see that tuning in will lead to some such conclusions. Work with alcoholism provides another example. Denial defences as a first move by the alcholic client coerced into treatment by crisis or by spouse may be visualized at this stage and will thus point up members' acknowledgement of alcohol problems as a short-term goal for the group (Ogren, *et al.*, 1979; Levinson, 1979; Sterne and Pittman, 1965).

Prediction of Process

Where the worker is well informed about the individual clients concerned, he may find it helpful during tuning in also to reflect on their probable behaviour as group members. This will often suggest ways of aiding them to use the group situation more constructively, either by supporting them in particular ways or by trying to limit them or by helping them to form or to avoid particular kinds of relationship. For example, such evaluations may be made concerning clients known to be either very submissive or very dominant, as in example 5. Where highly defended but active people are concerned, a decision to offer membership will necessitate some thinking about how to help them while preventing their damaging the group. Similarly it has on occasion been both possible and useful to predict alliances between dependent and protective clients or other potentially symbiotic pairs and these have been variously regarded as possibly nourishing relationships or as relationships inhibiting growth and treatment.

Such predictive reflection must never be more than tentative, lest the well-known self-fulfilling prophesies arise, but they are never-theless useful contributions to sensitizing the worker early on to some possible dynamics of the group-to-be.

SUMMARY

In this chapter the planning stage of group work has been described. A model has been developed, proposing that planning be regarded as a process consisting of six separate but interrelated sets of evaluation. These are:

'Who?' – the question of composition;
'Where to?' – the question of aims;
'Why group work?' – the question of choice of method;
'How many?' – the question of group size;
'How does one offer?' – the question of motivation and contract;
'How will it be?' – the many questions of tuning in.

NOTES: CHAPTER 3

1 Readers engaged in child abuse prevention should note that these ideas have subsequently been more fully described and developed in Wayne and Avery (1980).
2 Case examples and discussion of group work with parents of children with leukaemia or other carcinomous conditions include Knapp and Hansen (1973), Kartha and Ertel (1976) and Ross (1979).
3 Readers unfamiliar with crisis theory and treatment may be referred to many texts. Parad (1970) gives an excellent introduction and overview. More specifically for crisis treatment in nursing, Aguilera and Messick (1974) is recommended, whilst Rapoport (1970) and Golan (1969, 1978) are among many authors on crisis theory whose main interest is in social work and allied fields. Basic features of crisis treatment are recognition and catharsis of feelings engendered by loss; identifica-tion of realistic areas for worry and appropriate areas of grief; working through these in a structured and supportive situation; planning for future; and brevity. Strickler and Allgeyer (1967) wrote one of the earliest papers on the application of crisis theory to group work. Falck (1978) has made the most recent contribution – clear and creative.
4 A helpful summary of the advantages and disadvantages of 'open-ended' groups is found in Shulman (1979), well illustrated by group work on a gynaecological ward where cancer of the uterus was treated. Hartford (1971), who treats the subject more thoroughly, builds upon a yet earlier work, one of the few theoretical studies on this subject, Ziller (1965).
5 A helpful study of the relationship between spouses in this situation is Fengler and Goodrich (1979). The use of group work in support of the caretaking spouse is documented by Beaulieu and Karpinski (1981).
6 The literature on group work as method of choice is not extensive. However, a review by Lang (1978) is warmly recommended.
7 Group work in medical settings is frequently directed to problems associated with renal disease. Examples include a mothers' group for dialysis and transplant patients (Glass and Hickerson, 1976), groups of wives of home haemodialysis patients

(D'Affliti and Swanson, 1975; Roy *et al.*, 1982), a therapy group for patients on haemodialysis (Hollon, 1972) and for both the patients and their families (Mott and Taylor, 1975).

8 Preventive group work with the recurring challenges and problems of family life is increasingly referred to as 'family life education'. An extensive literature now exists on this method. Readers are recommended to the Family Life Education Workshop Series, published by the Family Service Association of America, 44 East 23rd Street, New York, NY 10010.

Chapter 4

———•———

THE FIRST MEETING

So, enough people said 'yes'. We have planned and prepared as well as we can, and we and our butterflies are now going to meet the group. It is both possible and valuable to consider the first meeting of the group separately from subsequent meetings. There are tasks and aims specific to the first meeting. There are recurrent themes in its possibilities and problems. There is an identifiable set of dynamics.

MEMBERS SEEK COMMONALITY AND MEANING

While it would not be true to say that the subsequent potency of the group process is decided here, it is certainly true that the ease and the tempo with which group process may be moblized is strongly influenced by the qualities of the first meeting.

Behaviour in the first meeting of any kind of group is exploratory in nature. In new social situations we need to orient ourselves in relation to the others present, the range and nature of permitted behaviour and the degree to which the group's aims are compatible with our own. Some authors have stressed that this exploration is a 'search for commonality', a hope of discovering sufficient likeness to facilitate mutual acceptance, relationships, and common objectives (Sarri and Galinsky, 1975 – discussed in Heap, 1977b). Other authors, though agreeing with the observation that exploratory behaviour predominates, attribute this to our reluctance to commit ourselves to affiliation until we are assured that the conditions and sacrifices of membership are not unreasonably high compared with its gains (Kolodny, Jones and Garland, 1965).

THE WORKER AIDS INVOLVEMENT AND EXPLORATION

These interpretations are not mutually exclusive. Both imply tasks which are in practice common to the first meetings of client groups. The worker's function here is both to aid the search for commonality and to help members perceive the gains of involvement in the group.

This takes several forms. For example, it is common practice, early in the first meeting, for the worker to suggest some way for members to get to know one another. This might be a traditional 'round' of introductions; or it might take the form of some kind of joint action or activity necessitating exchanges; or it might – more rarely – involve some more structured exercise or game (Drum and Knott, 1977; Schroeder and Pegg, 1978). But, whatever form the introduction takes, one use made of it by the worker is noting similarities, analogous problems, like experiences, common anxieties and other areas of potential fellowship and commenting on these in ways tending to increase members' awareness of them.

During the meeting, other opportunities of furthering cohesion arise. Members' awareness seems initially to be focused either on their private distress or on their attempt to place the worker and to relate in some individual and personal way to him. It seems to require both time and freedom for members to register and relate more to the others in the group. The worker, however, being oriented towards the group as a whole, hears many signals about commonality which the members, who initially are inwardly directed and guarded, tend to miss. He comments on these by 'linking' them together, indicating commonality and aiding the exploration and discovery necessary for the development of the group bond.

'You and not I', he tells them, 'have both the problems and the answers, and since you are in similar positions you may both understand and help one another.'

EXAMPLE 7

An open counselling group of post-operative mastectomy patients was commenced in the cancer department of a large national hospital. The group was led jointly by a social worker and a physiotherapist. The main aim of the group was to help the patients express and work on their extensive and intense feelings – horror, fear, traumatic change – and bring to a manageable level their anxiety about returning home.

During the early part of the first meeting the members were silent and inhibited. They exchanged but few words with each other and seemed very dependent upon the workers' directing the situation. They had had surprisingly little contact with each other on the wards. To the extent that they were able to comment on the group situation they drew attention to differences in their ages and in their backgrounds, some coming from cities and others from the remoter rural and coastal districts. During the first half-hour, members' remarks were addressed exclusively to the workers.

During the first hour the workers had helped all members to say at least something about their situation. While this was for the most part reticent and limited comment, a number of important things were said – 'This whole thing is so fearful and distasteful to talk about'; 'I daren't even look at myself or even think about it'; 'We only have one child, we'd meant to have more, but now that I'm like this God only knows how it will go'; 'I am the youngest and only single one here. Most of my money goes on clothes. They interest me, I work in the trade and style matters to me. Maybe I'll have to find something else.'

In a silence late in the meeting one of the workers carefully and reflectively said: 'I've been sitting here and thinking about what has come up so far. Several of you have remarked on how different you are from each other and that is of course to some extent true. But, at the same time, you have all in different ways brought up similar issues that clearly distress you all. Much of what has been said, whether it has had to do with marriage or clothes or children, seems to start from a feeling that you have all been changed so drastically that life can't be the same again. You cannot be loved any more, cannot look good any more – as if one is less woman after this. Isn't that what you have all been saying? Aren't these things you can talk to one another about and help one another with?'[1]

BUILDING ON MEMBERS' STRENGTHS

Such help in the search for commonality and stimulus to identification brings the group into the beginnings of co-operative work. This is because this function also gives the worker an opportunity to indicate recognition of members' strengths and to begin the conscious abrogation of his or her own central role.

It is hardly possible to overemphasize the importance of helping the group to gain confidence in their own ability to solve problems and to take decisions. This is part of the same process as decreasing their dependence upon the worker. There is an almost paradoxical situation here, since the worker may in the first meeting or meetings use precisely the authority with which the group invests him to direct them to an examination of their own resources. When he believes that the group concerned is rich in resources and well able early to take responsibility, he may combine this stimulus with an indication of the limits of his own function. He thus contributes to the clarification of contract. These themes give form to all first meetings and it is frequently possible to work on them together, as in the following case extract. This extract also exemplifies the process of 'linking'.

EXAMPLE 8

In the first meeting of a group of parents of mentally retarded, multiple-handicapped children, Mrs A (22 years old) said that she was 'at her wits' end'. She 'just couldn't manage any more'. She did not know whether the child's continual crying and sleeplessness were to be expected from all babies, or whether her baby was particularly in pain, or whether it needed something special because it 'is the way it is'. While she felt it was right to continue to pick the baby up, maybe it wasn't right according to the experts? What was more, she was sometimes so tired that she was worked up and desperate by the time she picked up the baby and then there was no chance at all that she could soothe it. The baby 'caught her mood'.

The child care worker leading the group said that she could see that Mrs A was in a dreadful situation. She could 'see that it must wear you down. And then you feel desperate and alone – especially during the nights, perhaps.' After a pause, she went on: 'What you have said reminds me very much of what Mrs B described earlier this evening. I remember, Mrs B, that you said that although you have successfully brought up several older children you feel helpless with your new baby. You know, I think something you can all gain from the group here is to listen and talk to each other, ask each other, compare experiences, ways of doing things – learn from each other, rather than asking me or other 'experts' for advice. It seems to me that the experts on raising and living with seriously handicapped children – if there are any at all – are to be found among you parents rather than social workers, doctors or psychologists. I'll come in whenever I think I have something useful to add, but the main idea of bringing you together is our strong belief that you can help each other.'[2]

INFLUENCE AND ACTIVITY SHOULD BE SHARED

Another important feature of first meetings is also present in the foregoing case extracts. It will be noted that the worker in example 6 drew attention to the worth and relevance of a number of diverse contributions from very dissimilar members. In example 7, another worker responded directly to an individual's pain, then quickly 'linked' her with another member, whereafter she drew the whole group's attention to their ability to contribute usefully. This has also to with the task of maintaining open structure.

This term refers to work with another regular occurrence in group process. A common observation is that the uncertainties of the formative stage of group life leave available positions of influence and initiative in the informal structure of the group. Leadership is up for grabs. Tensions and feelings of both inadequacy and protest often bubble under the passive awkwardness of the first meeting in client groups. There is then a strong tendency for informal leadership to be accorded to somewhat aggressive, domineering or perhaps over-compensatedly active members such as the 'life and soul of the party'. This certainly helps the group to get started. But it also has the undesirable effects both of inhibiting the less secure members and of establishing early a hierarchical group structure. This is as difficult to change as it is effective in limiting openness, acceptance and freedom in the group. For these reasons, the worker demonstrates continually – but with particular emphasis in the first meeting – his respect for and acknowledgement of all contributions, especially those from members who seem quickly to be accorded low status or who clearly find difficulty in manifesting themselves. Sometimes it is necessary to respond somewhat differently to contributions from early active and early passive members. It is not necessary to focus group process on the former: their activity will continue. But if the self-effacing members do not receive a response to their few timid contributions they may well accept a low-status definition of their role for the remainder of the group's life. Thus they will gain less from the group and at the same time their potential contribution will be lost.

This is a serious restriction on the use of group process, since it is likely that the initially reticent members include the most pained, conflicted and self-critical. In the context of group work with social and health problems these are often precisely the members who have most both to gain and to give. In our competitive culture a tradition has established itself of affording influence and prestige to the active and the articulate and of ascribing low status to the passive and reti-cent. Un-learning this well entrenched custom is quite a challenge, but it is a prerequisite for the group worker if he is to be able to acknowledge the potential and encourage the activity of the initially passive members.

This problem of uneven contribution by members is sometimes compounded by the worker himself. Our own uncertainty, our need for response and our inability to tolerate silence may cause us to collude with the initially dominant members. We may actively enter into dialogues with them in order to maintain a high level of activity. But we thereby convey the message that we especially prize their contribution and are correspondingly unimpressed with others.

Coping with this requires, more than anything, the security which comes of having survived some difficult times in groups. Until we have this apprenticeship behind us, we will at times lean for support on those group members who in fact should be stimulated least, and neglect those who most need our acknowledgement.

RELATIONSHIP OF WORKER TO GROUP

This of course introduces the whole area of our feelings about our clients and our attitudes towards them. I shall not add very much to the many volumes of words already written about treatment principles and the nature of helping relationships.

I shall limit myself to noting that the notions of acceptance, respect and non-manipulation and an approach based on active and sensitive listening and understanding are as vital to the outcome and value of group work as they are to any other treatment method.[3] The worker's relationship with the members must continually reflect these qualities. Members' confidence in the worker, their ability to express painful feelings and impulses, the maintenance or growth of their self-esteem, and their possibilities for being open and honest with each other – all of these important qualities are conditional upon the worker demonstrating unambiguous respect and acceptance and manifestly giving his intense and undivided interest to what members say and do.

While this is true of his relationship with the group during its whole life, it is of paramount importance in the first meeting.

It is in the nature of group norms that they become established very early in group life and that they quickly become subject to control. Certain attitudes and forms of behaviour are possible and approved. Others are frowned upon or forbidden. This being so, the worker's preparedness to listen and his use of his initially central role in actively demonstrating attitudes of acceptance, respect and understanding serve not only to establish his relationship with the members but also to influence the norms which will become established in the group. It is this process which lies behind such oft-heard remarks from clients as 'I could really say what I was thinking without feeling stupid or bad' and 'Everybody listened and seemed to want to help each other'.

THE ROUND OF INTRODUCTIONS

There is an important instance of this influence of norms and development of relationship which is peculiar to the first meeting. I am thinking of the use which may be made of the initial round of introductions.

What often happens is that the worker, after introductory remarks including some reminder of the provisional aims, invites members to introduce themselves. Members in turn then say who they are and something – much or little – about what brings them to the group.

It is commonly the case that the worker nods his thanks in acknowledgement and then invites the next person to take his or her turn. He misses an important opportunity in doing so. Let us consider an alternative. The concept of 'active listening' is important here. When members present themselves they usually say more than just their name, and indeed are often invited to say more. This 'something more' differs from member to member and seems very often to represent, if we can see it, a glimpse of each member's most pressing concern at the time of entering the group. Worries and experiences produce pressure which is slightly relieved by mentioning the problem in this way, and at the same time the member also indicates indirectly what he or she feels that they need help with. The 'something more' which members add is *not* determined by chance.

EXAMPLE 9

In the round of introductions in a discussion group of pensioners meeting for the first time at a service centre for the elderly one member said: 'My name is John Smith, I'm only 65 but I've already been retired two years because of the way the fishing industry has gone'. Another member said, 'I'm called Jane Hansen, I've been a widow now for about a year.' And so it went on around the group. These old people were not just saying *who* they were. They were also telling where it hurt and were taking the risk of exposing some of their private pain to strangers. Had the worker nodded and said 'next please' she would have rejected a gift and given the impression that she could neither listen nor understand. But she indicated that she had registered the importance of what had been said and gave a response showing empathy and an initial attempt at understanding. Thus she hoped already to help each member to feel a sense of meaning, hope and belonging in the group. To John Smith she said simply, 'It sounds as if your working life ended earlier than you would have liked.' To Jane Hansen she said, 'So you're still trying to get used to being alone.' These were contributions to the establishment of group norms which would come to include mutual understanding and acceptance, response to others' contributions and the relevance of feelings.

It should be observed that the worker's comments in the above episode were brief and simple. In the context of the round of introductions they should be so, since it is not intended that the round of self-presentations should be halted for a deep and detailed discussion of one member's situation. The aim of these brief responses is simply that the members should understand that the worker is saying to them, 'I hear what you say, I wish to understand you and I respect you.'

In all of these exchanges and contributions a large part of the spectrum of problems represented in the group is displayed. The worker may well find this bewildering. He may even wonder if his planning was at fault, where composition in accordance with common need was a guiding principle. But it is in fact desirable that this rather confusing and frequent shift of focus from one individual problem to another should occur throughout the first meeting. It means that each member has used the opportunity to present his or her problem as it is currently experienced; it gives the worker the material necessary to aid members in their search for commonality; and it facilitates the review, confirmation and perhaps modification of the contract provisionally entered into during the offer of group service and intake.

THE CONTRACT IS REVIEWED

This affirmation of contract as a collective activity is another of the recurrent themes of first meetings. It will also be brought up subsequently, but during the first meeting this occurs by prior decision at the initiative of the worker. He will probably include an invitation to discuss this in his introductory remarks and will throughout the meeting help members to make their expectations, motivation and wishes as explicit as possible. He will attempt to link work with the issue of commonality with that of contract. Finally, he must gather and try informally to sum up the many problems raised and suggestions made at the end of the first meeting. While a broad display of problems and experiences is desirable in the first meeting, this should not be allowed to appear overwhelming and unmanageable in its diversity. The group needs evidence that the worker has managed, even if they themselves have not, to gain an overview of the issues raised. Thus, all are assured that their contribution has had some impact and may become an active component in the group's subsequent work. It is also desirable that members in this practical way are given evidence of the worker's competence, since they have usually a fairly high degree of dependence upon him during this formative stage of the group. Finally, this review may be used to help the group affirm what they are going to work on and how they are going to go about it.

SUMMARY

In summary we may say that the recurring themes and tasks of first meetings are the following:

   short, clear self-presentation by worker;
   self-presentations by members;

review and perhaps amendment of aims and working agreement (contract);

identifying and articulating main problems and motivations;

ordering overview of problems and needs presented;

worker conveys to members: 'I listen to you, accept you, try to understand';

worker facilitates interaction, aids search for commonality and for meaning;

worker contributes to establishing purposive norms;

attempt to maintain open structure;

worker begins abrogation of 'central person' role;

worker observes group and seeks supplementation, confirmation or rebuttal of previous diagnostic thinking.

Having survived the first meeting, we shall now go further and look at the working phase of the group.

NOTES: CHAPTER 4

1 For other examples and discussion of group work with mastectomized patients see Euster (1979) and Feinberg (1980).

2 For case studies of further group work in this area see Mandelbaum (1970) and Murphy *et al.* (1973).

3 Well regarded sources on helping relationships include Keith-Lucas (1974), Ferard and Hunnybun (1962), Irvine (1979), Brammer (1973) and Salzberger-Wittenberg (1970). In my own authorship, I have discussed this a little further in Heap, 1979, pp. 56–66.

Chapter 5

———◆———

THE WORKING PHASE — RESPONDING TO NEEDS

The group is of course working from the moment of its formation, but I use the term 'working phase' to distinguish this main goal-striving period from those dominated by the exploration, anxiety and competition characteristic of formation and by the ambivalence and separation of termination.

THE WORKER'S ROLE AND TASKS

There are many ways of describing this main phase of group work and of trying to convey the nature of the worker's task. His functions are certainly many. He may at different times with the same group be confrontive, supportive, interpretive, informative, enabling, and limiting; or he may, rather passively, observe. Emphasis on these various ways of behaving will also vary widely from one group to another, depending upon their particular needs and their capacity for autonomous work. Not only the worker's role but also the group process has many and diverse characteristics during this phase. It is thus difficult to present an overall picture of group work process in this phase which is valid, dynamic and yet systematic.

Some authors, particularly in earlier years, have made attempts to describe group work process as a system of categories of intervention by the worker (Saloshin 1954; Pernell, 1962). Others have drawn our attention to certain 'core competencies'. These comprise the central skills which are the worker's main contribution and are seen as mobilized differentially in accordance with aims of groups or with different stages of their development, (Vinter, 1962, 1974; Northern, 1970; Sarri and Galinsky, 1975).

Other authors, notably Bertcher (1979), have contributed to our understanding of group work process by the application of role concepts. Bertcher achieves a most useful application of established social science theory to group work practice. Schwartz (1961, 1977), also using the role concept, is particularly occupied by the importance of the worker's role as 'mediator'. He emphasizes that the worker's experiences and observations in bringing service to clients give him knowledge of the need for improving and extending services. Thus, they imply new obligations. This new knowledge must be conveyed to the agency or upwards in the planning or legislative system, whose subsequently improved service the worker again conveys back to the client systems. Recently, Shulman (1979) has extended his own and Schwartz's earlier formulations of this 'mediating model'. He has clearly described his conception of the specific skills which the worker must develop in order to fulfil the mediating role. These include *inter alia* 'contracting skill, elaborating skill, empathetic skill, sharing worker-feelings skill, demand for work skill, pointing out obstacles skill, sharing data skill and sessional-ending skill'.

Particularly in the recent European literature, there has been a movement away from this type of attempt at systematization, as if in reaction to the risks of rigidity and of excessive emphasis on the worker as central resource, which may be the price paid for so high a degree of conceptual organization. Thus the works of Sigrell (1972), Røren (1976), Axelson and Thylefors (1976), McCaughan (1978), Douglas (1978), Brown (1979), among other Europeans, either invite the reader to draw his own generalizations from sensitively and systematically described case studies or to consider and integrate a pot-pourri of material on values, aims of groups, dynamics of groups at work, democratic organization and clinical tradition. Combined, these sometimes give an excellent impression of the nature and the issues of group work process, but they are perhaps not always as pedagogically coherent as the new group worker could wish. Brown *et al.* (1982) have recently published a serious attempt to identify the common strands characterizing the possibly emerging model of British group work. They found this complicated by the range of practice settings, the differing areas of theory used as a base for practice, and the number of unexamined issues of important principle.

In time, a coherent common framework for the many approaches to group work will emerge. But it is a difficult task, and all authors on the subject must meanwhile choose their particular priorities of emphasis, well knowing that the picture is incomplete and that the student must also learn those parts of different authors' visions and ways of conceptualizing which look right to him and which illuminate his particular practice.

In this chapter, I shall try to convey my own view of this central part of group work method. I hope that this will be another of the many useful 'bits' which readers may integrate into their own approach to practice.

I find it useful to regard group work skill mainly as a response to what is happening in the group. This should already be apparent from the preceding chapters. The worker's functions are to facilitate and mobilize group process and to contribute and respond to it in useful ways. (To some extent, this approach may be compared with that of Hartford, 1971, and of Klein, 1970, 1972, two important American authors who are also concerned with the 'primacy of group process'.)

This conception of group work skill presupposes the ability to observe group processes and to understand them as well as is possible. If what we do as group workers is a response to such understanding, we must return to the subject of group diagnosis. Understanding of what is going on in the group is the main indicator of group members' needs and thus of the ways in which the worker may contribute. In the following, I shall define group diagnosis and use this as a basis for indicating an approach to group work skills by considering the treatment implications of selected aspects of group process during the working phase.

SOCIAL DIAGNOSIS – ITS DESCRIPTIVE AND DYNAMIC ASPECTS

I have already used the term 'diagnosis' rather freely in preceding chapters and it is necessary now to say something about its use in social and mental health contexts before discussing the more specific term 'group diagnosis'.

The term 'social diagnosis' was introduced by Mary Richmond in 1917. It refers to the attempt to understand the needs, the resources, and ways of coping of people seeking help with social and personal problems. Its purpose is to provde the basis for the way in which the worker attempts to help. Mainly, it has been used in the context of one-to-one or family treatment situations. However, the term 'social diagnosis' is currently in disrepute. 'Old hat,' it is said; 'we don't play that kind of music any more.' The arguments are, first, that 'we work with clients in their present social reality' and, second, that 'it is arrogant and futile to hang labels on people'. These comments are valid and important. But they are quite invalid reasons for rejecting social diagnosis, since social diagnosis does not consist of 'hanging labels on people' and does consist precisely of attempts to understand clients in their present social reality. It is most important to clarify this issue. Rejecting the term 'social diagnosis' is perfectly permissible; it doesn't matter what we call it. But doing so seems increasingly to involve rejecting also the principle of understanding need as the basis for help with psycho-social problems – and this is entirely inadmissible. Why this confusion? An analogy with the development of psychiatric diagnosis is helpful here.

A few generations ago, by chance or mischance, the treatment of mental disturbance emerged as a new *medical* speciality. There was evidenced a strong tendency by the early psychiatrists to adopt a diagnostic approach which had characterized a much more primitive historical phase also of somatic medicine. I will call this approach 'static' or 'descriptive' diagnosis and I wish to contend that the futility of so much psychiatry has since then had its roots in the continued misapplication of the descriptive diagnostic tradition.

This has involved a search for apparent similarities of symptom, the conferring of classically derived names on similar symptom constellations and the empirical search for treatment specific to that symptom,[1] so that one has tried cutting chunks of it out, subjecting it to massive electrical shocks and driving it down with various drugs as though the symptom like some malignant growth had had an existence separate from the person who manifested it – with his feelings and thoughts, his life, family, job, hopes and fears and the myriad influences for good or bad which have either made him ill or which have got him through the night.

In the postwar years, however, we have seen the development of an interpersonal psychiatry. Interest in the life processes in which patients are involved, where many causal, precipitating and curative factors potentially lie, represents a major leap forward by this generation of psychiatrists. It is a courageous and creative break with an archaic tradition of descriptive diagnosis. The movement towards understanding mental illness as part of an interactive life process and towards finding its amelioration or cure also partly in interactive situations requires understanding which embraces social, psychological, cultural and political factors and which is directed towards perceiving how the continuing interplay of these forces produces illness or health. Such understanding perceives the patient as at all times interacting with and being influenced by his particular systems. We may, then, call this approach to understanding 'dynamic diagnosis' or 'diagnostic process'.

The foregoing is an almost indefensibly simplified overview of the development of diagnostic approaches in psychiatry. It is no doubt familiar, but it is useful to remind ourselves of it since something very similar has happened in social work and neighbouring fields.

When social workers reject social diagnosis because they 'won't hang labels on people', they are appropriately rejecting an approach which their profession has long since already rejected. Something corresponding to psychiatry's earlier descriptive diagnosis has certainly been practised and collective nomenclature such as 'unmarried mothers' and 'problem families' has been used in a manner implying that something significant has been achieved by putting people in a typological pigeon-hole. But designation by categories does not increase understanding one jot and undoubtedly has in earlier days led to stereotypic and simplified responses to need. 'The' unmarried mother was a moral and economic problem. 'She' therefore needed moral guidance and economic relief – most effectively given by placing her baby for adoption. 'The' elderly were frail, dependent and withdrawn. 'They' wanted a quiet life, with neither cultural, political nor sexual stimulation and 'they' preferred to be freed from responsibility. 'They' were best helped therefore by uniform caretaking services which provided optimum and predictable material aid, which removed conflict and the discomforts of choice from their lives and which provided sedentary and spectator pleasures as distractions from the losses, passions and challenges of old age. Mute withdrawal and confusion was explicable only by the standard and hopeless diagnosis of incipient dementia; no one entertained alternative explanations, that many of 'them' were in fact resigned and depressed after a painful and lonely struggle with accumulating unresolved crises, for which help might be given. And so on.

DIAGNOSIS AS AN ATTEMPT TO UNDERSTAND

It took time also for our profession to move from such descriptive to dynamic diagnosis. It took time for us to see that 'the' unmarried mother does not exist any more than 'the' old age pensioner or 'the' neglectful parent does. Each client, every living person, is a product of and is continually influenced by a complex battery of cultural, familial, economic, physiological and political forces. The task of dynamic diagnosis is to attempt to understand as well as possible how the interplay of these factors, in their particular manifestation for that particular client, have brought him into a situation of need. This involves using what we know of his history, his resources and his hitherto successful ways of meeting problems, as well as what we see and hear of his present unsuccessful attempts to regain the ability to cope.

This observation of both past and present experiences from the widely societal to the narrowly personal and the attempt to use these as a basis for the understanding of need is extremely complicated. It becomes even more so when we recognize that interest in clients' ongoing work with their problems and relationships deepens and often modifies our provisional understanding. Thus, diagnostic understanding is never 'achieved', but is continually subject to partial reinforcement, partial abandonment and continual supplementation. It is not a finite once-and-for-all job. It is an open, interested, questioning process.

Further material for social diagnosis is found also in the client's ways of co-operating with the worker, as well as in his interactions with significant others during the course of the helping process. The latter is particularly relevant in work in client groups.

SOCIAL DIAGNOSIS IN GROUPS – A DILEMMA

Since difficulties in relationships play so large a part in the kind of social and health problems met in group work, it is to be expected that they are also reflected in members' relationships in the group itself and with the worker. While such observations are not necessarily always to be shared with members, they are always informative to the worker.

The group situation does not only provide more diagnostic material. It also multiplies the task of understanding. Because of the number of persons present, more needs and resources are at play in the group, so that members' interactions and mutual influences are important additional forces in the total picture of each member's life situation. The number of factors to be considered is therefore very high. Their possible combinations and variations are almost infinite. And here we meet a dilemma.

The task of gaining and maintaining insight into this complex interplay involves very many variables. It is not surprising, then, that formulation of diagnostic method has time and again resulted in the compilation of long lists of factors to be observed and considered in relation to each other. Thus, despite the assertion of dynamic principles, 'group diagnosis' has commonly come to expression in detailed descriptive dispositions – perhaps well suited for examination purposes in training programmes, but of questionable utility in practice. Indeed these extensive diagnostic essays, because of their very size and complexity and because of the work invested in their production, tend to be regarded as almost inviolable delineations of the individual client and of the group. In this way, the weight of information necessitated by the idea of dynamic understanding has compelled both theoreticians and practitioners back to static descriptions. It has produced a kind of categorization which is more extensive than the earlier diagnostic labels, but which retains the old limitations of being impervious to new impressions and of ignoring both the nuances and the effects of experiences occurring after the formulation of the initial 'diagnosis'.

How may we solve this dilemma? When we nevertheless lay claim to a practice of dynamic diagnosis which succeeds in circumnavigating the problem, what do we in fact do?

I believe that key words are selection, concentration and empathy. I will incorporate these in the following attempt to systematize what I believe to be my own practice and something like that of other colleagues who have struggled with this problem.

GROUP DIAGNOSIS IN PRACTICE

Let us return to the process of 'tuning in', discussed earlier. By the time the worker has completed the planning stage and is prepared to meet the group for the first time, he is already in the process of group diagnosis. By the commencement of the group's life he has developed a provisional conception of the problems, needs and resources in the group and has some ideas about how the group is likely to function. He has developed this conception on the basis of the understanding available at this point and it enables him to begin his co-operation with the group in a manner which is likely to be relevant. But it is to be emphasized that we talk here of 'beginnings' and 'likelihood'. No matter how systematically he has planned and how sensitively he 'tunes in' to the group, his understanding is hypothetical and in-complete. For the rest of his time as worker with the group he will be amending, confirming and rejecting features of this hypothetical basis for understanding. He will do so in the light of new observations, new information and new insights. He will, with humility, be aware at all times how tentatively and imperfectly he understands and that even valid understanding loses validity as the client and the group change, work and grow.

However, the more the worker invests in planning and tuning in, the higher is the probability that his original diagnostic conception has validity. In practice, what does this conception consist of? It seems to me to have three components.

THE THREE COMPONENTS OF GROUP DIAGNOSIS

The first of these is generalized professional knowledge. We meet each group possessing a sum of knowledge which we have already gained during our years in the social and health fields, and which has a high degree of validity as general understanding of the kind of life situation common to the group members. This general knowledge is gleaned from our original training, from our experiences in the agency over a period of time, from our continuing reading of the literature and from our study of the research. For example, before a particular group is formed, a worker in an agency providing service for the elderly knows a great deal about facilities for the aged, about social legislation concerning them, about psycho-social crises in old age, about inter- and intra-generational social patterns, about communica-tion with and between elderly persons, about prevailing cultural attitudes to the elderly, about ways of attempting to provide the elderly with appropriate and acceptable service, and so on. Such knowledge will hold a high degree of relevance for all groups of elderly people which he might form. In whatever sector of the social and health services the worker is engaged, he will have such a reservoir of relevant general knowledge and understanding.

The worker also possesses knowledge specific to the one group now in question. Unique features of this special group and its individual members supplement and refine his more general understanding. This influences greatly his thinking about the aims of the group and its possible focus and ways of working. Some of this specific knowledge relates to the group as a whole; some concerns the individual members. Let us continue with the example from services for the elderly.

EXAMPLE 10

Here in Norway, the worker might find himself in a rural coastal district with fishing families living out on numerous small islands. The present depopulation process is selective, in that young people are attracted by the wages, conditions and apparent security of the distant industrial cities and offshore oilfields. The old people remain. They struggle to maintain their boats, their nets and their income; they struggle to survive and remain in their familiar surroundings although services are removed or atrophy; they struggle to retain the independence which is so vital a cultural norm at the same time as the welfare state bureaucracy presses upon them with wholesale solutions of institutionalization or rehousing on the mainland. Were the worker to engage in a collective enterprise with this population, these specific traits and needs would provide further sources of understanding, supplementing his general knowledge of the elderly. He would expect this particular group to experience realistic anxiety, anger and disorientation. Though direct expression of these feelings would perhaps seldom occur, they would probably strongly influence members' ways of approaching their common problems. Their growing poverty brings them hunger, cold winter nights and humiliation. The flight of their children isolates them and also calls into question the values and culture which have determined their lives and their forefathers' lives. Eventual removal to the mainland, voluntary or otherwise, is a future certainty which members will currently deal with in different ways, perhaps commonly with denial defences. The worker will also be aware that such a group would include a very high level of resources. In his planning and thinking about the group, he would be very conscious of these and would reflect about how they might be mobilized.

The worker's diagnostic conception of this particular group

would also include some knowledge about the individual members. (From agency to agency this of course varies very extensively.) Reflection about the strengths, relationships, work situations and problems of the individual members gives a more focused idea of probable group needs and resources. It also invites to a first tentative reflection about some probable dynamics in the potential group. Certain members have always been active in the district's social, political and organizational life while others have taken more passive roles. Some members are currently suffering other difficulties such as ill health or recent widowhood and will function in the group in a manner determined by their relation to these other crises. Such knowledge about individual members sometimes has predictive value and always helps the worker better to understand, evaluate and intervene when the group has come into being.

I earlier proposed that selectivity and concentration are important features of dynamic diagnosis in practice. This applies particularly to the component now under discussion. A very large number of facts may be available about the group under planning and about its individual members, and these will have been of value to the worker in forming his initial understanding of the group. But it is not intended that the worker attempt to hold in his memory during active work with the group this immense amount of detailed information. The intention is that he achieve an initial analysis of the problem on the basis of that information, that he synthesize this into diagnostic hypotheses relating to the group as a whole and that he also judge certain salient features of the individual members' social histories and self-presentation as being centrally relevant for them. The result of this work is a concentrated, selective set of hypotheses based on present information and previously acquired knowledge and on skill in analysis of psycho-social problems.

This is still primarily cognitive and lacks the third and final element, the affective process. No amount of facts and findings is of value in understanding others in distress unless we are able also with our feelings to envisage the impact upon them of their problem. This emotional component of understanding, for which I will use the customary term 'empathy', is difficult both to achieve and to describe. It is, however, vital that we invest continually in the development of our empathetic ability, for without it we do not know what a particular problem means to a particular client and are therefore unable to help in ways which are maximally relevant for him.

Empathy involves awareness, at the level of one's own feelings, of what clients are experiencing with their feelings as a result both of their particular problem and of needing help. It involves compassion, acceptance and understanding – the kind of closeness which Truax (1971) has called 'non-possessive warmth'. It requires of the worker that he be able to recall and to project into the present situation his own feelings in comparable situations of distress and to use this insight as a basis for understanding 'where the client is' in relation to his problem.

The concept of empathy and the necessity for contact with one's own inner experiences which it requires is vitally important. Indeed, without it we could not reasonably claim ability to understand others whose particular handicap or problem we do not share. Thus, it is not necessary to have maltreated one's own child in order to approach a group of abusing parents with openness, helpfulness and understanding.[2] But we are required, as a condition for empathy with such a group, to recall and re-experience the range and intensity of feelings with which an abusing parent is overwhelmed at the explosive and fateful moment of beating his child. We, too, have all suffered unreasonable demands. We, too, have felt desperate and hopeless. We have known our resources grow less as challenge and threats have remorselessly increased. We have felt that we cannot accept one more demand for concern for others. We have felt fury or resentment when our own needs are both engulfing and unmet, while we are expected to give immediate and dedicated response to others' trivialities – such as the filled nappy or the spilled porridge. We have felt, at some time, exactly what the abusing parent feels. We have been fortunate in being able to act differently, but we know – if we can face it – what he has felt, because we too have been there.

This ability for self-confrontive recall and imaginative projection into the client's world is the core of the empathetic process. It is this which enables social and health workers to work with so wide a range of psycho-social problems, since while we have not necessarily experienced the problems themselves we have experienced at some time, at some level, all feelings which may possibly be felt. Admirable though we well may be, we have all felt hate, fury, envy, loss, inadequacy, terror, resentment, greed and despair. Winnicott (1959), in an important early paper on empathy, stressed the importance of our also being able to 'forgive ourselves' the strong and often ill-regarded feelings which we must continually rediscover in this way.[3] The recall and re-experience of such feelings is a prerequisite for an accepting and non-judgemental attitude to our clients, just as it is a vital component of the type of understanding which I have termed social diagnosis – or, in our present context, group diagnosis.

Thus, our understanding of our group of isolated and elderly islanders in example 10 is seriously incomplete if it does not include an empathetic vision of the impotence, resentment, dependence, fear, confusion and anger which they feel and which will strongly influence their perception of the common problem and their ways of dealing with it. In turn, our ability to include this dimension of understanding depends upon our being able to recognize the normality, reasonableness and universality of these feelings and recognizing them also as part of ourselves.

THREE COMPONENTS WHICH PROVIDE A REFERENT

In summary, I have proposed that group diagnosis in practice consists of a synthesis and concentration of three related areas of knowledge and understanding. These are general knowledge of the problem and client population concerned, information about the particular group concerned, and empathy with members' affective experience of their situation. A distillation and fusion of these factors provides a source of diagnostic understanding, a referent, for our observation of the ongoing behaviour and interaction in the group.

We have constructed a tool, an instrument, illustrated in Figure 4. What use can we make of this tool?

GROUP WORK METHOD AS RESPONSE TO GROUP PROCESS

This diagnostic awareness, this synthesis of knowledge, facts, ideas and feelings about the group members and their situation is the aid to understanding. Such understanding serves at all times to determine the worker's choice of a particular intervention or of containment. It is a tool. It is, however, an imperfect tool. It is continually supplemented and modified as new observations confirm, refute or elaborate the impressions and hypotheses of which it is formed. But it is at all times held in the worker's consciousness; it is a continually active feature of his approach to the group. He maintains, cultivates and questions it. Its function is that of referent. His myriad observations of group discussion and behaviour vary widely in the degree to which he can understand and respond to them, but they are all explicable. The more he can understand, the better he is able to take a role in the group which contributes to its work. Thus, as he observes this behaviour, registers that verbal exchange, notes these concerns, or perceives a certain development, he strives to understand how these features of group life reflect members' preoccupations, problems and attempts at problem-solving. In doing so, he considers what he sees and hears in relation to the image of group needs and experiences which is his diagnostic referent.

We might then expand our model to show that the awareness and understanding which has been developed provide the referent for the

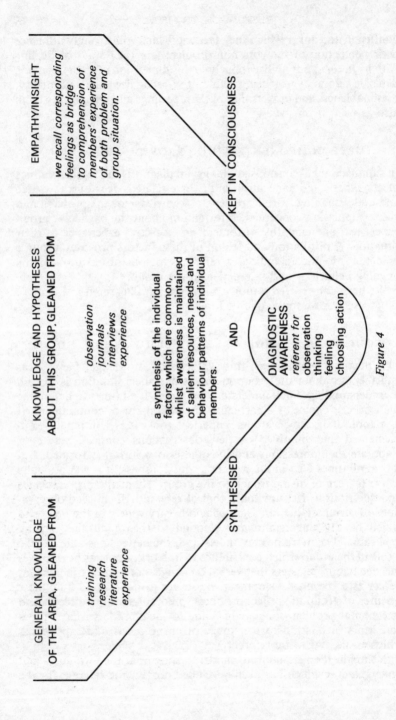

Figure 4

GENERAL KNOWLEDGE
OF THE AREA, GLEANED FROM

training
research
literature
experience

KNOWLEDGE AND HYPOTHESES
ABOUT THIS GROUP, GLEANED FROM

observation
journals
interviews
experience

a synthesis of the individual
factors which are common,
whilst awareness is maintained
of salient resources, needs and
behaviour patterns of individual
members.

EMPATHY/INSIGHT

*we recall corresponding
feelings as bridge
to comprehension of
members' experience
of both problem and
group situation.*

KEPT IN CONSCIOUSNESS

AND

SYNTHESISED

DIAGNOSTIC
AWARENESS
referent for
observation
thinking
feeling
choosing action

worker's observation and understanding of the life of the group in which he takes part. Figure 5 illustrates this.

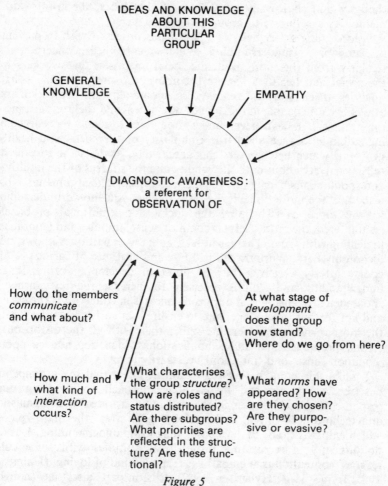

Figure 5

The attempt in practice continually to understand group needs – whether we call it diagnosis, problem analysis, or whatever – commonly takes place in something like the manner I have described here. In conception it is simple, but becomes increasingly complicated with the size of the group, with lack of clarity about group aims and with the incidence of indirect means of communication in the group. But, however certain or tentative the worker's hypotheses, with whatever incisiveness or caution he acts in the group, the consideration of what he sees in the light of this systematically assembled framework of understanding provides the continuing theme of his thoughts and choices. It is in this sense that I describe group work method as a response to group process.

Before going on to give examples of this process I wish to prevent one possible misunderstanding. We frequently hear concern, particularly from the more academic social scientists, that workers in the social and health fields are becoming 'too professional' – that qualities such as warmth, genuineness, spontaneity and dedication are at risk because people in these fields wish to expand their understanding and skill. I have never understood this. It seems to reflect an incredible ignorance about the complexity of the social and health problems which fieldworkers encounter daily, at the same time as it reflects naivety about both the validity and the sources of the intuitive and spontaneous behaviour which are so prized. The argument seems to be that the more difficult the task, the less you should understand it; the more overwhelming the social and emotional problems encountered, the more useful is common sense, impulse and ignorance in dealing with them. There is in fact, as every practitioner knows, no dichotomy here. Warmth, authenticity and attitudes of caring are of course utterly decisive. But the point of developing professional understanding and skill is precisely to increase the relevance of spontaneity, to ensure that our genuineness is in concern for the client and not for our own image, and to ensure that caring is expressed in the most relevant way possible rather than with all the distortions, errors, prejudgements and simplifications which dependence upon 'common sense' and 'intuition' necessarily involve.

I make this point here since I think it likely that my attempt to describe a realistic and manageable approach to choosing our response to group process might well be interpreted as mechanistic and technical. I will, in anticipation, again stress the major place which empathy holds in developing diagnostic understanding. I have no difficulty in reconciling professional attitudes with some colleagues' contention that empathy is really 'a kind of loving' (Halmos, 1965; Irvine, 1964; Hybertsen, 1982). It is, in part, also that, though Irvine's question 'What kind of loving?' brings us back to the need to temper the subjectivity, distortions and investments of personal loving relationships with the selflessness, insights and disciplines of professional behaviour. This accords with my own belief that closeness and relationships of respect and trust are more soundly based on mutual attempts at understanding than on ignorance deliberately maintained in the service of some vaguely defined, highly valued and usually manipulative intuition.

After which rather impatient parenthesis, I wish now to give examples of group work method in the working phase of the group and to show how response to group process may be based on the approach to group diagnosis which I have sketched here.

It will be most manageable if I try to show how selected features of the group process may be understood and how the worker may respond on the basis of that understanding. In practice, of course, these features of group life are closely interwoven, but they may for the purpose of exposition be dealt with separately. In the following, therefore, I will deal with the worker's observation of and response to communication, to group structure, to norms and to group development. Other features of group process such as interaction or decision-making could equally well have been discussed. Considerations of space have, however, necessitated making choices and priorities.

Before moving on from the working phase to termination, I will also discuss the use of activities and the growing practice of coleadership. Both of these subjects are in fact relevant to the whole group process, but since we are most aware of them during the working phase they will be discussed in that context.

NOTES: CHAPTER 5

1 Descriptive diagnosis is seductive. Kahn and Earle (1982) discuss the 'magic of naming'. They remind us that both patient and doctor draw greater comfort from having a name for a condition, irrespective of its prognosis, than from being in an uncertain state. Irrespective, also of whether or not the 'name' refers to a condition about which neither party has one jot of understanding!

2 Examples of group work in this area include Paulsen et al. (1974), McNeil and McBride (1979), Kruger et al. (1979) and Burch and Mohr (1980).

3 Other earlier papers on empathy include, Grossbard (1954) and Irvine (1964) – still well worth attention. More recently, Keefe (1976, 1980) on empathy in social work and Kalisch (1971) on empathy in nursing are to be recommended.

Chapter 6

———————◆———————

THE WORKING PHASE – RESPONDING TO COMMUNICATION

COMMUNICATION IN THE GROUP

No aspect of group process is more apparent and important than communication in the group. Some kind of communication is continually in progress and it provides and reflects the major content of the group's work.

Members communicate in order to give and seek information, to impart experience and reactions, to elicit responses and clarify contributions, to demonstrate attitudes and opinions, and to support, differ with, or influence each other. Words, actions, grunts, signals, facial and bodily changes – all of these, directly or indirectly, consciously or unconsciously, provide the communicated content of the group's work towards its goal. The worker must always respect its seriousness and meaning, and must continually improve his skill in observing and understanding its many expressions.

The worker's understanding of communication and of the group's goals will often help him to see that the group is functioning well and communicating in effective and purposeful ways. Thus he will restrain his own wishes to be actively 'useful'. In recognition of and respect for the resources inherent in the group process he will instead assume a recessive role. He then partly observes, in order to supplement his understanding, and partly facilitates in order to ensure that both the physical framework and the emotional atmosphere remain good enough to enable the group process to continue functioning efficiently as long as possible. This exemplifies what Phillips (1957), in one of the early standard group work texts, termed the 'principle of containment'. Today's colleagues, with their more robust usage, seem to be calling this 'the art of keeping your mouth shut'. Whatever we call it, this quality predicates the worker's belief that members have something very worthwhile to give each other. It also presupposes his skill in deciding when he should be active and when he should simply let the group process enfold itself. This choice does not only involve respect and self-discipline, however. It also requires that the worker perceive accurately the quality and relevance of the group's communication, as in the following case extracts.

EXAMPLE 11

(a) A radical voluntary service offered crisis help to men. With time, this was expanded to include open discussion groups focused on the problems of separated or divorced fathers. These men were seen to provide a fairly predictable and to some extent homogeneous nucleus of the crisis centre's clientéle.

The group leaders, a social worker and a lawyer, had anticipated reticence and embarrassment. They had assumed that active stimulation would be necessary to help the group members overcome their initial anxiety. They had prepared alternative approaches through materials and 'trust games' in case the group's initial awkwardness made discussion impossible.

In fact, before the first meeting was one hour old they had felt compelled to adopt a rather formal type of leadership. They became joint 'chairmen' for a while, in order to deal with an unexpected flood of experiences, protests, comparisons, proposed solutions and expressions of sympathy, understanding and support. Members raised only relevant issues and were active and responsive to each other. In fact they needed little help from the leaders. Apart from structuring the discussion, the leaders felt that for long periods they had no function other than preventing the group from getting stuck in a mutual reinforcement of unproductive 'blaming' of wives or of the 'system'.

The group has now continued for some time and the members' exchanges and relationships have been so productive that one co-leader has withdrawn to start another group. The remaining leader now perceives his role as that of 'facilitator' rather than that of 'therapist', as was initially envisaged.[1]

(b) In work with children suffering from chronic arthritis, muscular dystrophy, and other immobilizing and progressive diseases, group work with families is being used as support to both parents and children. One programme of such groups was initially led jointly by a pediatrician and a social worker during one-week residential experiences. This proved to be unsuccessful, as members exhibited dependence upon the doctor and insisted upon his retaining a central, advisory and authoritative role. It was decided that he should withdraw from active participation and limit himself to a role as resource and support for the social worker. The latter quickly found that members had enormous potential for mutual help, once the omniscient leader was absent. Work in these groups has subsequently been characterized by the early identification of important subjects, in which she is active and gives information. This then gives way to intensive, practical and supportive discussion and activity by the group which allows the worker more to adopt an observing and facilitating role.[2]

In both of the above observations, we see that the workers' recognition of members' ability to communicate effectively enabled them to adopt less active roles, thereby facilitating a high level of use of the groups' own resources. However, despite all the advances in education in modern society and in the elaboration of our languages, we are on the whole far from maximally skilful in communicating with each other. Much of what we convey is ambiguous, indirect, unconscious or incomplete, leaving the impact of our messages in the care of quixotic factors such as interpretation, varying sensitivity, selective perception, guesswork and chance. This is true even in quite benign situations. How much more true it becomes when we are under pressure, anxious, or in conflict, as in the client role. The worker leading a client group must therefore assume some responsibility for helping members to communicate more effectively.

His contribution to this aspect of the group process may well be the most important support he gives to the group. We shall look a little closer at this.

INCOMPLETE COMMUNICATION

Where members' communication is incomplete, it must become less so. It is, however, not always immediately apparent that an unfruitful discussion has this cause. It is up to the worker to be continually aware of this possibility and to consider incomplete communication as an explanation of inconclusive, repetitive or frustrated discussion. The worker questions himself: 'Did that member say all that he wished or was able to say?' and 'When the group are going around and around like this, getting nowhere, is it because they have been unable to state the problem completely and to describe alternative solutions thoroughly enough?' and 'Is some of the anxiety in the group a result of the uncertainty which results from incomplete exchanges and from ignorance of important facts?'

Incomplete communication may result from lack of necessary information, from inarticulateness, or from anxiety about the possible reception which a more complete contribution could receive.

In the first instance, the worker will first help members to pool their separate knowledge in the hope that the necessary information will prove already to exist somewhere in the group. Where this fails he will either help the group to find the information they need or will provide it himself. In the latter case, he must avoid excessive eagerness in procuring information. The group members may grow in social skill and self-esteem by 'finding out for themselves'. Every autonomous action is a step further from infantilization. The worker's question here is 'Is it necessary that I do this myself or am I showing off my muscles, and in which case to whom?'

In many cases, of course, lack of information is itself a factor motivating members to enter the group, perhaps a major one. The treatment agreement will thus often include an expectation that the worker will actively provide needed information. This might include information about available facilities and resources, about rights, or about certain aspects of the group's focal problem – such as an illness or handicap. For example, we see how the increased use of group methods in medical social work has integrated crisis theory, with its emphasis on ensuring an informed factual basis for decision or adjustment to loss. Felt lack of vital information is a strong motive for membership in these groups, and this points to a central task for the worker. Where incomplete communication results from inarticulateness, the worker accepts the task of helping the member or members concerned to formulate more fully and clearly. This often involves a patient, respectful, step-by-step process of helping the members to find ways of stating their point which are more satisfactory than the half-sentences, catch-all terms and guessed meanings of much everyday speech. This is particularly relevant to groups whose members are underprivileged and uneducated clients not accustomed to refining ideas into precise verbal formulation.

EXAMPLE 12

'Well, you know, I got this – like – thing, and showed it to this bloke, you know, and he got proper – well, I don't know how to say it really. ... But that was that, wasn't it?'

This 'incomplete communication' was quite typical of the contribution in a particular group of probation clients. The worker, seeing the speaker's evident distress and the potential importance to the group of what he had tried to say, helped him to define the 'thing', to complete the 'proper ...' and to say a little more about 'that was that, wasn't it?'. This proved to be an attempt at describing the common experience of the released prisoner who is an acceptable job applicant until the prospective employer sees his discharge papers, whereupon with more or less concealed mistrust and contempt he rejects him. In these situations the client is powerless and increasingly frustrated, angry and anxious. Having more completely communicated his experience to the group, this member was then actively supported and sympathized with. Thereafter, the group entered into a useful discussion of ways of dealing with this burdensome and common problem. They exchanged suggestions, ideas and experiences; they discussed thoroughly the pros and cons of trying to conceal their background; and they later went along with the worker's rather foreign suggestion of role-playing a number of such interviews, to find ways of increasing their chances.

Getting ideas out of our heads into others' heads is never easy. In group work with particularly inarticulate clients the worker should consider the possibility that reliance on verbal facility may be unrealistic and he should reflect on the use of activities as an alternative or supplementary means of communication (this will be discussed in Chapter 10).

AMBIGUOUS AND UNCLEAR COMMUNICATION

Much communication is ambiguous and unclear. This is particularly so where participants are burdened by conflict, insecurity, and feelings of inadequacy or perhaps guilt. This, of course, is common. In these situations, the worker's task is both to relieve, by acceptance and generalization, the painful feelings which inhibit clear communication and to invite the group or individual clients to restate or clarify what has been said. How far this succeeds will of course depend upon the strength of the defences which are involved. Where the worker finds that unambiguous restatement is difficult for the member, he will concentrate more on relieving anxiety or guilt than on directly increasing the effectiveness of communication, since these are probable sources of the ambiguity.

EXAMPLE 13

Four pairs of parents whose children were under the child care committee's supervision because of behavioural problems found difficulty in becoming actively engaged in their weekly group meetings. By the third meeting the worker was still very active, the members' participation in clarifying group aims had been resistant and limited, and no clear statement of members' perceptions of common problems had been made. However, many unclear and ambiguous contributions had been put forward. Examples of these were: 'Children all over the world are in trouble these days', 'When we were kids these things were easier to deal with', 'Nobody is really to blame', and so on.

The worker's earlier attempts to help members expand and clarify these possibly important but unclear contributions had been unsuccessful. The members were not markedly inarticulate and she increasingly believed their lack of clarity to result from confusion, anxiety and guilt feelings.

This hypothesis was consistent with her general understanding of family dynamics, her knowledge of the economic and other stresses of these particular families and her empathetic experience both of members' sense of parental failure and of their probable interpretation of the group's somewhat spurious voluntary nature.

From this point, whenever opportunities arose, the worker invested in relieving anxiety and guilt by generalization and by giving clear evidence of both her acceptance and her own attempts to gain understanding. Thus, she said: 'How painful it is to see one's children in such trouble and to feel so helpless' and 'Yet it sounds to me as if you blame yourself just the same' and 'I have never met any perfect parents, either in my work or my private life'.

This approach seemed helpful in increasing members' security. This in turn increased their openness and their ability to describe experiences more clearly and to exchange views.

The simple and helpful comments made by the worker in the above example reflect her understanding of her field and her empathy with the parents concerned. We should also note, however, that where members express themselves ambiguously or unclearly the worker's own understanding of the content of the discussion may at times be coloured by his or her own interpretations and fantasies.

EXAMPLE 14

A psychiatric nurse who worked in an out-patient clinic recounted the following episode, rather against herself. She led a group of young single women who had in common that they were unhappy, isolated and anxious. She felt her sympathies and a certain protective indignation aroused by one member who disclosed that she had in fact been married for a matter of days before leaving her husband on their honeymoon. The reason for this was his 'perversion' and his 'bestial sexual habits'.

Fantasies blossomed in the group, not least on the part of the worker. One member's curiosity caused her to ask what the husband 'actually did'. The original speaker explained with unbated distaste that since they 'couldn't manage it' in the hotel bed her husband had tried to persuade her to make love on the balcony under the stars. In horror, she had refused and left him. Thus she had in fact never consummated her marriage with her husband, whom she experienced as a 'perverse beast'. The worker's and the group's understanding of this member's difficulties became substantially modified as a result of this simple clarification.

CLOSING THE SEMANTIC GAP

It is not only such oblique references or special and circumscribed experiences that may be communicated ambiguously or unclearly. This is a pervasive problem. A great many everyday expressions are also likely to be encountered in a client group which are capable of widely differing interpretation. Unless the worker has reasonable grounds for presuming that he knows the speaker's meaning, he must invite further definition so that all present know what they are talking about, rather than believing mistakenly that they do so while in fact making erroneous interpretations based on their own associations. This source of error is often referred to as the 'semantic gap'. Thus, for example, 'bad nerves' might mean mild and sporadic irritability or deep and permanent psychosis. It depends upon who is saying it and in what situation. 'My husband drinks' may mean a couple of pints on a Saturday which dismay a temperance spouse, while in another marriage it refers to a massive and incurable process of self-destruction. What do 'bad', 'nice, really', 'a bit tired sometimes' or 'put up with' mean in the context of the speaker's life situation? We all put our own interpretations on these common phrases, but they may be very far indeed from what the group member is trying to convey. A great deal of communication would be more helpful if possible ambiguities were checked rather than ignored.

Often, simply repeating the word or phrase concerned in a questioning manner is enough to encourage the speaker to make a clarification.

Consider these alternative sequences.

ALTERNATIVE 1

Worker: So how have things gone since last week, Charlie?
Member: Not too bad, really.
Worker: Well that's nice to hear. Anybody else got anything to bring up?

ALTERNATIVE 2

Worker: So how have things gone since last week, Charlie?
Member: Not too bad, really.
Worker: Not too bad?. Not *too* bad?
Member: Well, bloody awful really. You see ... etc.

Alternative 1, based on the worker's associations and usage, displays his subjective and optimistic interpretation of the member's answer. His response increases rather than decreases the obstacles to problem-clarification in the group. In alternative 2, the worker achieves a quite different result. Whatever his own interpretation of 'not too bad' may be, they have nothing at all to do with the member's use of the phrase. He merely repeats the phrase questioningly, indicating both that it is unclear and that he and the group are really interested in hearing how things are going with Charlie. It becomes easier for this member then to disclose the difficulties he has experienced 'since last week'.

INCONSISTENT AND CONTRADICTORY COMMUNICATION

The gap between intended meaning and the listeners' interpretation is not always so easy to bridge as in alternative 2 or so wide as in example 14 above. However that may be, closing the semantic gap is always a helpful contribution to group process wherever misunderstanding is possible. Thus, the worker attempts continually to register ambiguous and unclear contributions and in these ways to check both his own and others' interpretations and their degree of accord with the speaker's intended meaning. In addition to increasing clarity, this technique often draws the group's attention to inconsistencies and contradictions in their communications. Since contradictory communication usually arises around areas of unresolved difficulty and conflict, identifying inconsistency is particularly useful in the working phase of the group.

EXAMPLE 15

The first of a series of foster-parent groups has been briefly described in Heap and Tvedt (1971). All members had maladjusted school-age children in their care. The aims of the groups included increasing understanding of the children's needs, solving problems arising in their daily care and solving problems in both the children's and the foster parents' relationships to the natural parents. All members of the groups were smallholders in a sparsely populated mountain province. Substantial cultural differences existed between them and their foster children's backgrounds, which were predominantly urban.

An episode early in the working phase of one of these groups exemplifies the clarification of inconsistency and underlying conflict as a result of the workers' concern for clear communication.

During the first meetings, the group had worked very well in discussing the ways in which the children probably experienced their situation. They had discussed ways of dealing with some of the children's problems as outsiders in the district and at school. They had also clearly stated judgemental attitudes in relation to the natural parents, which suggested for the workers an important subject for further discussion. In contrast to the natural parents' alleged attitudes, the group members had given unanimous expression of their own uncomplicated and loving relationships with the children, which were agreed to be virtually without difficulties.

Early in the third meeting, where the children's reactions to their unstable life situation were being discussed, one foster father briefly made the cryptic remark that he 'needed to go for a walk in the woods pretty often'. This seemingly meaningless comment was not picked up by the group, who were about to go further with their child-centred discussion. One of the workers intervened, saying 'Could we stop there just a moment? Mr Olsen just said something I didn't really understand. I don't know whether others did? What was that about going in the woods, Mr Olsen?'

The member, thus encouraged to explain, clarified his remark by saying that even though he understood that the children behaved badly because of the upsetting lives they had led, he nevertheless became so furious with them sometimes that he had to go for a long walk to cool off, so as not to hit them in his anger. This clarification introduced the hitherto inadmissible issue of members' own anger, disappointment and frustration with the children, just as the obscurity of Mr Olsen's communication was shown to reflect the members' conflicting feelings towards the children.

These issues proved to be of great importance and were discussed over several subsequent meetings. The workers' contributions thereafter aimed at reducing members' demands upon themselves for perfect parenting, at generalizing and legitimizing their feelings of anger and frustration and at encouraging members to exchange and consider different ways of dealing with the foster children's provocative behaviour.[3]

INDIRECT OR 'LATENT' COMMUNICATION

Such clarification as in example 15 is a relatively simple technique. However, the demands on the worker's diagnostic understanding and group work skill are much greater in relation to indirect or 'latent' communication in the group. Much everyday conversation includes latent communication, in the sense of implied or concealed meaning which supplements or modifies that which is actually said. It seems that our reliance on latent communication increases when anxiety, guilt or conflict are associated with the subject under discussion, since painful and emotionally fraught subjects are those we find most difficult to talk about directly. Thus we 'pack in' this important material and include it as submerged and unspoken content in communication which apparently conveys other meaning or which may even seem to concern quite other issues.

The ten-year old, suddenly interested in her arithmetic and asking her parents what the percentage of, 'for example', divorced parents is in Norway, may really be asking, 'Am I safe?' The working-class wife, nagging that her husband has not noticed the perm she has saved so hard for, may really be saying, 'I'm terrified that you no longer care about me and the kids. Tell us that you do.' In group work and treatment contexts, reflection about such hidden and latently conveyed meaning is a continuing task. It may lead the worker to intervene in many different ways with a view to facilitating the more direct delineation of problems, and to providing opportunities for the demonstration of acceptance and non-judgemental attitudes in relation to guilt-provoking material. These are prerequisites for the solution of psycho-social problems.

Important concepts here are those of 'group-focal conflict' (Whitaker and Lieberman, 1965) and 'common group tension' (Ezriel, 1950). Both terms refer to the existence of central recurring themes in the work of groups and to the possibility of increasing understanding of group members' exchanges by relating what is happening or being said to one or other of these central themes. Both concepts assume that a group whose motivation and commonality is a shared problem will reflect their work with that problem in a sequence of central themes whether directly or indirectly expressed.

I have found this notion to be of real value in practice. It has been particularly helpful in gaining understanding of the many situations in which groups are apparently occupied with peripheral or irrelevant matters. It seems strange that groups of people, assembled to discuss and work on painful personal problems, should so often use their time in talking about quite other things. We might become irritated here. Do they have trouble or don't they? Have they no group discipline at all – no concern for procedure? But models of group leadership from organizational life and politics are irrelevant here. It is inappropriate to criticize the digression and to 'bring them back to the subject' as we would do in an organizational context. The notion of group-focal conflict helps us to see that their behaviour is not necessarily flight or evasion, which the worker should point out in order that they should work 'relevantly'. On the contrary, it is often latent communication, rich in meaning, about aspects of common group problems which are simply too painful or difficult to talk about directly. Thus, far from intervening to halt such apparent digressions, the worker should try to gain insight into what they convey indirectly about the common group problem and on that basis decide how or whether to intervene. There are several alternatives.

Perhaps the worker should invest in indirect supportive help to resolve the feelings which inhibit direct communication. Or he could reflect aloud about alternative ways of understanding what is going on, so that the group may choose whether or not they wish to approach their common concerns more directly. Or he might be sure enough about the latent content to propose an interpretation. Or he could believe the latent content to be so overwhelmingly painful that it would be premature to try to help the group at that stage to articulate the issue more directly.

The keys to understanding this aspect of communication are sensitivity to association, and recognition of defensive behaviour. Much digressive discussion consists of projection or affect displacement, in defence against strong feelings. The relevance of its content to the real problem may again be understood by considering its associative quality.

In my book on group theory (Heap, 1977b) I illustrate understanding of latent communication with two case extracts (pp. 91–4). I shall now take both of these somewhat further to show how different response to the process in different groups grows out of this kind of understanding. In examples 16 and 17 below, the reader should have in mind our model of group diagnosis, to which we could add the component of sensitivity to association. The worker observes apparently irrelevant communication, refers it back to his core referent of diagnostic awareness and tries to understand it as indirect, associative statements about the group's real concerns. Figure 6 illustrates this.

EXAMPLE 16

An adoption agency initiated a program of group work services for future adoptive parents. This included several groups of applicants who had waited six years or more without having yet received a child. The agency had little or no contact with them since accepting their applications. These applicants could now expect to be offered a child within a year. It was believed that they could profitably come together to discuss general questions about child and family development, role and activity changes following adoption and

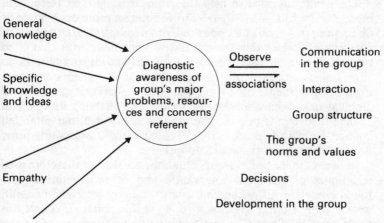

General
knowledge

Specific
knowledge
and ideas

Empathy

Diagnostic
awareness of
group's major
problems, resour-
ces and concerns
referent

Observe
associations

Communication
in the group

Interaction

Group structure

The group's
norms and values

Decisions

Development in the group

Figure 6

their feelings about these, and in some cases perhaps to re-evaluate the decision to adopt made several years before.

One social worker in the program was aware of a certain cautious formality in her group. She quite reasonably attributed this to members' anxieties, both about the group situation and the imminent offer of a child. At the third meeting, however, the worker was delayed a few minutes and arrived to find the group already in heated discussion. The topic was the new Shop Closures Act, an issue apparently far removed from their joint aims and problems. The discussion continued in her presence. It became clear that the main issue was their common anger at legislation which extended freedoms to shopkeepers in deciding when they should open and close. Members' experience was that many grocers, bakers, butchers, etc., were already choosing to close at precisely the time when the public found it most convenient to shop.

The worker noted that the central element in this curious exchange was anger and resentment at the whims of possessors who had the power of both dispensing and withholding valued commodities. She also registered that this was shared by all members, although it was manifestly related to a matter entirely outside the area of the group's common aims and problems. In reflecting on aspects of the common group preoccupations to which this could be associated material, she thought it probable that she was witnessing latent communication of group anger and resentment at the powerful and manipulative adoption agency which withheld children from them. Direct expression of this was threatening, owing to members' fantasies about the possible consequences of criticizing the agency.

The worker decided to help the group to state their resentment more clearly. She hoped thereby to facilitate a more open mode of discussion, to provide an opportunity to demonstrate the quality of acceptance vital in this group, and to contribute to a change in members' role images from that of dependent supplicants to autonomous citizens with the right to make complaints and decisions. She wished also to use the group's indirect reference to ambivalence about adoption as a means of enabling members to change their minds because she thought it possible that some felt committed by their much earlier decision without necessarily being now as strongly motivated to adopt.

In her response to the group situation, the worker therefore used techniques of reflective observation and of interpretation. Her initial comment, after she had listened quietly for some minutes, was: 'I think I'd like to say something at this point. Of course this business of the Shop Closures Act is irritating for many of us and I can well understand that you all get steamed up about it. But I can't help finding it strange that you choose this place and time to talk about it, since what brings you together is something quite different. And then it occurs to me that what you are all saying about the Shop Closures Act could also be said about this agency. We, too, just like the shopkeepers, have something that everybody wants. We, too, take pretty arrogant decisions about when and how children are to be made available and even who is going to get them. And with all that power, we also decide that you can wait for six or seven years before the shop opens, as it were. I think we ought to talk about that.'

The group responded quickly to this, using the opportunity to express long-suppressed resentment. This encouraged the worker to go further later in the meeting and to make a tentative interpretation:

'Earlier, when you were criticizing the Shop Closures Act, one of the things that clearly bothered you was that the shops were open at a more convenient time before. This has got me wondering whether there might also be a parallel there – that earlier, when you decided to apply for adoption you were in a different situation from now, and that perhaps for some of you it may no longer be quite so certain that this is what you want to do.'

While no one responded to this with agreement, members were later well able to express some ambivalence and in doing so referred back to this interpretation. (It is to be noted that one pair, initially very impatient to adopt, in fact used their participation in the group to make a decision some weeks later to withdraw their application.)[4]

The worker may, however, find it inappropriate to disclose to the group what he has observed and may simply add this to his store of understanding of the group. This will be the case where the contract and the aims of the group preclude entering into this kind of discussion or where members appear to be so dependent upon their defences that attempts to facilitate more direct communication would be premature and would probably heighten their anxiety rather than reduce it. It needs to be said from time to time that one does not gratuitously confront the group at all stages and times with the understanding one has acquired or the observations and reflections one has made. Whether or not to do so, and how to do so, are decided by the group's needs, aims, contract and stage of development. It is a diagnostic question. Understanding is as likely to lead the worker to silence as to explication or some other active intervention.

EXAMPLE 17

A group of parents of mentally defective and physically handicapped infants found in an early meeting a topic of apparently intense common concern. This seemed not to be their own problem at all, however. They took up a recent newspaper article about the 'problem' of gypsy families who gathered in the city during winter months. The group united in strong moral condemnation of the gypsies' way of life. Gypsies 'brought unwanted children into the world' and, having done so, 'did not even care for them properly'. It was a 'well known fact' that 'half of the poor mites had to go into homes' where they were 'yet another burden on the ratepayer'.

This topic was apparently irrelevant to the common life situation of the members and to the very painful preoccupations motivating them to membership. This suggested to the social worker that the content of this curious discussion was associated with the chronic problems which the group members had in common. She perceived the discussion as being pregnant with latent communication which (in Whitaker and Liberman's terms) reflected a possible focal conflict between the members' wishes to express some of their resentful and rejecting feelings about their own children and their fears of meeting condemnation from other members or from the worker if they did so. The worker's hypothesis was that the group's behaviour represented projective defence.

She therefore provisionally understood the latent communication as meaning 'We understand and believe it morally right that irresponsible and rejecting parents are condemned. But our own lives have been so changed with the birth of our defective children. Our disappointment and grief are so great that we wish, partly, that we did not have them. Are we therefore "bad"? Perhaps some kind of home exists? But then we should feel even worse – not only guilty about "having brought unwanted children into the world", but also making "the poor mites" a "burden on the ratepayer", and thus being as "irresponsible" as the gypsies. This is how we see ourselves, and no doubt others would regard us similarly if we exposed our feelings.'

Although believing in the viability of this hypothesis, the worker decided not to attempt to encourage more direct communication at this point. This decision was based on several factors: the group was still in a very early stage, where it is on the whole inadvisable to bring up material of this intensity and depth; she felt that more observations were needed to strengthen her hypothesis before she could justify raising such guilt- and taboo-laden ideas. She also believed that the group could be of most use to its members if it were for a time more supportive and encouraging than confrontive, since work with such issues as ambivalence and rejection presupposes security and good relationships in groups.

However, as a future investment in the development of accepting and non-judgemental norms in the group, she decided to enter the discussion about the gypsies and clearly stated her disagreement with the group's condemnation of them. She said she could understand that gypsies – or indeed anyone who lived lives of great stress and insecurity – could find it impossible to be as good parents as they wished, and that giving up their children to others' care was one of several solutions which we should be able to accept. Thus, while overtly discussing the 'irrelevant' subject chosen by the group, she responded to the underlying need for acceptance and understanding of their forbidden feelings of rejection and ambivalence. She hoped that this would later make it easier for them to clarify these painful questions more openly. Later work confirmed that these were in fact central preoccupations in the group and the parents seemed able to discuss institutional provisions, among other subjects, with apparent confidence in the worker's understanding and acceptance.[5]

It is one of the clichés of communication theory that all behaviour is communication. It is self-evident that behaviour always says something about intent, about wishes and about attitudes. Indeed, our behaviour seems often to be a more reliable signal of our meaning than what we say. In fact verbal signals and behaviour sometimes contradict each other. This is a particularly fruitful field for the worker and the group to explore in order to identify unresolved conflicts or postponed decisions.

EXAMPLE 18

In one of the foster parents' groups referred to in example 15 above, the issue of control/limits/punishment was raised late in the third meeting. Discussion was active and unusually open about the members' anger and disappointment with the children. Ideas and practices concerning limiting and punishing were exchanged. At the close of the meeting all expressed satisfaction with the evening's work. At the following meeting two of five pairs failed to attend. The same subject, among others, was discussed. The absent pairs returned for the fifth meeting but two other pairs who had been active during the fourth meeting were absent this time.

The worker thought it appropriate to comment reflectively on the divergence between the members' expressed delight with the group and the sudden spate of absence. Discussion of this incongruity brought to expression the members' feelings of inadequacy and defeat in the face of the foster children's difficult behaviour, as well as what was termed 'shame' at their angry and sometimes punitive behaviour. It was a heightened experience of these feelings that was causing their absence from the group with which they were so 'delighted'.

SILENCE IN THE GROUP

There is one particular aspect of behaviour as communication which I wish to deal with at greater length. This concerns silence and passivity.

Few group phenomena arouse more anxiety among group workers than silence. Only seconds of silence are necessary before we begin to worry: 'What has gone wrong?' 'Will they just go on for ever in silence?' 'What can I do to break it?' And sometimes 'I wish I'd never got into this.' Until some years ago, group workers and therapists were in fact taught to equate silence with hostility. I certainly was and this did little to aid me in dealing productively with it during my first years of practice. But even without this indoctrination there is something about silence which produces for many of us a type of persecutory anxiety. Silence leaves a space which we fill with feelings of fantasy about the group's anger, stubbornness or power. Or we fill it with our conviction of their disillusion with ourselves and the group. 'We are hopeless and they know it' is the essence of this feeling. We panic and quickly regress to the primitive stage of professional functioning which Reynolds (1942) and Killèn-Heap (1979) have termed 'acute consciousness of self'. The survival of one's own image swiftly comes to supersede interest in and identification with the needs of the group.

Spontaneous reactions on the basis of these feelings and fantasies are seldom fruitful. Such reactions may take the form of admonishing the group. Or the worker often hectically increases his own activity in the hope of increasing members' active interest or, simply, with the intention of filling time. Or he may try to seduce the group into 'co-operation' by evading challenging material or even by joking. The worker may also misuse confrontive techniques in an accusing way as an outlet for his counteraggressive impulses. This serves only to increase the gap and is experienced as a futile challenge representing projection of the worker's own feeling of inadequacy.

I think we can do better than this. First, it is probably necessary to have survived some silences. We can get some of that behind us by using role play during training or in our agency teams, but the threat of silence in 'real' groups must also be experienced before the worst of our paranoid fears are proved groundless. Thereafter, when we are less burdened by our own anxiety, we can begin to see that silence is also a form of communication. Certainly it is very easy to misinterpret, but something is being conveyed about the group's experiences and needs when they behave in this way. What this 'something' is varies, of course, widely. The worker's task is to develop the best possible hypotheses about the reasons for the silence and to contribute to the group process on the basis of that tentative understanding with a view to facilitating resumption of clearer and more direct expression. In short we are back to the basic principle of differentiated response to the group process on the basis of differentiated understanding.

I have tried over the the years to identify different kinds of silence and to develop a repertoire of appropriate ways of dealing with them. I shall try to summarize these ideas as briefly as I can. I shall name each kind of silence, propose its probable cause and indicate an appropriate response. Where response is concerned I will in particular emphasize whether or not I believe that the silence as a phenomenon should be taken up with the group or whether it should be dealt with indirectly. I emphasize this point since there is a current tendency to deal with all group silences with confrontation. This seems to be an uncritical and perhaps aggressive generalization of techniques from reality and Gestalt therapies. It reflects a withdrawal from the demands of adapting response to different groups' different needs and a flight into stereotypic and routine 'technique'.

While the following observations are my own, some of the terminology is derived from other authors whose work on silence has helped clarify my understanding. My main acknowledgements here are to Slavson (1966) and to Lewis (1977).

I shall distinguish between six types of silence. These are transitions, reactions to new understanding, reactions to isolation and poor inter-action, passive dependence, passive aggression and use of silence as a therapeutic device. I shall describe these in note form, so as not to give disproportionate emphasis to the subject, hoping that readers who find it helpful will by discussion and practice make their own associa-tions and elaboration.

SILENCE IN TRANSITIONS

Transitions in the life of the group are often marked by periods of silence. Two kinds of situation produce such transitions.

1   Change from Non-Group to Group (Formation)

Probable cause. Commencement of group life demands adjustment to change, requires exploration, involves insecurity and disorientation. Silence represents safety until the rules and expectations are clearer.

Appropriate responses. Silence need not be commented on. Worker actively orients and takes up discussion of aims/expectations/con-tract. He invests in creating non-threatening atmosphere. Stimuli to pleasant or reassuring interaction and to the discovery of common-ality are needed.

2   Change of Subject/Focus/Style of Working

Probable cause. Realignment of thinking, reflection about new contributions takes time. Collective silence results, reinforced by uncertainty about new direction.

Appropriate response. Silence need not be commented on, but any comment should be positive: worker acknowledges achievement, summarizing that which has been completed/achieved/clarified. Worker aids group to the extent necessary in finding an approach to the new task/subject.

SILENCE AS REACTION TO NEW UNDERSTANDING

There are two contrasting versions of this type of silence.

1   Following Insight − Suddenly or Gradually Achieved

Probable causes. Time is needed to adjust to something new and to consider its implications. Sometimes such silence reflects a pleasurable and conscious experience of growth.

Appropriate responses. Silence is either not commented on or is commented on positively. Important that worker avoids premature disruption of such 'good' or 'necessary' silence. Worker helps to articulate/increase consciousness of the new understanding. He may initiate discussion of its implications.

2   Following Shock

Probable causes. Unexpected disclosure in group of attitudes or behaviour which deviate strongly from group norms produces shock state. Acute confusion in relation to member(s) most involved. Silence expresses anxiety, disorientation and often disapprobation. Also constitutes defence.

Appropriate responses. Silence may profitably be commented on with aim of inviting clarification of shock reaction. Some tentative interpretation of silence by worker may be necessary to facilitate discussion. Contribution which 'shocked' may reflect forbidden attitudes or behaviour which are present but denied or suppressed in group. Worker is active in demonstrating acceptance in order to reduce guilt, to legitimize the hitherto forbidden material and to increase reality-orientation. Contribution which shocked may also represent real deviance from group mores. Worker supports deviant as demonstration of acceptance. He then invites consideration of prevailing norms. Attitudes to conformity and to common group problem may be sharply focused here, often with rich potential for development and growth in group. Rejection of a member or other disrupting reactions may, however, also occur here. Sharp dilemma for group worker if the 'shocking' contribution in fact deviates from basic human values, as in disclosure of abuse of children or dependent aged. Acceptance of violent feelings but not of violent behaviour must then be shown.

SILENCE AS REACTION TO ISOLATION
AND POOR INTERACTION

Where members' exchanges are few and relationships have not developed, silence occurs with increasing frequency and duration.

Probable causes. Members' decreasing expectations of response from others reduce motivation to contribute. Resignation, frustration, loss of hope.

Appropriate responses. Silence may well be commented on, perhaps interpreted. Role expectations, aims and contract are taken up again.

Worker invests in strengthening members' self-esteem – they *have* something to give each other. Resumption of earlier aid to search for commonality (see Chapter 4). In groups where contract is formally articulated, worker may extend norm-set to include 'rule' that all contributions receive response – as in 'LTD model' for learning and deciding in groups (see Hill, 1978). Worker should also re-evaluate both group's style of working and its composition, where errors of judgement may have been made.

SILENCE AS PASSIVE DEPENDENCE

Some groups remain dependent upon worker as central person and as authority. Silence arises when worker refrains from active leadership and initiative.

Probable causes. Low levels of social functioning both in and outside the group. Insufficient understanding of or confidence in the idea of the group. Members bear chronic feelings of inferiority, a history of failure and sometimes guilt. The feeling is 'We can't manage without the worker's leadership and expertise'. May also arise in response to unresolved conflict in group. This kind of silence may reflect lower-class traditions of submission to middle/upper-class expertise and dominance.

Appropriate responses. Silence may be commented on. Responses as for foregoing type of silence, with exception of possible formalization of rule about response. Major emphasis is on increasing members' self-esteem. Worker points up strengths and achievements, furthers feelings of solidarity and commonality. Worker encourages and responds positively to all initiative; invests in furthering member–member interaction. Use of activity/action as alternative to 'talk' often productive here. If caused by unresolved conflict, worker must reduce anxiety about being in conflict, and help members find productive ways of tackling and solving conflict.

SILENCE AS PASSIVE AGGRESSION

This is the one that has been generalized into the 'all silence is hostile' spectre.

Probable causes. Members feel manipulated or diminished, which produces hostility towards agency and/or worker. Suspicion concerning agency's motives and worker's role. This kind of silence occurs also where worker is authoritarian, judgemental or offensive. He may also be recipient of displaced aggression because of his availability. Arises also where group is allowed to work unproductively and to protract frustration while worker remains passive.

Appropriate responses. Silence should be commented on. Worker invites collective reflection about meaning of group's silence. If not successful, may propose alternative meanings. If this is not successful, indicate own favoured interpretation. *Must* show willingness to receive criticism of self and agency. Worker conducts self-critical evaluation of own functioning in relation to group needs and considers possibility that agency framework and group's style of formation is repressive or provocative. Vital that worker recognize possible rationality of group's aggressive feelings; it must never be 'assumed' that it is a result of projection.

SILENCE AS A THERAPEUTIC DEVICE

This refers to the intentional staging of silence or to the conscious prolongation of an occurring silence as a device in group work or treatment. This, too, seems to fall into two categories.

1 Creative Use

Probable causes. Worker determines that tension or anxiety is necessary in order to create movement or to raise consciousness of certain phenomena in the group.

Appropriate response. Worker, allowing silence to continue, must be very sure that he has a clear and defensible diagnostic, ethical and contractual basis for this manipulative technique. Aims are clear and he has thought through his possible responses to the group's alternative ways of relieving the tension. (This device is rarely appropriate in treatment and problem-solving contexts and is more frequently encountered in various kinds of groups concerned with sensitivity, growth and 'human potentials training'.)

2 Negative Use

Probable causes. Worker's uncritical application, without differentiation as to need, of a dramatic style. Worker's enjoyment of power. His narcissism.

Appropriate response. Review agency's treatment philosophy. Intensify supervision of or fire worker.

In the foregoing I have sketched some aspects of group work method in the working phase of the group, where the worker's response to communication in the group has been the main theme. This has included response to unclear and ambiguous communication, to latent communication and to behavioural communication with particular reference to silence. This is of course incomplete and needs further exposition and illustration. However I must now move on to describing response to other aspects of group process. Next, structure.

NOTES: CHAPTER 6

1   Men's groups are a recent and important innovation. Experiences and reflections to date are helpfully reviewed by Stein (1983) in a symposium on gender issues in group work.
2   Case literature on group work with families of children with disabling illness includes Bice (1955) on cerebral palsy, Bergofsky et al. (1979) on spina bifida, West et al. (1979) on Williams's elfin facies, and Glass and Hickerson (1976) on kidney disease. On group work with the child patient see Sheridan (1975) on amputation, heart surgery, etc., and Morse (1965) on rheumatoid arthritis.
3   Other reports and discussions of group work with foster parents include Carter (1971), Ball and Bailey (1971), Hilson and Heaton (1971) and Nyman and Nyman (1971). Ludlow and Epstein (1972) and Mayfield and Neil (1983) discuss group work with the foster children themselves, while Lee (1978) describes group work with mentally retarded foster adolescents.
4   Other reports and discussions of group work in adoption services include McWhinnie (1968), Wickström-Stormats (1972), Brown (1971), Sandgrund (1971) and Munk (1975).
5   Mandelbaum (1970) and Murphy et al. (1973) have written excellent papers on this application of group work, while Olshansky (1962) displays profound empathy in a brief paper on 'chronic sorrow' which is vitally useful background material in the planning of such groups.

Chapter 7

THE WORKING PHASE – RESPONDING TO STRUCTURE

DEFINITION

The term 'group structure' seems to be used in a number of different ways, sometimes so widely that it embraces all group life and thereby loses usefulness as a concept. I have found it helpful to limit my use of the term to refer to the patterns of status, role and subgroup formation which characterize the organization of groups. These features of group life are usually highly visible. They are very important for the effectiveness of the group and are often amenable to influence – both reinforcement and change. For these reasons, this aspect of group process is of great interest to group workers and much of our contribution in groups is response to the development of structural phenomena. In this, as in all group method, the starting point is in trying to understand what we see.

UNDERSTANDING AND RESPONDING TO GROUP STRUCTURE

Observation of group structure involves a continual interest in who is doing and deciding what, who is rejected or chooses passivity, who gains influence and takes initiative, and what patterns and criteria for alliances arise. We see these things and we know that they are important in all groups we belong to, whether as private persons or in our professional capacities. Their importance to us as group workers is brought sharply into focus when we remind ourselves that group structure usually develops in a functional manner and thus may reveal to us a great deal about members' needs. I will say a little more about this. (My book on group theory (Heap, 1976) illustrates this aspect of group process more extensively, but does not deal with the worker's intervention.)

The distribution of roles and the apportioning of status is not decided by chance. Each group we belong to has certain aims which may be more or less conscious and articulated, but which clearly reflect both the purposes for which the group was formed and the relationship and tensions existing between the group and its environment – either in the sense of immediate surroundings or of the wider society. In order to meet these collective aims of the group it is necessary that members each contribute according to their ability. The varying abilities and resources of members come to expression in differentiated role behaviours. These are in turn accorded varying status according to the priority which the group's aims confer on different kinds of contribution. Thus, observing the criteria for high or low status – that is to say the degree of initiative and influence accorded members in different roles – we may see a clear expression of the felt needs and the priorities of the group. As group workers, our function is not to judge a particular choice of leader or a particular episode of scapegoating as more or less fortunate or cruel, but to consider what these particular choices reflect about the group's needs and ways of dealing with their problems at each point of time.

The question of time has also some importance here, since we see that the same group confers status according to different criteria at different times. Observation of such changes also brings important material to our attention, reflecting as it does the group's conclusion of a stage of work, or its awareness of new needs or shifts in alliances in important areas of the group's organization.

EXAMPLE 19

A common history of alcohol problems was the central criterion in the composition of a new group of male psychiatric in-patients led jointly by a psychiatric nurse and a social worker. Attendance was mandatory, as was all group treatment at the hospital. Groups had hitherto been composed on the arbitrary basis of admission sequence and this selection by common symptom was a new departure.

During the first meeting, members were passive and demonstratively indifferent, with the exception of Sigurd. After a few minutes of tense silence he openly challenged the workers on the rationale for the group. Why were they being picked on ('on', not 'out') in this way?

The nurse responded with an explanation about the common difficulties of people with alcohol problems, his belief in their ability to increase each other's insight and control, etc. Sigurd was not helped by this and with the silent approval of the others he increasingly expressed anger and suspicion about the workers' 'special attitudes' to alcoholics. The same worker, unsuccessfully, responded to this with repeated rational explanation. Sigurd increased the pressure, with yet more evident support from the others in the group, one of whom leaned over and clapped him on the shoulder.

During this sequence the workers gradually became aware of the status accorded to Sigurd on the basis of his accusatory and suspicious manner. They concluded that this reflected his expressing views common to the group, which others were unable or were too anxious to put into words. The workers saw that group members' ability to accept and use their own rational explanatory response was blocked by the intensity of these feelings. In continuation, the social worker then said: 'I can see that you are angry and suspicious, Sigurd, and I think I am beginning to understand that better. At the same time I have the impression that what you are saying could equally well be said by others here. Isn't that true? Can some of you others come in now and say what you think about these things that are worrying Sigurd? I don't think he's alone in this.

With this response the workers achieved several aims. Their understanding of the group's support of Sigurd helped them to see that members' immediate needs were not for 'explanation' but for the expression of strong feelings. In addition, response which frees individual members from the role of spokesman for the group intensifies interaction between members and increases the number of members who actively contribute. At the same time, such responses prevent the development of the common situation where a spokesman for negative feelings himself becomes viewed negatively at a later stage when the group's needs have changed. Such progression from initial spokesman to scapegoat is in my experience common, and may be prevented in this way.

EXAMPLE 19 (continued)

By the close of the second meeting of this group, the atmosphere had changed, following lively collective ventilation. Members were generally more active and markedly less suspicious and hostile. While Sigurd was not yet ready to abandon his attack upon the system, he no longer received support and stimulation from the group. Two other members were now most prominent and both were accorded high status. One of these, Torgeir, was an expansive and witty man who invested in 'keeping up the atmosphere'. He had a long history of alcohol problems, several periods as an in-patient, and was a 'sophisticated' and experienced member of therapy groups. He was highly defended, in the style of 'drunk and proud' (Ogren *et al.*, 1979). Bernt, who was also highly active by this time, was a younger man with considerable resources, both intellectually and socially. He represented a contrast with Torgeir. He was very serious and troubled – 'terrified', he said, of turning into a 'revolving door' patient, in and out of institutions and clinics the rest of his life. He was sceptical about the use of antabus and similar preparations and believed that to control drinking you 'had to reach deep into yourself ... and to take and hold to some tough decisions'. He said that he believed strongly that they could help each other with this.

Observing the status conferred on Torgeir and Bernt, the workers saw this as reflecting an important ambivalence in the group: on the one hand, the need to deny and defend and thus keep the symptom; on the other hand, to confront themselves with the problem and the great demands which its solution required in order to be free of the symptom. Since it was productive for this ambivalence to come to expression, the workers assumed a less active role around this period. In this way their 'containment' allowed the group process to manifest even at this early point a vital conflict for the members.

GROUP STRUCTURE AND DEFENCES

It is important to note from example 19 that functional development of structure does not always result in creative mobilization of the resources present in the group. It is equally consistent with a functional analysis of structure that defensive and inhibiting behaviour or attitudes are accorded status at times where members feel threatened or guilty. Thus, again, it is not the worker's job simply to 'regret' that an overcompensated and defensive member is accorded influence and the right to initiative. The worker's job is to mobilize his diagnostic understanding of the group's overall problems and in that light to understand that the elevation of defensive members to high status is an expression of common anxiety and defensiveness by the group as a whole. His own contributions should then be directed to alleviating the anxiety, guilt or feelings of inadequacy which give rise to defence and thereafter to aid the group in moving from a 'restrictive' to an 'enabling' solution,[1] from inhibition to freedom.

SCAPEGOATING

One common version of defensive status ascription is worthy of special comment. This concerns scapegoating. We frequently witness group situations where a member is isolated, ridiculed, or in some other manner defined as both deviant and reprehensible. For the observer, it is tempting to fall into one of several oversimplified ways of regarding and responding to this situation. We might simply accept the truth and rationality of the group's disapprobation and thus regard their rejection of the member as valid. Or we might give priority to protection of the isolated member, since he is distressed and being treated harshly. We might attempt to mediate between the parties in the hope of re-establishing cohesion and harmony. In most cases these responses are wasted time.

We frequently see a particular dynamic in scapegoating, which points to a more hopeful way of contributing to the group process. What seems to happen is that some groups develop a set of dysfunctional norms. Attitudes and values arise which are at variance with the group's needs and with impulses, behaviours and concerns which are present though not admitted – perhaps not even conscious. The group's control system, serving conformity to the approved norms, thereby both suppresses important material and introduces or increases guilt about the suppressed concerns. Both of these may be relieved by the defence of collective projection. A member who is vulnerable, or new, or less identified with the group, or who has in fact done or said that which is forbidden, is chosen as scapegoat. By clearly ostracizing him, the group as a whole both relieves the tension of suppressed conflicts and vicariously punishes and asserts their disapprobation of that which they in fact feel but which is forbidden. (I have dealt more thoroughly with the dynamics of scapegoating in earlier publications, notably Heap 1966, 1969 and 1977b).

Our response to these situations might or might not include direct protection of the scapegoat. That is decided both by his own ability to deal with the pain of exclusion and by the extent to which he has colluded in and attracted the group's projection. However that may be, it is consistent with understanding scapegoating as a projection to respond to it as group process, as a collective manifestation of both a problem and a restrictive way of dealing with it. Thus, the most liberating contribution is one which is aimed not at protection, not at mediation, not at judgement of the scapegoat, but at relief of the feelings of guilt, deviance, inadequacy, fear or whatever qualities arouse the need for projection and expiation. The worker attempts therefore to legitimize the suppressed and disturbing feelings. In doing so, he will find the use of generalization most helpful.

This is where we say 'I'm sure that most people in X's kind of situation feel the sort of feelings he is describing, though it is common to disapprove of them', and 'There has surely never been a parent, not even of the most attractive and successful child, who has not frequently wished that they had thrown the baby out with the bathwater', and 'In my work here I have heard countless people say what Y is saying now, and I'd be surprised if he alone in the group felt like that. But I can see that it is difficult and painful to admit it, when popular attitudes appear on the surface to be so different', and so on.

Where that is not successful or acceptable as a means of reducing guilt or anxiety and thus of scapegoating, the worker may go on to a reflective observation of the group process as he sees it and try to increase members' consciousness of the way in which they use each other. As members become increasingly able to permit themselves what they have hitherto suppressed their need for the scapegoat diminishes. Their projections are then gradually withdrawn and the scapegoat may take either his earlier place or some revised role in the group.

This is a complex process to condense into one brief case extract but I hope that the main elements are made clear in the following. This material is abstracted towards the end of the first year from an extensive weekly process record prepared for supervision over two years.

EXAMPLE 20

Background of Group

A small psychiatric hospital serves a geographically extensive area, where main occupations are forestry, deep-sea fishing and small-holding.

The hospital invests some resources in preparation for discharge and aftercare. One feature of this which has now functioned for a year is an open pre-discharge group, led jointly by the social worker and the head nurse (female and male respectively). Patients with more than 6 months' hospitalization must attend the group, while patients with shorter stay may attend and are encouraged to do so. Membership has varied from three to twelve. Average participation during this first year has been four attendances per patient, though this average conceals a wide distribution.

At the period from which this material is extracted the group was in an active phase with from five to nine members each week. With few exceptions, the same patients continued to attend. Thus a process developed which made observation of structure more possible than is usual in open groups. A certain polarization had developed between two patients. These were Mrs Olsen and Petter.

Mrs Olsen

Thirty-five years old. Middle-class mother of three children. Married to dental surgeon, 38 years old. Their marriage was 'without problems' until a few months ago. Mrs Olsen had accepted her role as her successful husband's admirer and handmaiden. She believed that his criticism of her passivity, ordinary appearance and lack of creativity was justified, though at times hurtful. Her decision a year ago to take up dinghy sailing, sculpture and politics was, consciously, intended only to gain her husband's approval.

However, Mrs Olsen quickly evidenced considerable latent

talents, and became daring and expressive in a number of new ways. Mr Olsen showed that he could not cope with the wife who had become as exciting as he thought he wished. He appointed an attractive young girl as receptionist, rented her an apartment and announced to his wife that he would live with them alternately – 'one for excitement, one for the children's sake'.

Mrs Olsen's explosive reaction to this – tears, fury, blows, bitter protest – was countered by summoning the doctor. Sedative injection 'there, there'. After the effects of sedation wore off, Mrs Olsen again took up her protest. Another visit from the doctor. More sedation. She was quickly defined as sick, Mr Olsen and the (male) doctor agreeing that so extreme a reaction was pathological. Pills prescribed, Mr Olsen to ensure that she took them.

After a few weeks, Mrs Olsen ceased to eat, became virtually mute and was hospitalized as depressive. She seemed to accept hospitalization and the sick role as a refuge. The hospital team however, rejected the 'sick' interpretation of her behaviour at the same time as assuring her that she could use the hospital as a refuge while working out her family situation. She was referred to the social worker, with whom she had fairly frequent interviews during the first weeks.

In the following episode, we meet Mrs Olsen after six weeks, now a member of the pre-discharge group. At this point her husband had the children living with him and his girl-friend. Both in letters and during his (few) visits he had pointed out how unsatisfactory a solution this was. Why could not Mrs Olsen and his friend amicably share him? In that way, Mrs Olsen would still be able to keep the children whilst 'many would otherwise doubt her continued suitability as a mother' after her mental illness. Mrs Olsen was now in the course of alienating herself from this hitherto highly idealized husband. At the same time she was very afraid of embarking on life as a single mother. Wonder and reflection about her own maturation and liberation had not yet begun.

Petter

Forty-one years old. Married to the manageress of a fishmonger's shop; two teenage sons at school. Petter was a semi-skilled worker and had been in the timber/pulp industry since he left school. Active in his trade union, and had been committee member until three or four years previously, when his increasing instability reduced his workmates' confidence in him. Not at this point clear whether he was entering some kind of pervasive paranoid development or whether his inappropriate behaviour was a result of his periodic heavy drinking. Petter's family relationships seemed curiously formal. Members maintained a polite distance with neither overt conflict nor any apparent real engagement between Petter and the others.

Petter had an excellent work record before the decline in the paper industry. As former deputy chairman of his union branch he had dealt competently with many conflicts and negotiations. However, he seemed to have been without interests outside work and union activities and he was probably already severely threatened by the first closures five or six years ago. His aggressive public protests brought him into conflict with employing bodies in the district. Some of his workmates turned from him at this point, apparently through anxiety about being identified with him. But, coincidentally with this, his own anxiety-derived militance was further stimulated by a new extremist faction in the union. Petter became increasingly isolated and disoriented.

With increasing anxiety he became excitable and behaved in an inappropriate way, and his drinking increased seriously. When drunk he threatened employers and foremen, proclaimed bloody revolution on the street corners, denounced employers' radar surveillance and their spies in the union. His employer suggested to Petter that he take sick leave. Petter misinterpreted this and attacked him violently. It was this episode which led to Petter's entering hospital.

We meet Petter after three months as an in-patient. He had had a good deal of psycho-pharmaceutic treatment during the first weeks. Subsequently he took part in group therapy, occupational therapy and the daily decision-taking on the ward which derived from the prevailing 'therapeutic milieu' philosophy. In these activities he manifested himself strongly, though with no bizarre behaviour. He said that he 'was himself again' and was looking forward to going out 'with this lot all behind him'. He had very little contact with his family during his stay in hospital. His wife had said that she was anxious about his discharge and had become afraid of him. He did not believe this and laughed it off.

Current situation

The past two meetings had been markedly influenced by Petter's contributions. It had often seemed that he had engaged himself actively in others' issues, but had then moved by association from these to his own concerns, on which the group had then focused. He was articulate about the inherent inequalities and dangers of capitalism and described himself and all fellow patients as impotent victims of the system — 'When we have abolished capital's dominance over the means of production and distribution we will be able to close both psychiatric hospitals and prisons.' But at the same time he expressed confidence in his future and was quite sure that everything would go well for him both at home and at work. He strongly advised the group to regard their illness and hospital stay as a closed chapter in their lives and to avoid thinking and wondering about it. Group members listened to him, agreed with him and encouraged him to talk, even though some expressed reservations about his political views.

Mrs Olsen had other opinions, much less popular. She had become increasingly able to express her views and raise issues. She was occupied with the incredible number of choices which we make during our lives. She had a 'picture of her past' as a long succession of wrong choices culminating in her hospitalization. She was burdened by the recognition that we are all 'always alone with irrevocable choices' – 'life consists of choices'. She had recently decided to postpone her discharge for another two weeks.

The opposed poles of projection and privatization confused the group, as did the increasing tendency to sharp exchanges between Petter and Mrs Olsen. Increasingly, members allied themselves with Petter, who thus gained influence and became correspondingly rejecting of Mrs Olsen and increasingly hostile to her.

The workers understood this as a scapegoating episode, in our sense that a member was being rejected for demonstrating attitudes common to the group but denied by them because of anxiety. The workers first tried to deal with this by generalization, remarking how uncomfortably near the truth they found Mrs Olsen's picture of life: 'It is surely a common experience?' The group was not helped by this. The workers then offered further support by showing their understanding of the anxiety which is raised when one allows oneself to see the extent of independent choice and coping which society demands. At this point, projections were about to be withdrawn from Mrs Olsen, two members being able to say that they too were scared of being unable to cope. They quickly submitted, however, when Petter and a follower again urged them to 'make as little of it all as possible'.

The group got stuck at this point. The workers again intervened and found it most hopeful, generalization and anxiety-relief having failed, to invite consideration of what was happening in the group. They pointed out that valuable things were being contributed which the group was unable to use, that two active members had become antagonists and that members had dealt with this by taking sides, and that they had chosen a position which relieved them from looking at the tough situation with which they were all faced.

The confrontive quality of this intervention seemed to provoke thought, but the group maintained silence. The workers then suggested that while both Petter and Mrs Olsen were saying some very useful things, perhaps both of them were also giving extreme versions of their views, as so often happens in conflict. What about looking at the strengths and weaknesses of the respective arguments, instead of siding with one against the other? After some hesitation, and with reduced leadership from the workers, the group were able to say how much they were encouraged by Petter's optimism and drive, while not really agreeing with him that problems go away by pretending that they have not existed; similarly, they could see that Mrs Olsen was of course right about all the choices and challenges but had been provoked and made anxious by her insistence that we are 'absolutely alone' with our choices.

By withdrawing projection from Mrs Olsen, the group established a structure which facilitated a more productive and realistic way of helping one another clarify common problems. At the same time, the two members most involved in the episode were given a new opportunity to modify and extend their perception of their own situations.

The workers' understanding of the defensive development of structure during this episode was also a useful indicator to them both of the extent of members' ambivalence about discharge and of specific tasks of clarification and decision which the group could be invited to work on.

DYSFUNCTIONAL STRUCTURE

It would, however, be naive to suppose that structural aspects of group life always logically and tidily express the group's priorities and needs in the way so far described. We have all had life experiences marked by quite other tendencies, and these occur also in groups in the social and health fields.

I am thinking here particularly of two related aspects of status and role. Certain factors often bring into positions of influence members who in fact are not well qualified for it. Similar forces prevent other members from making useful contributions when in fact they are potentially well able to do so.

This arises particularly in connection with the phenomenon of ascribed or transferred status, sometimes called the 'halo effect'. Members may enter the group with expectations of high status, being accustomed to this in other contexts. They may, for example, in speech or dress clearly demonstrate membership of a higher social class. They may belong to high-status professions or enjoy and reflect other kinds of eminence. There is then a strong tendency for less privileged group members to accord them high status whether or not their views, experiences and proposed solutions are in fact purposive and relevant in the group. They may of course be so, but this is only by chance. It is equally likely that their contributions reduce the effectiveness of the group's work, yet they are nevertheless deferred to and accorded influence. I think of this situation as dysfunctional structure and believe it to occur commonly.

Conversely, many members are placed in or enter recessive positions who have in fact useful contributions to make. These members may be viewed by others and may also view themselves with little esteem, although the explanation for this lies in quite other areas than their potential ability to contribute creatively to the group. Again, this might be a question of social class, appearance or speech where these outward symbols of 'value' automatically relegate the bearers to low status, however rich in ideas and motivation they may be. Or their passivity may result from painful and anxious contact with their problem. This is a quality which the group in fact needs, but many groups will not initially recognize its value and will not actively encourage the passive members' engagement. Such a member then quickly becomes defined as a low-status non-contributor and both the group as whole and he loses by this.

This is an aspect of the group process which usually calls for intervention from the worker. Since ascribed status has roots in both cultural norms for influence and in the less rational areas of members' perceptions of themselves, the group structure tends to crystallize around these criteria, unproductive though they may be. The worker's interventions may therefore have to be carried out over a period of time before producing effect.

The interventions are not necessarily complicated, however. It is mainly a question of seeing the need for them and having the confidence to carry them through. The latter requirement is not to be lightly dismissed, since the worker's role here runs counter to the norms and structure of the group. I believe that I have seen a number of colleagues and students stand aside from this whole issue in order to avoid possible conflict with group members or from anxiety about losing the facile acceptance which comes from sharing the group's prevailing views.

The kind of interventions I am thinking of contribute to a less hierarchical structure, reducing dominance at one end of the status spectrum and enhancing prestige at the other. It is by no means always necessary actively to oppose the annexation of leadership by members with high ascribed status. My experience points to the contrary conclusion, that the most decisive factor in avoiding this kind of dominance is that the worker himself must consciously refrain from actively stimulating it. The worker, too, picks up such members' signals about their anticipated status and may play almost as readily into it as does the group. When the worker is anxious about whether the group will function and worried about passivity and silence he is particularly prone to stimulate such members in order to ensure a certain level of activity. Where such members nevertheless do enter dominant positions and the worker needs to intervene, it is important that he does so as early as possible. There are two reasons for this. One is that structure in a group very rapidly crystallizes and it becomes increasingly difficult with time to effect change in status and role distribution. The second reason for intervening early in this kind of development again has to do with the worker. He must not wait until he is irritated or worried about the uneven activity in the group, since it is necessary that he intervene without hostility and with respect when he points out to a member that he is filling a disproportionate amount of the group's time and content. There are innumerable ways this may be said, but is is always important in doing so to include some acknowledgement of the impetus which the member has given the group and of the relevance of the issues he or she has introduced.

Just as important as containing such dominant members is the function of stimulating recessive members who have defined themselves as 'one down'. Thus, the worker will use every possible opportunity of showing his interest in the low-status member's hesitant contributions and of encouraging the others to work on them. This is a conscious and constructive use of his own high formal status in the group, since respect tends to be accorded to the views for which he evidences particular regard. This, in turn, enhances the status of the hitherto marginal member and contributes to a more functional structure. If the low-status members have become so passive that they give him no opportunity for showing recognition in this way, he may need more actively to encourage them to contribute. It is desirable that this should be based on a clearly demonstrated belief in the potential worth and relevance of the member's contribution, rather than on cajoling or on moralization about inactivity. The youth club member should not hear that he is 'not pulling his weight' but that 'this is the kind of thing I know you're good at — come and give us a hand'. The self-effacing, rejected lower-class mother in a parents' group is not helped by hearing 'It's a long time since we heard from you, Mrs Anderson'. But she might be helped and her status will very probably be enhanced by the worker saying, 'I remember that you had some experiences/ideas/suggestions about this that you brought in at our first meeting, Mrs Anderson. I think we are more ready to talk about that now than we were then.' This function has its roots in the tuning-in process, since the worker's reflections in the planning stage should on the whole make him aware of the various possibilities for ascribed status.

WORK WITH SUBGROUPING

Not only role and status distribution may be understood in this way, but also the development of subgroups. Also this may be understood in ways which increase our chances of taking a constructive role in the group process.

In any group of more than four or five members, the network of relationships − often called the 'informal structure' − will reflect varying degrees of liking and indifference, of attraction and rejection between the members. This results in the formation of clusters of members having closer relationships with each other than with the group as a whole. These are subgroups, an inevitable and natural feature of group life. Earlier approaches tended to overproblematize subgroups, as if they were in some way malign and both could and should be avoided or discouraged. But members will always like some fellow members more than others and the commonality of ideas and attitudes which this reflects often gives diversity and enrichment to the group.

Subgrouping first becomes a problem when members' identification with their subgroup is so intense that it prevents engagement in the group as a whole or when it results in the kind of commitment which produces inflexibility and resistance to change. Since many clients encountered in the health services and social work are already burdened with histories of rejection, deviance and unacceptability, such situations of rivalry or exclusion from subgroups would provide regrettable additional stress − which is hardly the intention of group work. Thus the group worker, while viewing subgroups as inevitable and potentially rewarding in their diversity, nevertheless invests in stimulating interaction across the subgroup boundaries and tries to keep alive the identity and cohesion of the group as a whole. To this end he continues to 'link ' members in different subgroups, drawing attention to similarities of concern and experience. He uses reflective observation and sometimes interpretation which focuses attention and work on the common group problem. He encourages and sometimes actively suggests appropriate activities which necessitate concerted action by the group or which presuppose use of resources drawn from different subgroups. (This latter point is illustrated in examples 28 and 31a.)

A closer look at the causes of subgrouping is worthwhile. It is not only differences in interests and abilities or spontaneous variations in mutual attraction or rejection which produce this aspect of structure.

Subgrouping also arises because clusters of members have different motivations for joining the group and thus varying expectations of its aims and ways of working. In such cases it is necessary that the group state this problem or be helped by the worker to do so. This should then lead to a collective review and renegotiation of the whole area of common aims and needs. Possible results of this include both major change in group content and, more rarely, abandoning or dividing the group. Where formed groups are concerned, this situation arises as a consequence of errors of composition or of insufficient investment in the preparatory phase of the group. Natural groups or other groups already in existence at the time of the worker's entry of course manifest this situation more frequently.

CONFLICT BETWEEN SUBGROUPS

In treatment groups a particular type of subgrouping seems often to occur. One frequently sees subgroups form because of differences in their approach to problem-solving or problem avoidance. One subgroup may be open to the expression of concern and feeling; another evades painful issues by projecting blame on to others outside the group; another denies or minimizes the problem; yet another is resigned and attempts to establish passive dependence upon the worker. Where this kind of division occurs, tension arises between the subgroups.

They may become committed to their positions and are therefore both provoked and anxious on finding that members of their group are equally committed to other – perhaps opposed – positions. What could have been fruitful diversity becomes conflict.

Where group members do not find their own rational way out of this, the worker must help them. There are several elements in such help. A calm and reflective manner in the face of conflict is important, as is a non-judgemental attitude to whatever evasive or irrational traits characterize the subgroups. This has value in reducing members' fears and fantasies about the destructive effects of conflict. The worker's intervention here also has importance seen in the context of his role as model. Throughout the whole contact with the group, the worker fulfils this role. Whether or not we wish it, and however imperfect we in fact may be, we inevitably represent models of 'a good parent', 'an adult', 'an efficient problem-solver', and so on. While we do not wish to encourage imitation, it is often helpful to remind ourselves that 'how' we are, the way we behave towards members, and the attitudes which we show are influences whose importance often exceeds that of the most carefully chosen intervention. This is also the case when helping a group in conflict. The worker consciously uses this role when emphasizing his belief that conflict may at times be productive. As well as helping the group to deal better with the current conflict, this may also contribute to valuable attitudinal change. Further, in helping the group to examine its conflict, he is, as model, reinforcing the important general truth that the recognition of problems is a prerequisite for their solution.

The worker's actual intervention in these situations of subgroup conflict may or may not be presaged by clearly calling attention to the conflict itself, though in most cases it provides a natural point of entry. His main contribution, however initiated, is to invite discussion leading to recognition of the common concerns and fears which generate each subgroup's different norms. His aim is to help members rediscover their commonality and gain a greater measure of acceptance of the inevitability of different reactions. This provides a basis for proceeding to an examination of what constitutes constructive or inhibiting reactions ('enabling' or 'restrictive solutions' in Whitaker and Lieberman's terms).

EXAMPLE 21

A group of four engaged couples met with a pastoral counsellor for a series of discussions called 'Marriage: growth and change'. They were on the whole rather conventional middle-class couples, all in their early twenties. The first two meetings were harmonious, much of the content involving declarations of similarity with regard to background, religion and views of marriage.

Change occurred with the third meeting. One couple had brought with them a copy of Gibran's 'The Prophet' and thought how beautiful were his lines on marriage:

> 'The pillars of the temple stand apart,
> And the oak-tree and the cypress grow not
> in each other's shade ...'.

Another couple were also immediately delighted with the image, while a third were not at all happy about it. They thought it 'all very well, but it really advocates reservation and avoids commitment to each other'. The fourth supported this view. The group divided over this issue into two subgroups each of two couples. They became increasingly heated, increasingly supportive of others in their subgroups and increasingly inclined to disagree with the opposing subgroup's members on other issues also.

This tendency to generalize disagreement to other questions caused a crystallization of the subgroups. Despite some concern about this, the worker decided not to attempt to repair this disharmony. He observed that the adversary attitudes between the subgroups in fact produced highly relevant work. It brought to the surface relevant disagreement and competing values and priorities. It clearly reflected in the group situation itself the dilemma of being 'together, yet apart' − the fundamental issue in marriage and the determinant of how far marriage may offer involvement and intimacy while enabling each partner to grow and change.

The worker was relatively inactive during the third meeting and the early part of the fourth, recognizing and respecting the productiveness of the group process (practising 'containment', Phillips would say). However, he involved himself more actively in this issue when during the fourth meeting members wished him to arbitrate between the subgroups. What was 'right', 'wrong', 'best', where 'commitment versus freedom' was concerned? He replied by saying that he had been rather quiet because he thought they had had very useful discussion around their disagreement. But he was glad, he said, to be pressed on this and wished to join in. Was it not the point, he asked, that there is no right and wrong? That the dilemma is never finally soluble between becoming 'a part of each other' and 'remaining yourself'? That they were each asserting one of these continually present tendencies as being the only valid one, while an open relationship in marriage required recognition of the right to be oneself as well as − not instead of − being committed to the other's interest? Finally, he expressed the opinion that it was not arguments or conflicts around this issue which most threatened marriage, but rather the pretence that the issue did not exist: 'Not difference, but inability to tolerate it, is the problem.' This led further into the question of open communication in marriage. The group worked productively with this, the division into subgroups disappearing. They found it exciting and useful. Later in the series, one member referred back to this earlier period marked by subgrouping.

He remarked that the group had functioned like a bad marriage − two factions, each of which knew what was right and was unable to concede without argument and anger that the other had a different but equally legitimate view.

NOTES: CHAPTER 7

1 These terms are also derived from Whitaker and Lieberman's (1965) model of 'psychotherapy through the group process' referred to earlier. They perceive the group as continually focusing on sequential 'focal conflicts' (common problems) and solving these by 'restrictive' or 'enabling solutions'. Enabling solutions make it possible for the group to focus on increasingly relevant material. The worker's role in the group includes indication of or interpretation of restrictive choices, support and generalization to reduce guilt, or other techniques which facilitate enabling solutions.

Chapter 8

———— • ————

THE WORKING PHASE – RESPONDING TO GROUP CULTURE

WHAT ARE NORMS?

All groups develop norms. Many volumes have been written describing the nature of norms and the ways in which norms are established, maintained and modified during the life of groups. This is often referred to as the 'group culture'. I shall add little new here to that fund of knowledge. I shall, rather, draw from it and show how group work method involves understanding and working with this aspect of the group process.

For our purpose we may content ourselves with a simple definition of norms as being 'the attitudes, values and forms of behaviour which are approved and accepted in the group'. From this definition alone, it is clear that the norms developed by a group are decisive for its chances of reaching its objectives. Much interaction between members is therefore aimed at supporting and rewarding conformity with group norms or criticizing and controlling deviance. This is true not only in football teams and administrative committees, where norms are reflected in rules and clearly articulated expectations of procedure. It is also true in treatment groups, problem-solving groups and growth-oriented groups in the social work and health fields where norms are usually more nebulous and implicit. Here also, members invest – sometimes most emphatically – in reinforcing norms although they may never have been actually stated, because they nevertheless represent behaviour and attitudes necessary for the attainment of the group's goals.

And here we meet a recurrent group work problem, for the aims which are perceived vary during the life of many groups and are sometimes seen to run counter to their long-term objectives. Thus, the control system of the group is engaged in reinforcing norms which are either productive or counterproductive depending upon when, under what circumstances, and under which members' influence they have become established.

In a group of meths drinkers living in packing cases by the Oslo docks no member is welcome during a period when he is trying to remain dry. He is therefore pressed to conform to the group's self-destructive norms. The same behaviour, however, would place him in a central and influential role in another group with other norms where others too were struggling to achieve control. Similarly, in group work in social and health settings, a group which has developed purposive norms will support and encourage a member who is able to confront his problems, to be open and to contribute to the group's work. The same behaviour on his part would bring him into conflict with the norms of a group which had developed irrelevant or defensive norms, which may well also happen even in groups which have been formed to attack common problems.

It is not in itself sinister that norms may develop which are counter-productive or which focus on maintaining more peripheral aspects of group life. There are a number of reasons why this occurs.

SOCIO-EMOTIONAL VERSUS TASK-ORIENTED BEHAVIOUR

One explanation is that different needs are perceived and different aims given priority at different stages of group life. At some periods the stresses of the group situation itself are so demanding that priority has to be given to coping with these. Where this occurs, behaviour directed to these problems rather than to the long-term tasks of the group is normatively approved.

The socio-emotional and the task-oriented interaction which occur at times compete for priority, but both are essential components of group process. They are interdependent, as has been stressed in so much literature (in particular, see Bales 1970, Goffman 1961, and Heap 1977b). The task cannot be performed if the atmosphere is not 'good enough'. If the socio-emotional atmosphere is not at least minimally satisfying who wants to perform that task in that lousy group anyway?

For example, during the first meetings – which we will later call the 'formative stage' – members might be so burdened with the strangeness and tensions of the group situation that resolving these in fact temporarily overshadows the needs which brought them to the group. Norms of easy social superficiality are then established, rather than of work and problem-confrontation. Or a group who are compelled into attendance or who have accumulated a store of resentment, suspicion and helplessness in relation to organized welfare and authority will early establish norms of aggressive or subversive behaviour. These may be greatly at variance with the norms envisaged by the worker as being relevant and purposive. Also, at later stages, relationships in the group may become so complicated that norms develop which are well suited to relieving the socio-emotional situation in the group but which appear to have little relevance for its goal-striving.

It is, however, vital that the worker recognize that such norms are in fact functional. They deal with real and immediate needs. The task of the worker here is not to cajole the group into some more 'sensible' or 'agreed' way of working. His task, in accordance with the diagnostic principles discussed earlier, is to understand this behaviour as being purposive. It indicates – sometimes with highly focused specificity – areas with which help is needed before the group can work more directly on their long-term tasks. (Short-term aims as a recurring theme of the tuning-in process and of first meetings, discussed in chapters 3 and 4, are again relevant here.)

EXAMPLE 22

The social worker leading a newly formed discussion group of long-term prison inmates registered feelings of suspicion and resentment which did not come to expression. Members said almost nothing to one another, and very little more to the worker. There was, however, a strong sense that co-operation was to be frowned upon, and the rare members who made hesitant attempts to introduce something positive either were ignored or met with offensive and rejecting gestures. A norm of silent collective non-co-operation was becoming well enough recognized to be reinforced by control.

One member, Ron, broke through this barrier of passive hostility during the third meeting with an explosion of accumulated accusation, suspicion and scorn. The others reacted to this with a tense and watchful silence, some looking from Ron to the worker and nodding slightly, while others looked entirely away from the group. The social worker said, first to Ron. 'I'm glad someone finally put that little lot into words. You know, I don't think you're alone in being suspicious of me and fed up with this place. I can't believe other than that everybody in this room resents the situation that brings us – in fact, forces us – together.' Then, to the group as a whole, he said: 'I have a strong feeling that Ron is really talking on behalf of the group. I don't think it's just his own opinion he gave us. Isn't it the whole group's?[1]

In the above example, the worker's recognition of the relevance to immediate problems of emerging norms which were apparently at variance with the intended purposes of the group would, with luck, have several effects. It would strengthen group bond since it emphasized members' common feelings, encouraged solidarity around them and avoided subsequent scapegoating of the aggressive 'spokesman' for group norms. It would increase the likelihood of members' recognizing the worker's ability to accept and respect them and his attempt to understand them. It would also aid the group in the further development of norms characterized by open expression of opinions and feelings and thus by use of the group for relevant work on common problems. Clearly, then, the emergence of these apparently inappropriate norms in fact offers therapeutic advantage, since it may facilitate constructive work with situational problems, underlying feelings and the worker's relationship with the group. Their emergence is only a real problem if they become crystallized and thereby determine also the long-term behaviour and attitudes of the group. Interventions by the worker as seen in example 21 also contribute to preventing such a development.

DEFENSIVE NORMS

Diagnostic observation of the development of apparently unhelpful norms does not, however, always reveal this kind of purposive work towards immediate situational aims. It might also reflect group members' needs to defend themselves against the pain and threat so often involved in working towards change. Optimal recognition of needs or problems is a norm which in general should characterize the kind of groups we are discussing here. But that isn't always easy.

Charlie Brown's all too perceptive friend Lucy once said, 'No problem is so big that it can't be run away from!' Group workers in social and health services have frequent confirmation of this. Many burdensome and acute problems are avoided by groups even though the purpose of membership is to work on those very problems. There are many reasons for this – anxiety about losing an adjustment which 'works', guilt about one's own role in a family or community problem, the fear of change in lifestyle, the possible loss of some secondary gain, and the sheer pain of beginning to talk about certain subjects. But problems cannot be solved or relieved without their being recognized, and it is essential that members develop group norms which enable as much problem-confrontation as they are capable of. The group worker has a role to play in helping to establish this norm. In doing so, however, he does not relentlessly pursue a confrontive 'policy', as may be the case in certain 'human-potentials' or sensitivity-training groups. He is continually sensitive to the degree of members' dependence upon defences, and – where problem avoidance is shown by the group – will not go faster in initiating the norm of problem-confrontation than he can achieve by supportive methods.

THE WORKER AS MODEL

The worker's most useful tool here is, again, the conscious use of his role as model. In establishing norms, group members often strive for ways of tackling the complex and burdensome situations which bring them to the group. Where anxiety is high, defensive norms may be established even in a well motivated group because alternative modes of group behaviour are unfamiliar and because they lack models from everyday life for more direct and problem-confrontive approaches.

From the beginning of the group's life the worker may contribute to a more direct approach to problems simply by ensuring that he himself represents a model of one who sees advantage in recognizing the problems which exist.[2] No problems may be solved until they are recognized and the worker should use opportunities as they arise for demonstrating this. Often the context of the group in itself offers simple practical problems which may be used in this way. The meeting room, seating arrangements, the question of 'coffee or not' and timing of meetings are among common issues which provide an opportunity for saying: 'Well, there is clearly a problem here: let's discuss it and find out what we are going to do.' The issues are simple and unthreatening, and not least for that reason provide a situation where the worker's modelling function is both acceptable and productive in terms of influencing norms.

There is another common issue, though more complicated, threatening and richer in potential, which may be used in this way. I am thinking of the frequency with which the group worker has a double role. In addition to leading the group, the worker often exercises power over members in some other context so that the group has difficulties in developing an open, unambivalent and trusting relationship with him. He might, for example, also be the leader of a residential agency in which the group takes place. Or he might have influence over money payments or release dates, so that group members' dependence upon him in such other contexts complicates their relationship to him as a group worker. So, too, does the formal authority lying behind the worker's leadership of non-voluntary groups.

Compulsory membership is a feature of group work practice which is met with particular frequency in European practice, according to Brown *et al.* (1982). In all such situations, complicated though they undoubtedly are, the worker is provided with a means of influencing norms in productive ways by utilizing his 'model' role. He must call attention to the problem of authority and suggest directly and undramatically that it should be recognized and discussed in order to solve it. The following example shows two ways of dealing with such a situation. These two episodes were frequently recounted in the early days of group psychotherapy. (I cannot guarantee that the events described actually happened – but it is a good story and has an important point!)

EXAMPLE 23

Students of group psychotherapy at a military hospital where war casualties were treated observed two therapy groups from their first meetings onwards. Uniforms were worn in the group, and also by the group leaders, who were psychiatrists and therefore commissioned officers.

At the beginning of the first group the leader said, 'Look here, chaps. You're patients here, not soldiers. And I'm a doctor, not an officer, when I'm together with you. So let's ignore all this up here' – and he touched his shoulder insignia – the glorious scrambled egg of a full colonel.

At the beginning of the second group, its leader – also a medical colonel – referred in a different way to his crown and stars. He said, 'I think we ought to talk about these before we try to do anything else. They're a problem, aren't they?'

Both of these openings by the group leaders were likely, through modelling, to influence the norms which would evolve in the group. Not having recognized this, the psychiatrist in the first group was inviting the development of defensive norms, strongly reinforcing from the outset the tendency both to avoid difficult problems rather than to confront them and to establish patterns of communication which avoided recognition of both feelings and conflict. The second group leader, however, would conduce to norms which made it possible to confront problems with less anxiety, to recognize and therefore resolve conflict, to perceive the relevance of feelings and to respond to them. The quality of the relationships between the workers and their groups which were commenced here could also be expected to differ widely along such important parameters as understanding, openness, acceptance and confidence – unless of course the first leader consciously invested in repairing the unfortunate start he had made.

Similarly, the worker's influence on defensive norms was also seen in Examples 16 (adoptive parents) and 22 (prison inmates), where invitation to identify with the workers' calm recognition of problems was a feature of both workers' contributions to the group process. It is to be emphasized that the function of this kind of intervention is not the solving of problems, but their identification and recognition and the development of norms which facilitate this.

The influence of modelling on norms, which is of real value in reducing defences against situational anxiety, seems to be less where defences have their roots in guilt and feelings of inadequacy. Where this appears to be the case, more hopeful means of developing norms of problem-confrontation and open communication are generalization and group support through reassurance and recognition. Examples of generalization in such contexts may be found in example 13 (parents of children in care) and example 15 (foster parents). Both of these cases were cited earlier primarily to illustrate aspects of communication and it is an indication of the interdependence of norms and communication styles that they may also be studied in the present context. A brief further illustration is useful here.

EXAMPLE 24

Few groups are more burdened with guilt and inadequacy than those whose members are abusing parents. In Kruger *et al.* (1979) there is a vivid example of how the workers' generalizations and their openness – demonstrated not least through their own active role play – enabled group members to give up their self-abnegatory behaviour and become more assertive in constructive ways. For example, when the workers urged the importance of consistency in child-rearing, the group were able to challenge the workers with their own inconsistency since 'how can parents develop consistent upbringing practices when the children are removed from their homes?'

Group support through recognition and reassurance is a potent factor in group work and has many times both impressed and moved me. Of many examples which could be given, Mandelbaum (1970) is most eloquent in his description of group process as a source of help to parents of retarded children.

'Feelings toward the retarded children gradually emerge. Some parents see the children as grotesque objects to be hidden from public view and from friends and relatives. As such feelings come to light, they become attached to the parents' self-image. The parents feel inwardly grotesque and are afraid of being regarded as genetically imperfect, contaminated, and inextricably identified with the damaged child ...

'As the parents describe the cruelty of others toward them in their misfortune, many reveal their own harsh and punitive views of themselves. These are gradually modified by the gentle, kind, perceptive judgments offered by other members of the group ...

'Eventually, the group enters a period of alternating grief and solace: themes of loss and death alternate with themes of how gentle and lovable retarded children are and the solace they offer the family. The parents' fears that the children have other congenital defects add to the difficulty of caring for them and fill their parents' days and nights with apprehension.

'The parents praise each other's children, and during the expression of such positive feelings they slowly venture to speak of their anger and fright at the persistent intrusion of intense death wishes. Many say in effect, "Having a retarded child is like having a death in the family, only worse; at least you can get over a death, but this is never behind you. You have to learn to live with this − for the rest of your life." '

The value of norms facilitating expression of feelings is well seen in this quotation. Gain is not only in the relief of releasing feelings, though that in itself may be truly helpful. Identifying and expressing feelings also increases the ability of group members to proceed further. Mandelbaum saw here that the relaxation of defences against guilt enabled generosity and warmth to unfold in the group, enabled members to face both the probability of and their ambivalent wish for the child's early death, enabled them to give renewed expression for positive feelings for their children and for praise for each other − in short, enabled members to set about the task of 'learning how to live with it'.

It is a general truth that clarity of feelings is a prerequisite for commitment to decision and change. Vital guidelines for evaluating the relevance of norms in groups are therefore the extent to which they reflect acceptance of feelings and facilitate work on the realities of the problem which members bring to the group.

Where norms relevant to the aims of the group are emerging or have become established, the worker invests some of his contributions in increasing consciousness of them and in reinforcing them. Conversely, where irrelevant, restrictive norms have become established or are emerging, the worker accepts some responsibility for helping the group find their way to more productive criteria for mutual approval and identification.

There are, however, important reservations here. Personal growth is never served by unquestioning subjection to group control. Integrated and productive change cannot be achieved by members in groups where normative pressure merely replaces other tyrannies and repressions. The important notion of individualization in the group emphasizes that each member must take his or her solution from the group, adapted to his own needs, resources and lifestyle, rather than

attempting to achieve some common collective 'solution', undifferen-
tiated as to individual needs and valid for all. Thus, the group norms,
while relevant, must also be flexible. Indeed, the solution of problems
in the group and the growth of its individual members presuppose the
possibility for comparisons, for considering alternatives, and for
reporting and reflecting on different experiences. Where group control
is too energetically and restrictively applied, these important
possibilities are crushed in the demand for sameness and solidarity.
The worker therefore tries to help the group maintain flexibility within
a range of norms in which the widest possible logical interpretation of
relevance is permitted.

CONFLICT

This, however, reintroduces the question of conflict in the group,
since the flexibility of norms and the recognition of individual
differences introduce the possibility of conflict. (This has already been
touched upon in connection with tension between subgroups.) The
point is not to avoid conflicts. The point is to help the group grasp the
possibilities for growth and clarification which intragroup conflict
often offers, while attempting to prevent it from reaching a degree of
affect which seriously threatens the life of the group.[3]

Norms must exist in relation to conflict which accept its existence
in group life as both natural and inevitable. Sometimes it is appropriate for the worker as early as during the offer of service or at
formation to prepare members for the probability that conflict will be
encountered. Whether or not this is so, it is desirable when conflict
arises to be able to talk about it and to try and see what it represents.
One may be more direct about this in a treatment-oriented group than
in groups whose main aims are of providing social contact for isolated
or anxious clients, but, however that may be, the guiding principle is
to face conflict in some way rather than ignore it or hope that it will
go away. The conflict may be seen to concern rational difference of
opinion and aims – or misunderstandings about these – which may be
resolved by a clarification of the issues, by compromise, or by
integrated solution. Or conflict may simply be found to be acceptable
difference which is not amenable to change or mediation. Concerning
this, there is no reason to suppose that groups may achieve harmony
and understanding on every possible issue and there is important
learning for life outside the group as well as in it in understanding and
accepting this. Conflict may, however, also arise from irrationality
and affects which may require other solutions, such as examining and
locating the source of the affects. Not infrequently, this is shown to
be a magnification of unresolved disagreement from an earlier stage

of group life. This emphasizes the need to ease the airing of differences at an early stage and thus to prevent their gaining both pressure and temperature during unnecessarily prolonged storage.

EXAMPLE 24

The intensity of residential agencies and the protracted intimacy which necessarily characterizes them brings conflict into focus as a central theme of residential work.

A long-term residential agency for physically handicapped teenagers carried out a difficult adventure living project in a mountain area. One child-care worker from the agency, one nurse and one physiotherapy student, all experienced in mountain living, accompanied the six teenagers.

Unexpected tensions and antagonisms arose early in the group. Quite trivial matters and relatively minor challenges split the group in different directions over different issues. The workers were not able to understand this until the third day, when one of them picked up the remark 'It's the same every time, it's always been the same'. Exploring this, the worker was told that members found it unfair that they were praised when they overcame their handicaps and did well, but were never praised for trying and failing. Thus, when one member was praised it made the others 'mad at him ... but it's really you "teachers" we're mad at and haven't dared to say so. It's just the same back at the home.' The group went on to explain that they 'stored up hatred' from when they were 'on the receiving end' and then 'really had a go at the others when it was their turn'.

The workers were thus able to see that present conflicts echoed earlier unresolved conflicts, whose roots lay in deficiencies in their own understanding of members' needs.

We often see that conflict in the group reflects analogous conflicts in life outside the group, particularly in connection with the problems motivating to membership. In groups whose aims involve some gain in insight, consideration of such situations — which usually requires a direct initiative by the worker — is another way in which conflict may be used productively.

EXAMPLE 25

In a parents' group of psychiatric out-patient teenagers, Mr and Mrs Anderson were increasingly in conflict with Mr Beck, a single father. Both had sons, now at home, who had been hospitalized for acute episodes following drug abuse. Relationships in both homes were very strained, and both the Andersons and Mr Beck had remarked upon the uncompromising stubbornness of their sons – 'You can't talk to them', 'They won't listen', 'Won't budge an inch', 'Nothing but conflict', etc.

The Andersons and Mr Beck were, however, in sharp disagreement about another issue, namely their own drinking and smoking habits. The Andersons had completely given up both alcohol and tobacco, as an example of self-discipline and in solidarity with their son. They were critical of other parents who did not do likewise. Mr Beck, on the other hand, felt equally strongly that liberal and trusting attitudes should pervade the home and that parents would be better examples if they could take their moderate pleasures, 'without making every single thing either a threat or something to be ashamed of'.

The worker became aware that these members strongly rejected each other's viewpoints, infusing the question with accusatory issues of 'responsibility' and 'parental morals'. Having observed that neither party had considered or responded to the content of the other's arguments, simply rejecting them out of hand, he commented: 'I'd like to point to something that I have been noticing. A number of valuable things are being said from both sides here, and opinions are being put that are most important to discuss. But I note that neither of you responds to what the other has actually said. Instead of considering and arguing the merits or weaknesses of Mr Beck's or Mr and Mrs Anderson's opinions you simply reject each other. Let's talk about that in the group.'

After some discussion of this point, it was fairly well agreed by members that the worker had in fact pointed to a general tendency in the group. It was agreed that members would try to be more conscious of this and would both give and ask for response to the content of contributions.

The worker then took the further step of remarking how similar members' behaviour in the group was to the behaviour they complained about in their teenagers during conflicts at home – 'Managing conflicts is always difficult and the most common way of dealing with them in our whole society is to regard them as contests to be won or lost. We have agreed that we have seen that in the group. And now I am wondering whether this also happens at home and whether it is only your youngsters who are 'uncompromising' and who 'won't listen'. What does the group think about that idea?

With some initial resistance, members were able to discuss this. They accepted that their anxiety about their sons and daughters caused them to be particularly competitive in their conflicts with them. This prevented them from hearing the valid things their children no doubt had to say as well as limiting their possibilities for rational discussion of issues on which they disagreed. Recognizing this caused the group to discuss in concrete terms more productive ways of dealing with conflicts, with particular emphasis on giving response to content. Reporting conflict and discussion 'from the home front' and evaluating the way it had been dealt with became a feature of the group.

Learning about dealing with conflict in life situations on the basis of experiences in the group was also illustrated in example 21 on family life education in a church setting. This common feature of group work method, where actual group experience is related to life situations and coping mechanisms outside the group, is often referred to in the literature as 'use of present reality'.

Whether or not the worker uses actual group conflict in this particular way, his attitudes to conflict must always be serious, reflective and – above all – impartial. In terms of our earlier model of group diagnosis, the worker observing conflict should consider it in the light of his prevailing conception of the dynamics of the group. He should ask himself what the conflict can be telling him about members' needs, feelings and ways of coping. This understanding determines his way of helping the group deal with the conflict and thus the extent to which it may be used constructively in the service of growth and change.

Needless to say, all this assumes that the worker has himself developed a fairly relaxed attitude to conflict and aggression, accepting both his own and others' as inevitable and constant features of the human landscape. Acting rationally and purposively under conflict and when exposed to aggression is advanced social behaviour. Most of us retain some difficulties in this area far into adult life. Clarifying one's own attitudes to conflict and developing a less anxious attitude to aggression is an important feature of developing group work skill and most of us – sporadically – need to work on this for some years.

INTERGROUP CONFLICT

So far we have discussed intragroup conflict. We should not leave the subject of norms concerning conflict without also commenting on intergroup conflict.

It is desirable that group norms facilitate engaging in conflict with bodies and forces outside the group where this is necessary or advantageous. Some group therapy seems to aim at so high a degree of cohesion and at so much introspection that the group could be seen to exist in a social vacuum with only its internal dynamics, resources and problems. In group work, whose long-term function is always to aid members in functioning better in the wider society, such insulation is both unnecessary and unfortunate. Group life gives many opportunities for dealing directly with the environment in which the group exists and to which members return. Conflict with forces in the environment provides an important example of this. This is of course already apparent at the planning stage of groups in that overlapping area between group work and community work, where intended aims include from the outset making some kind of impact on the environment through planned action, demonstration, the formulation of protest, and so on. But many groups offer similar opportunities even though other aims and ways of working provide the main core of the group's work. The need to direct group resources outwards will in such cases become apparent as the group process unfolds. Thus, it will often involve creatively seizing an opportunity for *ad hoc* action, rather than reflecting long-term planning. Group norms should as far as possible facilitate such appropriate externally-directed activity – inclusive of conflict – in all groups, rather than limiting concern with the environment to discussion and to the clarification of attitudes.

Where group members are in some way disadvantaged by forces in the environment, resignation inevitably damages self-esteem. Collective outward manifestation of protest, whether or not it is successful in achieving actual change, may on the other hand be expected to increase members' sense of worth, autonomy and dignity. Intensification of group bond may also be expected to result from assertive collective activity. Possibilities for such creative use of intergroup conflict are often present in groups whose members have chronic problems and who experience a high degree of dependency upon help. Such clients are vulnerable to manipulation and discrimination. Engaging in appropriate conflict is an antidote to this, conducive to growth and to increased self-esteem.

EXAMPLE 26

Again, from a residential setting ...

In a hospital for patients with rheumatic illnesses and other progressive degeneratory diseases a group of teenage and young adult patients was led jointly by the social worker and a senior nurse. The patients had all had, intermittently, very long periods of hospitalization. For some, this had been the case since early childhood.

The group was open, loosely structured and called itself a 'discussion group'. Over the years, its gradually appearing and disappearing membership had focused usefully on such problems as coping with pain and increasing dependence, experiencing deviance, concern for the interruption of education, family life and friendships, and the abiding uncertainty of future plans for training, work and independence.

The workers experienced the members as continually working on underlying problems of self-esteem, which were painful by-products of their condition, their dependence and their semi-institutional lifestyle.

A generalized resentment of the medical staff was often indirectly evidenced as the counterbalance to the periodic idealization of certain doctors. This produced a confusing and ambivalent relationship with these powerful resource persons, on whom they were so dependent. During an active phase, with high membership and attendance, this relationship arose as an important new subject. It was gradually discovered that most members had been informed indirectly and incompletely about their condition. It was found to be most common that members had for a period of years been given to understand that they had curable conditions and that they would become healthy. The discovery in early adulthood that this was not true had been a devastating experience. Members' common anger when they discovered that they had all been falsely reassured gave impetus to a demand for a confrontation with the medical staff.

Conflict was anticipated. The meeting did in fact occur, did in fact become heated, and was concluded with most of the staff accepting patients' criticism and agreeing to reassess their policy. Group members had been impressive, assertive and reasonable.

This experience of entering conflict and dealing purposefully with it was valuable both to members' self-esteem and to the identity and cohesion of the group.

INTERGROUP CONFLICT AND THE AGED

The importance of developing norms which facilitate purposive conflict merits special emphasis in gerontological services. Western industrial societies infantilize, de-individualize and alienate their aged, ascribing them roles of such dependence and passivity as to shatter their self-esteem and their social health. Many so-called 'problems of old age' are not the results of age in itself, but of the ways in which our societies regard and treat old people. This includes the assumption that they should be shielded from conflict and controversy. This protective interpretation of 'help' may be well intended, but we should bear in mind that younger people assume life to include degrees of conflict, which are to be dealt with. Our self-image as competent and autonomous beings is dependent upon our ability to enter and survive conflict in areas which are important to our survival or well-being. Even though we do not expect always to triumph in conflict, it is vital to us that we accept responsibility for confronting issues which concern our own lives. By removing conflict from the lives of old people we are removing therefore an important source of self-assertion and esteem. Forman (1967), an American social worker, has long since argued that appropriate help to the elderly includes aid in identifying and confronting conflict instead of assuming it oneself.[4]

In group work contexts, the collective power of the group may sometimes enable members to face very potent adversaries. The Grey Panther movement in North America is a dramatic example of this, showing how old people in their struggle against attitudes and policies may take issue with such powerful institutions as Madison Avenue and even the White House. Also small groups, such as we social and health practitioners work with, may similarly gain in self-esteem and social health and may improve their life situation if group norms make it possible for them to confront problems in their immediate environment.

EXAMPLE 27

A municipal service centre for the elderly provided a wide range of health and welfare services and was a social focal point. Cuts in public spending included the withdrawal of the part-time services of a keep-fit instructor who had two half-days per week at the centre. An imaginative, popular, and stimulating young woman, she had succeeded in engaging many of those attending the centre in actively keeping fit and in taking renewed pleasure in bodily movement — not least in dancing, with which she closed all her sessions.

When she was withdrawn, an elected council of members complained to the centre staff and asked them to protest to the social services department. A group worker prevented her colleagues from taking up this issue on behalf of the members. Instead, she was able to assure the support of members of staff 'if necessary', but otherwise advocated their taking up the matter themselves. Members organized an effective protest campaign, with letters to the authority responsible, following considerable internal discussion. The director of social services accepted their invitation to come and debate this question and was also accompanied by a local councillor who was chairman of the finance committee. Mutual understanding was reached, members accepting the necessity of some cuts and the officials accepting one of the member's alternative suggestions about less damaging areas for saving expenditure. Thus, not only did members achieve their goal through purposive joint action, but the successful conclusion of a chosen confrontation heightened their self-respect, sense of autonomy and participation in ownership of and responsibility for the centre.

OTHER DESIRABLE NORMS

In discussing conflict at such length and in drawing attention to its possible value, I have tried to make explicit one consequence of the important norms of acknowledging feelings and of flexibility in relation to group contract. These, again, relate closely to the worker's guiding concern for the relevance of group norms, which I have already mentioned. I would like briefly to make one or two other points about relevance before leaving the subject of norms. Certain general norms governing the style rather than the content of the group's work are seen to be essential in all well functioning groups dealing with social or health problems. I will very briefly define these.

One such basic norm is that of democratic organization. By this, I refer to the importance of all members recognizing their freedom and right to contribute, their equality one with another, and their common responsibility for the group to the extent that their personal resources make this possible. This norm has clear roots in the values and ethics of professional helping and of group work history, but it has also vital pragmatic significance. It provides the conditions under which each member may both contribute and receive maximally from the reservoir of experiences always present in the group.

This relates closely to other basic norms, which are expressed in giving both acknowledgement and response to each other. Acknowledgement here is to the achievement, courage, wisdom or tenacity which clients continually display, but which is usually overshadowed by both their own and their professional helpers' greater awareness of their areas of failure or difficulty. Response is to their contributions during the work of the group. In client groups, as elsewhere, many valuable contributions are lost because other members are busy polishing their own thoughts and formulations prior to presentation and have not really heard and considered what has been said by others. Encouragement of these norms of acknowledgement and response serves thus the purposes of increasing members' self-esteem, and increasing the satisfaction of contributing and thereby the degree of activity. Thus, mutual identification develops, ensuring a more effective use of the material presented by members.

Acceptance – both of differences between members and of painful or guilt-laden feelings which they share – is another of these desirable general norms. This too, has several purposes. Members work better, more openly and on more relevant material when they do not feel judged or regarded as deviant. Their self-esteem, often seriously damaged by prevailing social attitudes, is reinforced by acceptance in the group. Further, their need to take personal, individualized clarifications or decisions from the group presupposes latitude for diversity, also a condition which assumes a norm of acceptance.

SUMMARY

The worker's response to what is happening in the group will always be intended partly to contribute to the emergence of favourable norms, as discussed in the preceding pages. In this, as in all his responses and interventions, he will be guided by his consciousness of the group's aims, his evaluation of promising ways of attaining those aims and the best understanding he can achieve ('group diagnosis') of the relationship between the group's needs, background and resources and their behaviour.

Where favourable norms do not spontaneously generate themselves from a sound group process and the worker has actively to contribute to normative development, he has, as we have seen, a number of means at his disposal. Some norms – for example the giving of response – may simply be made the subject of agreement in the group. While this does not guarantee the integration of the norm it does increase the likelihood of its being implemented. Others again may be established on the basis of modelling and identification with the worker's own behaviour and attitudes. Acceptance and problem recognition are cases in point. Generalization and reassurance are also useful means here, as in several other contexts. Direct indication of certain forms of behaviour as being both possible and gainful is also another means of influencing norms, as in engaging in confrontation.

NOTES: CHAPTER 8

1 In example 22 a particular tension exists between the agency culture and the client culture. Schwartz's (1971, p. 77) concept of the mediating role is particularly apposite here and is specifically discussed in relation to group work in a maximum security prison by Forthun and Nuehring (1971).

2 The model role is performed both by consistently representing certain relevant values and attitudes and by making conscious use of unpredicted opportunities as they arise. Some group therapists have recently been developing a more methodical way of exploiting modelling potential in groups, based on behavioural theory. Although a directive leadership style is assumed, as in all behavioural therapy, I think it likely that we will in time learn to adapt this technique to the group-centred

method of mainstream group work as well. Bertcher (1978) has already formulated guidelines for this approach to modelling and related them to Vinter's (1974) well recognized exposition of group work principles. Other interesting sources in this context are Bandura (1971) and Bednar *et al.* (1974).

3 On the theme of conflict as a precondition for growth and change, Coser's (1956) sociological analysis is standard. His ideas are among those which influenced Bernstein (1967), who wrote clearly on the subject of conflict and group work. These notions of conflict as both potentially purposive and threatening and as amenable to therapeutically gainful 'management' in group work have more recently – and most systematically – been discussed by Cowger (1979).

4 At least one writer would talk of 'stealing' rather than 'assuming' conflict. The Norwegian criminologist Christie (1977) discusses 'conflict as property' and challenges our right to take it from others. His paper, though focused on penological practice, raises important questions for practitioners throughout social work and the health field.

Chapter 9

_____•_____

THE WORKING PHASE – RESPONDING TO GROUP DEVELOPMENT

GROUP DEVELOPMENT THEORY

Many group workers have noted the tendency for groups to develop in sequential stages. Such descriptions bear strong resemblance to each other despite differences in membership, purpose and setting. The way in which groups settle down to work or not, how they organize themselves, share or avoid responsibility and tackle or evade their problems are features of group life which time and again have been described as falling into identifiable stages.

Norms, structure, communication – all the group processes we have discussed here – are subject to change. These features of group life are inextricably interwoven. Structural changes influence or result from changes in perceived priorities, aims and, thence, norms. Intervening in group structure therefore effects the norms of the group and vice versa. The style, content and level of communication will vary with the group climate, the prevailing degree of acceptance, the amount of problem confrontation which is possible and, thus, with both leadership patterns (structure) and the rules for what is permissible (norms).

In so far as it is possible to describe stages of group development, we should then expect to see interrelated changes in all aspects of group process, change in one producing change in the other. Growth in groups does in fact seem to occur in this dynamic way. It is both interesting and convincing to see that authors who have made their various attempts to describe patterns of group development address themselves to all these aspects of group life.

I will here summarize some of the main features of group development theory and indicate their implication for the practising group worker. I am able to do this rather briefly since much of the material which normally would be referred to is already dealt with in other contexts in the present volume. To some extent this summary of group development may also be regarded as a gathering together of those strands of the preceding pages which have touched upon change and growth.

The implications of group development theory for the group worker are considerable. They must not be taken to represent predictions of what *will* happen in the group and thus become self-fulfilling prophecies. They represent, rather, general observations and probabilities. As such, they may help the worker to become more sensitive to change and more rapidly to register, evaluate and respond to movement in the group. Thus while group development theory may not always aid the worker in choosing specific interventions it frequently helps him to evaluate the 'strategy' – the direction and aims – of his contribution to the group process at different stages.

In the following summary I shall sketch some of the most frequently encountered features of group development patterns. I shall also indicate and give examples of some of the worker's functions in relation to group development. This summary is selective and cursory. It includes elements from the models of Sarri and Galinsky (1975), Kolodny, Jones and Garland (1965), and Caple (1978) as well as my own observations. Very many other authors would have to be included in a thorough treatise on this subject, but I hope to catch the main points here.[1]

It is convenient – and is a compromise between the sketchily impressionistic and the ambitiously elaborated models – to propose four overlapping stages of group development. I shall deal here with the first three of these. The fourth, the stage of termination, provides the subject of Chapter 12.

THE FIRST STAGE

This stage is characterized by the activity noted in Sarri and Galinsky's 'formative phase', in Kolodny, Jones and Garland's 'pre-affiliation phase' and in Caple's 'orientation stage'. There are important similarities and some differences between these models. My impression in practice has been that the differences in these formulations reflect not so much observations of competing validity as real differences in emphasis from one kind of client group to another. Thus we may expect one or other of these formulations best to describe the initial stage of one group, whilst another model best depicts the initial phase of the next group one works with.

Combining the main components of these models with one's own observations, an overview of group behaviour during the first stage would include the following recurrent phenomena.

Members' behaviour has its roots in initial uncertainty and disorientation. Activity is tentative at first, becoming increasingly exploratory. The somewhat anxious quality of this exploration is reduced as members gradually discover and confirm that sufficient common characteristics, background or needs exist to give a basis for affiliation. Some tentative alliances may be formed, but on the whole there tends to be little active interaction, in the sense of spontaneous mutual response. Members more commonly send out their own chosen signals, showing an edited version of who they are and what they want, otherwise limiting interaction to putting or replying to questions. What response does arise is rarely disagreement, some investment in a positive atmosphere being common at this stage. There is dependency upon the worker or workers who initiated the group, as well as testing out of his or their understanding and acceptance.

A provisional structure often develops at this early stage. It is readily visible and shows little differentiation. A member or a small number of members may take initiative and be offered status early. Such members tend to be less inhibited, less anxious and freer with both their aggression and their association than other members. It seems to be the case that such members are deferred to also because they represent attitudes and possess skills which aid the group in dealing with the initial problems aroused by the group itself and by the group's relationship to the agency, the worker or the wider environment. Thus, clowns, diplomats, or revolutionaries will enter this role in different groups. It is important to note that in addition to the norms ensuring an optimally pleasant atmosphere, and thus survival, other norms are established in this stage. These are a result of members' support and deference to the initial leader or leaders, whose attitudes and behaviour become norms by consensus (or by subjugation). These may well be highly functional in meeting initial needs, but may be poorly suited to governing the quality and direction of members' subsequent work.

Worker's Functions during the First Stage
This stage begins with the first meeting of the group and continues for an indefinite period thereafter. Some groups — highly motivated, secure in group situations and with a clear view of common aims — will rapidly leave this phase behind them. Others again will need quite a considerable time to come through the tasks and tensions of formation. However that may be, the worker's functions are those already dealt with in the description of the first meeting in Chapter 4. The functions discussed there are not, it will be recalled, exclusive to the first meeting but are those which are to be most highly emphasized during that meeting. In the same way, we may see that the functions concerned dominate the whole of the first stage, gradually giving way to others, though never entirely disappearing.

The main functions of the worker in the first stage include aiding the search for commonality. This is a phenomenon and a function emphasized in all literature on the subject. Performance of this function is shown in the extracts from the mastectomy group in example 6, and from the group of parents of multiple-handicapped children in example 8. Another important function in the first stage involves response to the hierarchical and primitive status pattern common to this phase. The worker attempts to facilitate an 'open structure' by helping passive members to be more active, by relieving members of the role of 'spokesman for the group' and by avoiding collusion with already dominant members. In some groups the worker may deal with this also by direct indication of unevenly distributed influence and initiative as a problem to be dealt with. One earlier case extract depicting work in maintaining open structure is that from the alcoholics' group reported in example 19.

Other important themes in the worker's contributions during the first stage are clarifying contract and 'instituting, supporting or stimulating norms favourable to the aims of the group' (Sarri and Galinsky, 1975). As stated earlier, norms and normative control do not exist as discrete characteristics. They come to expression in communication and in structure as well as in patterns of group organization and development. The worker's efforts at influencing norms may thus be indirect and may manifest themselves as work with communication or structure. Most of these first-phase functions are illustrated in the following case extract.

EXAMPLE 28

Background

A residential agency offers vocational and social training as well as general education to clients suffering multiple handicap combined with sensory loss or impairment. Extensive use is made of group methods.

One group was led jointly by a remedial teacher and a social worker. There were eight members, young men and women between 16 and 25 years. Most of these, prior to admission, had led extremely isolated lives. There were several reasons for this, including parental overprotection, upbringing in remote mountain and moorland farms, physical incapacity to move away from home, and extreme anxiety about doing so. Two members had not even been known to exist until quite late in their childhood. Members had serious communication and identity problems. There had been a long and difficult preparatory stage in reaching the clients, in motivating them to enter the agency (a long journey for most) and in securing the co-operation of the parents. It was intended that these young people should be admitted simultaneously. This was well achieved, only one week separating the first and last admission.

The first weeks

These eight clients met as a group two afternoons per week as well as informally during evenings and weekends. The group meetings were intended to provide support, social satisfactions and enrichment and opportunities for sharing tasks, for taking decisions and for experiencing responsibility.

At the first meeting and on subsequent occasions, the group workers discussed these aims with the group in such terms as 'to help each other get used to managing without your parents', 'to find out how much you can in fact do for yourselves/decide for yourselves', 'to find interests/pleasures together, both old and new ones', 'to have someone your own age to turn to and get through problems with'. This exemplifies negotiation of contract, both in terms of specifying aims and asserting members' participation in responsibility for the group. The assumption of members' ability to use their own resources not only exemplifies work with contract but also the beginning of the formation of respectful relationships and the workers' first steps out of the 'central person' role.

During the first weeks the members' feelings were strongly ambivalent. The new milieu was both stimulating and demanding. They were both more free and more confined. For the first time they were away from their parents. While they missed them, they also experienced a dawning resentment of the limitations they suffered because of overprotection. Rejection of dependency struggled with anxiety about inability to cope. Contact with members of the opposite sex was a new, exciting and threatening experience. The agency in general and the group in particular brought these young people new hope – and new conflicts.

Some of these conflicts were matters of unambiguous observation for the workers. Others were tentatively understood on the basis of empathy and of members' hesitant and indirect comments. The workers contributed to norms of open communication, expression of feelings and recognition of problems by facilitating clearer expression of members' common conflicts – 'It looks as if being here raises as many problems as it solves', 'It would be strange if you didn't have very mixed feelings about being here', 'Any big change/big new thing/challenge scares us all, even it excites us at the same time'.

After two or three weeks, members seemed to have overcome earlier inhibitions in seeking contact with each other. An increasing curiosity about each other led to an exploration of the group – 'Where are you from?', 'Have you been here before?', 'Have you lived at home or in a home?', 'How long have you had an el-chair?', 'Have you ever been to school?' During daily life in the institution friendships between pairs of members of the same sex developed at this time, and in group meetings there was evidenced a gradual increase in awareness of and reference to the group as a whole. The workers aided this 'search for commonality' both in the group and in the daily life of the institution. In the group, similarities were pointed out wherever appropriate, individual members 'linked' with each other, and discussion rather strongly led in the direction of issues known by the workers to be common to all members. Emphasis was given to recognition of the potential value of the commonality of their backgrounds and their struggles. In activities of daily living, the workers ensured that wherever possible members of the group worked together, particularly in activities which demanded interaction. These included the weekly discussion of the menu with the kitchen staff, the clipping, choice and editing of the wall newspaper maintained by the residents, the discussion of subject matter or activities for the one school day each week planned by the residents, etc. In leisure time, suggestions were made for activities which also presupposed co-operation and sharing pleasures – such as sightseeing by bus, visiting the cinema in the town, sedentary group games such as Monopoly, handline fishing from hired boats, etc. The physical handicaps from which members suffered entailed special transport arrangements. Negotiating these was also consistently made a responsibility of the group. Such activity served other purposes – increasing self-esteem through mastery, life enrichment, and emphasizing autonomy – as well as furthering relationships and the continued discovery of commonality.

The workers did not observe in this group the tendency to dominance by temporary leaders which is featured in so many descriptions of group development patterns. However, there were two or three members who were almost entirely passive initially, which also contributes to a hierarchical group organization in time. The workers therefore contributed to maintaining open structure by helping these anxious members to contribute and participate in various ways.

THE SECOND STAGE

I include in this second stage those recurring phenomena reported in Sarri and Galinsky's 'first intermediate' and 'revision phases', in Kolodny, Jones and Garland's 'stage of power and control', and in Caple's stages of 'conflict' and of 'integration'.

This is an exciting and certainly a decisive stage of development. It is mainly characterized by the opposing tendencies of consolidation of the norms and structure established in the first stage and movement towards optimally effective ways of using the group situation.

Developments in the first stage frequently result in ways of behaving in the group which are by no means optimally effective, seen in relation to the purposes of the group. These opposing tendencies – to maintain and strengthen initial structure and norms and to reorganize more effectively once the initial uncertainty and exploration is past – inevitably produce tension or conflict. The second stage is strongly marked by these tensions and their resolution. Commonly, there is a tendency to reinforcement of the norms which emerged in the first stage. They have been sufficiently clarified for conformity with them to be acclaimed and deviance discouraged. This also produces a further differentiation of structure, with more members enjoying prominence and others becoming more clearly defined as low-status, either because of non-conformity or passivity. Where existing norms are not purposive seen in relation to long-term aims, revision of both norms and structure must occur, however. This implies the threat of conflict or the discomfort of withdrawing support from earlier leaders. Groups at this stage often withdraw defensively from these threats into what has been called a 'honeymoon' situation. Problem confrontation is avoided and members collude in keeping up a benign and pleasant atmosphere, while being anxiously aware that a difficult reality has soon to be faced. The movement through this phase into productive 'revision' necessitates either extension or change of norms and either change in membership of high-status positions or demand upon incumbent leaders for a wider and more relevant repertoire of behaviour and attitudes.

This may be a critical stage of group development. There are real issues of competing aims and values which may be encountered here, and the extent to which they may be reconciled with each other decides the group's survival. Even where tension is less related to such real issues and more to social-emotional competitiveness, the group may be threatened at this stage. A successful completion of the second stage represents both important and praiseworthy achievement for many groups. Therefore, they may be expected to continue with very good chances of further survival and with heightened self-esteem as well as being more efficiently geared to their aims.

Worker's Functions during the Second Stage

The worker's functions in the second stage grow out of his evaluation of the relevance of the norms and the structure which emerged during the first phase.

If he assesses the group process as developing along relevant and purposive lines, he may enter into a contained and facilitating role, intervening mainly to prevent normative control from becoming repressive and impoverishing. Where the first phase has not been so successfully completed, he must help the group to avoid crystallizing irrelevant and inflexible norms. This involves contributing to the amelioration of normative control, giving active support to new and purposive behaviour and attitudes, and helping the group to confront the threatening task of revision. Where necessary, the worker also intervenes to safeguard the integrity of 'deposed' former leaders, particularly by acknowledging the importance of their earlier contribution and asserting their continued potential value to the group. The manner in which the worker responds to the conflict in the group, discussed earlier, will here have particular importance for the further development of norms, openness and communication style.

Most features of this second stage of group development and the worker's tasks in this stage are evidenced in the following case. It is a summary of process journals up to and including part of the fourth meeting. The beginning of the revision process and the tensions associated with it are particularly evident here.

EXAMPLE 29

Background of the Group
The agency is a school psychology service in a high-rise suburb on the edge of a Scandinavian city. A number of pupils in the 12–15 age-group, from four different schools in the district, exhibited serious learning problems. Some also evinced behavioural problems such as truancy, vandalism, sniffing or tentative drug abuse, shoplifting and – in one or two cases – school phobia. Several of these were already in therapy at the child guidance clinic or were the subject of supervision orders at the time of referral to the school psychology service for learning problems.

Because of the common elements in these problems, the school psychology service decided to offer group counselling to four parental pairs and one single (divorced) mother. It was planned that a social worker from each agency should lead the group jointly. All group members knew one of the co-leaders, some knew both.

There was doubt during planning about a feature of group composition. The single mother, Mrs A, had a school-phobic son and the co-leaders were in doubt about the suitability of group treatment. They decided to offer her membership since the group might serve the secondary purpose of alleviating her isolation.

Weekly meetings of $1\frac{1}{2}$ hours' duration were agreed. They were to continue through the winter, with a decision to terminate or continue to be taken at Easter.

Summary of Group Process up to the Fourth Meeting

The first three sessions were marked by active engagement by the members. Already at the end of the first meeting the group had abandoned its careful testing of the situation and entered into quite direct problem-focused discussion. A climate developed which initially impressed the workers as positive. Most members participated. It seemed likely that the group could develop into a setting in which the parents could engage and disclose themselves and from which they could gain.

By the end of the first meeting, and more markedly in the second, the workers registered a gradual increase of focus on Mrs A. She was 40 years old, divorced, and mother of a school-phobic 12-year-old boy. Mrs A talked quietly, in a well formulated way. She smiled much, occasionally inappropriately, such that the workers began to regard her smiling gaze as a social device rather than an expression of pleasure. She and her son had moved into the town from a valley farming district. Mrs A said that city living was unnatural and alienating – 'It must cause all kinds of problems for our children, no matter how much we love and care for them.' She herself could have 'screamed at all the noise and traffic on the roads and around the shopping centres'. She believed that 'also the schoolteachers are affected by it' – not that she wished to accuse them, but she was sure that 'city teachers just don't care about children or their profession as those in the country do'. Mrs A's concerned, clear way of expressing herself, her direct smile and her frequent contributions brought her viewpoints into prominence and gave them impact on the group.

There was an interesting episode in the third meeting. The only member who had remained silent throughout the entire second meeting was Mr B, whose wife clearly was accustomed to talking on their joint behalf. Mr and Mrs B were both 39 years old and had a 13-year-old daughter who had begun to sniff lynol. Mr B, an inarticulate dock-worker, seemed able to conquer his shyness only when pressed by strong feelings. He became briefly active during the third meeting, when he said that 'while much of what "the lady" [Mrs A] said was true' he felt that they 'were all busy putting the blame on everything and everyone but themselves'. The group were silenced by this, and clearly looked to Mrs A or the workers to do something with the suddenly tense atmosphere. Mrs A smiled with apparent warmth to both Mrs and Mr B and asked the latter if he would repeat what he said since his 'language is rather difficult to understand'. Mr B said that it wasn't worth it, but his wife repeated his point and shared his concern. Mrs A won several supporting nods and mumbles when she replied to the Bs: 'If we can't find out here who and what is to blame I don't see how we can help our children, and I assume that is also what you two wish, isn't it?'

Early in the fourth meeting, Mrs C took the initiative for the first time. She was 32 years old, worked irregular hours in the booking office of a night ferry service; her husband worked in a ski factory. Mrs C broke a rather protracted pause to say that she had been thinking about what the Bs had said at the last meeting: 'Could they say something more about what they thought?' They could not. Mrs C referred then to the workers. Didn't the workers 'also think that the group blamed uncritically all around them, as Mr and Mrs B had said'? The question 'bothered her'.

By this time, the workers had become aware ('belatedly', they said in supervision) of the development in the group. They believed themselves to have been too passive in allowing structure to settle around Mrs A's leadership. While she had given the group impetus and had identified a major problem area, she was strongly defended against recognizing parental involvement in the aetiology of the children's problems.[2]

Under her leadership, while serious work had been done, norms of denial and projection had become established. Mrs A's superior and insinuating behaviour towards the Bs received some group support and represented normative control which was counterproductive.

The workers were encouraged to observe the group's movement into revision. First the Bs then Mrs C, raised the forbidden question of the parents' own responsibility in their children's problems. This rejection of the group's normative limits and the introduction of greater problem confrontation represented relevant norms which the workers wished to support. In responding to Mrs C in the situation above as well as in subsequent contributions, the workers helped the group to confront the tasks and conflicts of revision. This involved agreeing to the relevance of the new questions raised, generalizing about the stresses of raising children in high-density, high-rise areas, and assuming that the milieu made problems for adults as well as children. They also involved themselves in influencing group structure. This was effectuated by actively encouraging group attention and response to the newly active low-status members (the Bs) as well as to the Cs. It also involved supporting the 'deposed leader', Mrs A, to ensure that the redistribution of status did not involve her being rejected. The workers asserted the continuing relevance of the environmental problems she had introduced and spoke of the new themes as 'additional' rather than 'alternative' issues. During a phase of conflict around these issues, the workers chose not to indicate the defensive aspects of Mrs A's contributions, but confined themselves to commenting 'how good it was' that the group could have strong disagreement and could keep working on it. This was a further influence upon norms and a contribution to ameliorating normative control.

THE THIRD STAGE

I include in the third stage of development those recurring features of group life which are embraced by Sarri and Galinsky's 'second intermediate' and 'maturity' phases, by Kolodny, Jones and Garland's 'intimacy' and 'differentiation' phases, and by Caple's phase of 'achievement'.

Much of Caple's 'integration' phase also spills over into this third stage. In short, we are here well into the working phase of the group. What characterizes this stage, in developmental terms?

The revisions and realignments of the second stage have been survived. While residual tension may never entirely disappear, power struggle will not again dominate the group and members are able to use it optimally for purposive and relevant work. Members' resources are available, initiative is welcomed, and status is more evenly and democratically distributed. All members participate in discussion and decisions and interaction occurs between all members – though not necessarily equally. Norms relevant to group purposes are accepted and while they are subject to some control it is neither so tyrannical nor so restrictive as in the second stage. The group seems to perceive the necessity for a considerable degree of flexibility in order to facilitate experimentation, growth and change. Thus, members experience greater acceptance of their individuality, at the same time as group cohesion (particularly interpersonal and functional cohesion)[3] is strong and supportive. Communication is more open and direct than hitherto. Conflict and stress, both internal and externally derived, may be resolved without serious threat to the survival of the group. Members are committed to the group.

The Worker's Functions in the Third Stage

By this stage, the worker should have moved out of the 'central person' position as far as the group's basic resource potential permits. The group, as indicated, is working well. The worker should be aware of the importance of practising as much containment as possible, but he must also be prepared in periods to increase his own activity level in response to changing situations in the group.

At this stage, the worker addresses his contributions as much as possible to the group as a whole rather than engaging in dialogues, no matter how briefly. He recognizes the identity of the group and helps the group to increase consciousness both of its identity and of its ways of working. He does not say, 'Well done, Charlie!' but 'The group got through that pretty well'; not 'You know something about this, don't you, Karen?' but 'I think the group have met this one before some time, haven't you?'; not 'This new regulation from the National Assistance is going to make life difficult for you, Jan', but 'These changes effect the group – perhaps quite seriously. I think you ought to be having a look at them together.'

Increasing the group's awareness of their identity and working procedures may be formal and direct or informal and implied, according to the contract with the group. But in either case it serves the purposes of strengthening the group bond and of either increasing collective awareness of improved mastery (and, thus, self-esteem) or aiding early awareness of the occasional need to attend to the group's level of functioning. While the worker will try to help the group regain its earlier higher level, he should prevent anxiety about periodic stagnation or regression and help the group accept this as a normal feature of development. Periods of growth are often followed by plateaux of inactivity. Increasingly, I believe this to be a necessary condition for useful integration and adjustment to the changed situation which growth has presented – for example, through having made a decision or through insight. So the worker says, for example: 'I'm not sure whether you're finding this silence uncomfortable or not. For my part, I think it's all right. So much happened yesterday/last time that it needs thinking about/getting used to."

In this stage, the worker is particularly interested in helping the group to clarify their norms – sometimes to articulate them clearly, depending upon the group. This is an aid to increasing the effectiveness of the group, since an assumption of the third stage is that norms are optimally functional. Such clarification has the concomitant effect of reinforcing normative control, which is of course desirable to the extent that the group have by now developed a serviceable norm set. The worker may often find it necessary, however, actively to aid the group in retaining flexibility and acceptance of degrees of deviance. Normative consensus must never be allowed to hinder productive experimentation or to prevent individual members from developing and changing in ways which differ from the majority in the group, provided that these ways are consonant with their particular needs, resources and life situation.

During this stage the worker will at times be active in aiding the group to survive turmoil caused by crises, which may arise from both external or internal threats. Individuals often regress in crisis, when faced with the threat of loss and when hitherto successful ways of solving problems no longer function. Similarly, some groups lose cohesion, confidence and effectiveness when overwhelming and unfamiliar demands and threats to the group are encountered. The worker's functions here are not dissimilar from those which are well established for crisis treatment in individual and family contexts. The worker moves into an active role and contributes structure and 'order' in the situation. He helps the group to identify the source of crisis and to name the threat. He helps members to express and reduce the pressure of strong feelings raised by the crisis and thereafter to identify and talk about the sources of worry and grief. In this he will particularly help the group to sort out areas of realistic concern from those which arise from fantasy, irrational worry, 'folklore' and low levels of information. It is also important, during work on crisis, that the group maintain its self-esteem in order to deal with threat more confidently. The worker should therefore invest in supporting the group's belief in their ability to cope, reminding members of earlier achievement and expressing confidence that they will also manage the current critical episode. He may give or help the group to find information necessary for dealing with the crisis. After these steps have been taken – feelings ventilated, realistic worries identified, information acquired, and so on – the worker will aid the group to the extent necessary in considering alternative ways of dealing with the crisis and in initiating actions or decisions. In these ways, groups not only survive crises but solve them in purposive ways so that they may often produce growth rather than inhibit it. Further, something is learned so that members' skills in dealing with crisis increase.

Again, an observation from residential group work is helpful here, reflecting these recurrent themes of crisis treatment.

EXAMPLE 30

A residential agency for teenagers with severe behavioural difficulties was organized as a therapeutic community. Several types of group work were featured, two of them being daily events.

Following a suicide attempt by one boy, subsequently hospitalized, the group regressed to a level of destructive, impulsive and rejecting behaviour which contrasted sharply with more recently achieved behaviour. The clinical team had initially dealt with the suicide attempt by informing the group in an undramatic but concerned manner, by promising to keep them informed of the boy's progress and by giving assurance of his eventual return to the agency.

The team recognized the group's regression as an indicator of continuing unresolved crisis. The crisis concept was helpful here since it sharpened their perception of the group's behaviour as a reaction to both actual loss (grief for their friend, for their joint progress, for their group pattern) and to the threat of further loss (fear for own mental stability, own life, etc.). It was thus decided to respond to the group by facilitating work with their worry and their grief, instead of attempting to correct and control their present behaviour.

Both reflective and interpretive comments were made about the group's evident distress. Members grasped the opportunity to articulate what was bothering them and quickly moved on from acknowledging this to expressing 'how sorry they were' for their comrade and, yet further, to saying that they were both 'scared' and 'angry'. (Such facing and naming of feelings is important in crisis treatment.) Both their fear and their anger had origins which were unclear to them. Some time was used in both freeing the expression of these strong feelings and thereafter in finding out where they came from. Throughout this stage, workers invested greatly in showing acceptance, concern and the wish to achieve understanding of the residents' feelings.

It gradually became clear that their fear was partly the reaction which we all experience when we are for the first time near to death, whether others' or our own, as if our personal mortality is briefly confronted. The normality of this reaction was emphasized by the workers. As so often in crisis, however, fears were also found to be grounded in fantasies, distortions and lack of knowledge. Here, members were afraid because 'suicide is catching', because 'he will be defective when he comes back, after all those pills', and so on.

Their anger was found partly to be self-reproach for not having been able to foresee their comrade's behaviour and to protect him from it. But it arose also from the feeling that the staff should have been better able to help him (and them) and thereby prevent such desperate and frightening behaviour.

Following this catharsis and clarification, members could better use the reassuring information they were given and they again became less destructive and hostile. With this background they were able to look ahead and to plan how to receive their comrade on his return. More important, they had seen the advantages in directly giving expression to fear and anger instead of storing it up for subsequent indirect and unproductive expression: 'If you are frightened or angry, it is both possible and helpful to say so.'

The sequence summarized here exemplifies regression in a group during crisis and shows how appropriate response to crisis reactions may result in new progress. The episode summarized developed over four or five days. The material discussed was taken up in plenary meetings and other group contexts, both as planned items on the daily agenda and as more opportunistic response to unpredicted situations and communications arising in the group. The team chose to deal with this in the group, rather than individually with the prominent 'troublemakers', since the latter were assumed to be expressing needs and feelings common to the group. This was, as noted, confirmed by the group's positive response.

Not only during such a crisis but throughout the whole of this phase the worker should reflect belief in the group's ability to manage the tasks which bring it together. He generates confidence and trust, through identification, even where the group is in turmoil and apparently at a dead end. This is but one aspect of modelling, a function discussed earlier, and one which is especially important during this phase.

Another important contribution to the effectiveness of the group's effort in this stage is aid to clarification. The purposiveness achieved by this stage and the intensity which often characterizes it may be unproductive despite such progress if the issues, aims and the feelings of the group are not kept clear. This is a 'maintenance' function which the worker will only very rarely be able to abrogate entirely. In many groups, clarification of these concerns remains a major part of the worker's task. Indeed, some such work is first possible in this stage since clarification of feelings between members presupposes a greater degree of security and shared experiences than exists in the earlier phases of many groups.

Similarly, clarification of communication – and, in some groups, its interpretation – will commonly require the worker's continued attention. Work with communication will in fact increase during this stage in some groups. This is because the early reticence has disappeared and members have gained trust in each other, such that the worker judges that the group may be helped to establish more direct and, if appropriate, confrontive ways of communicating with one another.

SUMMARY

I have attempted in the foregoing to summarize the main features of development in group process and to indicate the worker's main functions at each stage. This does not pretend to be a 'scientific' model. It simply builds upon my impressions over the years but I hope it gains some increase in validity by integrating features of three well regarded models whose observations are consistent with my own. The reservation is hardly necessary that these 'stages' are simplifications and represent tendencies. Groups in practice move to and fro, often exhibiting characteristics of two phases simultaneously. Phases may also be repeated – the 'revision' of the second phase especially, – just as it may be avoided entirely if an exceptionally mature and purposive group rapidly coheres and mobilizes efficiently in the first phase. However, the model presented here is a useful indicator of the most usual trends. In summary, I shall present it diagrammatically in Figure 7.

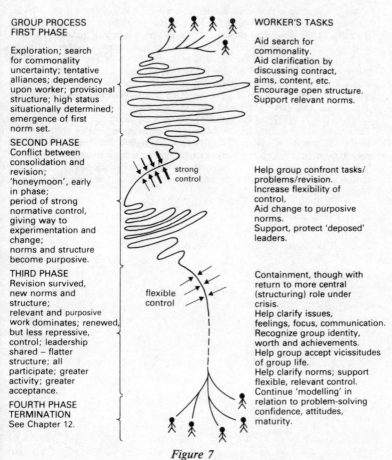

GROUP PROCESS
FIRST PHASE

Exploration; search for commonality uncertainty; tentative alliances; dependency upon worker; provisional structure; high status situationally determined; emergence of first norm set.

SECOND PHASE
Conflict between consolidation and revision; 'honeymoon', early in phase; period of strong normative control, giving way to experimentation and change; norms and structure become purposive.

strong control

THIRD PHASE
Revision survived, new norms and structure; relevant and purposive work dominates; renewed, but less repressive, control; leadership shared – flatter structure; all participate; greater activity; greater acceptance.

flexible control

FOURTH PHASE
TERMINATION
See Chapter 12.

WORKER'S TASKS

Aid search for commonality.
Aid clarification by discussing contract, aims, content, etc.
Encourage open structure.
Support relevant norms.

Help group confront tasks/problems/revision.
Increase flexibility of control.
Aid change to purposive norms.
Support, protect 'deposed' leaders.

Containment, though with return to more central (structuring) role under crisis.
Help clarify issues, feelings, focus, communication.
Recognize group identity, worth and achievements.
Help group accept vicissitudes of group life.
Help clarify norms; support flexible, relevant control.
Continue 'modelling' in relation to problem-solving confidence, attitudes, maturity.

Figure 7

The termination phase has not been discussed. This will be dealt with separately in Chapter 12. Before that, however, there remain two subjects which need to be taken up, if only briefly. The use of activities and action and the practice of co-leadership are aspects of group work method which have entered into a number of the examples used in the book so far. Both have considerable current importance – the former, because of revived use of non-verbal means in group work and the latter because it is an innovation which is both gaining ground and becoming the subject of increasing contention.

NOTES: CHAPTER 9

1   A more extensive review and a detailed analysis and illustration of Sarri and Galinsky's (1975) formulation is included in Heap (1977b).
2   It was this issue which had caused uncertainty about composition during planning of the group. The dynamics of school phobia include parental overprotection and binding, the production of anxiety, and projective defences. Few would argue that group work is the method of choice. Mrs A, like many school-phobic mothers, would probably have gained more from a long-term, caring relationship with one worker with whom she could have regressed and worked through the childhood dependency problems which caused her manipulation of her son.
3   Feldman (1967, 1969) and Gross (1956) have defined group cohesion operationally. They make a useful distinction between three different aspects of cohesion which they term 'modes of integration'. These are 'normative integration' concerning consensus on behaviour, 'functional integration' concerning consensus on aims, and 'interpersonal integration' concerning closeness of relationships. The rather complex relationship between these modes of integration has been summarized in Heap (1977b).

Chapter 10

◆

THE USE OF ACTIVITIES AND ACTION

Group work method, from its earliest days, has made extensive use of non-verbal means of help to group members. The initial direction of group work in the early years of our century strongly emphasized the use of activities as an alternative or supplement to verbal means of approaching problems. 'Doing' instead of, or as well as, 'talking about' was a cardinal feature of early group work which has in recent years enjoyed rekindled attention.[1] Why is action so valuable a resource in group work?

Solving or preventing problems requires courage, creativity, expressiveness and practice. These, among other qualities, may be both mobilized and developed through activities just as well as by verbalization – often better. For many people, actions are easier to initiate and to take part in than discussions. For many purposes, action is more appropriate and relevant than words are. 'Programme', as planned activity and action in groups was called earlier, has for these reasons an abiding place in group work method. Middleman (1982) described activity in group work as 'the vehicle through which relationships are made and the needs and interests of the group and its members are fulfilled'. The point, clearly, is not just to be 'doing something' or 'keeping out of mischief'. The point is to initiate actions which maximally serve the purposes of the group. This apparently obvious thought is by no means always realized in practice. We see clients or patients who need help in developing social skills being encouraged to perform highly individualized handicrafts which demand concentrated and silent attention. We see others, whose troubles include loss of self-esteem, being helped to 'kill time' with ritualized games – as if in confirmation of the expendability of both their time and their persons. So the question 'Does the activity fit the needs?' is decisive.

I shall now as briefly as possible show some connections between the aims of group work and the use of activities. I have earlier (Heap 1977a, 1979) formulated a categorization of aims which activities may serve in group work. The following is a revised version of that earlier formulation.

TWO PRINCIPLES

There are two guiding principles. The first of these is that activities share with verbal communications in group work the quality of being relevant and purposeful contributions to treatment, based on the best possible understanding of group members' needs which the worker is able to achieve. In other words, the introduction of action in group work is also diagnostically based. Here too, understanding derives either from knowledge of members' backgrounds and the aetiology of their problems, or from observation and interpretation of 'here and now' group behaviour, or – perhaps most commonly – from a combination of these sources.

The second principle is that it is not the quality of completed products which determines how well activities have contributed to group work goals. In group work, the value of activities lies in the process of pursuing them together and is to be evaluated by the extent to which that process has aided the problem-solving, problem clarification, improvement in relationships, or social learning which is the aim of the group. They are means by which the resources of support, control, recognition, generalization and integration may be liberated and used by the members.

AIMS OF ACTIVITIES

With these principles in mind, we may view activities in group work as serving the following aims:

Stimulating contact and interaction;
Conveying and confronting the problem;
Aiding social learning and growth;
Increasing self-esteem through achievement and life enrichment;
Contributing to environmental change;
Preparing for future change or crisis.

These aims will now be briefly discussed and illustrated in turn.

STIMULATING CONTACT AND INTERACTION

Our survival depends upon our ability to live and work together with others. Production, shelter, learning, defence, political assertion, most kinds of recreational and cultural experience – all require co-operation and sharing. But our need for emotional sharing is quite as great. How much we are loved and accepted by others is from infancy a major determinant of what kind of human beings we become. Even our self-respect is largely a reflection of the degree of acceptance we enjoy in groups whose membership we prize. We seek friendship. We marry. We work with others. And we look for love from those nearest to us and for regard from our colleagues. In their absence, even temporarily, we are dismayed and we doubt ourselves and our value.

Many people encountered by social and health workers are, however, seriously impoverished of human contact. Disability, old age, physical or mental illness, and membership of minority groups compel many clients and patients into leading very isolated lives. Such alienation further decreases self-esteem, which in its turn continues the erosion of the client's ability to function socially. Thus he is caught in a descending spiral of self-reinforcing social failure, which inevitably influences both his mental and physical health. Group methods are particularly well suited to dealing with such problems of alienation, breaking as they do into the spiral of isolation, rejection and social failure. Group meetings provide in reality a social situation which counteracts isolation and alienation.

There is, however, no guarantee that group meetings will function in this way. Whether or not they will do so depends upon the composition of the group, members' motivation and resources and the success or failure of the search for commonality. Another quite decisive factor is the extent to which the group pursues activities which are meaningful for members and which require or stimulate active interaction between them.

EXAMPLE 31

(a) A group of young adults with severe multiple disabilities was discussed in example 28. Members had led unusually isolated lives. Throughout the group's life much use was made of activities. Members were involved in collective planning of the week's menu, in editing and maintaining the wall newspaper, and in arranging transport facilities for both pleasure trips and other excursions. Since physical energy was severely limited, sedentary games were encouraged which involved the whole group in protracted interaction, such as Monopoly. At a more demanding level physically the group was encouraged to go sea-fishing with handlines – an activity which offered excitement and developed confidence but was primarily chosen because it involved collective transport, collective decisions of various kinds, and the sharing of boats, tackle, bait and sympathy about the ones that got away.

(b) A group of single teenage mothers, living alone, attending school, were shy and inarticulate at first, as much stigmatized by their commonality as supported by it. The worker believed their reticence to arise from feelings of failure and self-contempt (really, introjected moral disapprobation) combined with anxiety about forming new relationships for fear of yet more rejection. The worker therefore suggested activities which might both increase self-esteem and give a more familiar basis for inter-action. The group began to meet at weekends, instead of during harried week-day evenings. They met in the woods or at the beach, and had their children with them. They brought food and drink. They played games together and with the children. The actuality of the babies' presence and demands released a flood of exchanges, discussion and suggestions. The sharing of one another's food gave an opportunity for both generosity and appreciation to be expressed, as well as for exchanging useful information about buying and preparing food cheaply – a matter of central importance to these very disadvantaged girls.

In such ways as these appropriately chosen activities may be used to aid members of an inhibited group to enter into contact with each other.

The use of activities with this aim is not limited to severely handi-capped groups, however. As already emphasized, most groups experience a formative phase characterized by anxious exploration and a search for commonality. While verbal means are usually successful in furthering interaction at this stage, the use of action is an alternative which often offers advantage, in terms of both the ease and the tempo with which interaction between members may be established.

There are no limits to the activities which may be used here other than those imposed by the needs of the group and by the imagination of the worker and the members. Some activities may be demanding and confrontive if the strength and motivation of the members permit this. There come to mind some of the introductory processes developed out of encounter therapy training. These include 'trust games' such as the blind walk, games involving different kinds of mutual introduction, 'sculpturing' families, miming problems and so on. Robust or intimate physical games with some degree of bodily contact are also a part of this repertoire. (Brandes and Phillips, 1977, Schrøeder and Pegg, 1978, and Ross and Bilson, 1980, are useful sources in this area.) Many such procedures, however, have been developed in co-operation with highly motivated patients in psychotherapy or with students and therapists in training, for whom overcoming resistance to involvement in the group is welcomed as a feature of professional growth. But amid the privations, grief and tensions of group work in our own field there is usually too much insecurity and earlier failure, too little surplus of energy and daring, for clients to wish to enter into strange and demanding games. We must be most careful about uncritical application of training-group experiences to practical group work in the field. Here it is much more common to choose activities because they reduce pressure, rather than increase it. Activities are chosen which are pleasant, familiar or rewarding and which increase opportunities for interaction and self-presentation in some manner which is as little threatening as possible. In some groups, this may involve something as simple as sharing the task of making and serving coffee or tea; in another, the physical preparation for the meeting – arranging furniture, lighting fires, bringing out equipment, games or tools; in yet another members may have been separated in order to gather information or materials which they then come together to share. Some such activities may even seem banal; the point, however, is always to consider how well a given activity is suited to furthering interaction in a particular group, regardless of whether or not the actions concerned are intrinsically simple or sophisticated.

A final point here. Such activity may at times have a symbolic value which further increases its relevance.

EXAMPLE 32

Elderly widowers as a social group appear to be under-represented as users of community facilities for the aged. They appear often to become withdrawn earlier and to lose social skills and confidence more rapidly. One service centre for elderly people living in the community used activity group work as a means of overcoming this withdrawal.

Most men in the district had worked in fishing, boat-building, or allied trades. The centre wished to build a large model display of the earlier harbour installations and canvassed these old single men, inviting them to contribute work to the project. Many accepted. Some of the work – suitable for those who had lost their manual dexterity – was very simple. Some required refined skill in carving, joinery, wiring and ropework. While the first stages of the work could be done individually in the centre's workshop, it became increasingly necessary for members to co-operate and co-ordinate so that the whole would be in proportion and would function. All of the pieces had to fit and had to be tried together many times.

The process of the project from individual effort through adjustment to each other's structures and, finally, by assembly into an attractive and well fitting whole paralleled and symbolized the development of relationships between the members – from isolation, through limited co-operation to rich and protracted interaction.

CONVEYING AND CONFRONTING THE PROBLEM

Much group work involves describing, discussing and trying to solve problems which members experience in their lives outside the group. It is never easy to convey the nature of a problem – either to describe it, or to envisage it as described. This is doubly true of the burdened, disadvantaged and often inarticulate people who compose the kind of groups we are discussing. Here again, actions may provide means of conveying the nature of the problem, or clarifying some feelings about it and, perhaps, even proceeding some steps towards its solution. Some examples ...

In earlier publications (Heap 1977a, 1979) I described in some detail how newly adoptive parents, after many years on the waiting list, were invited to make paintings arising from the situation where they finally received their child. They could put 'anything' onto paper – pictures, words, patterns, anything. Their paintings brought to the surface vital aspects of their common situation which had been quite inaccessible to discussion. (One couple shot the stork. Another depicted all of their socially active, childless friends walking out of their lives leaving them alone with the baby, and so on.) It is as if there are fewer censors – or different censors – on what we do with our hands than on what we do with our tongues. Similarly, disaffected young people, whose inarticulate frustration seems only to increase when invited to discuss 'what is wrong with life', have time and again made vivid videotapes and films about their experiences of their place and time in history. Such films are not only highly specific communication about problems, but are also both a catharsis and a rich and accurate basis for treatment, planning or negotiation – as the need may be.

Music has many uses in the context of conveying and confronting inaccessible problems. In my earlier book, I described how tape-recordings of Watusi war-drums were used as background to a therapy group of inhibited, neurotic stammerers who were almost literally choked with long-suppressed aggression.

Comparably, Arnold (1980) has written a moving account of the use of quite another kind of music in group treatment of alcoholics. Arnold perceives the alcoholic condition as dominated by loneliness, overwhelming anxiety about the need for human contact, a pervading sense of unacceptability, defensive grandiosity and flight into self-romanticizing fantasy. In his dependence upon defences of denial and illusion, the alcoholic 'denies himself the one truly secure basis for human relationship – the admission of vulnerability and the need for interdependence'; yet 'only in the *act of communicating* "I am lonely: I need you", is there any hope that another will understand our need and be able to respond to it'. The night music of the juke-box – Sinatra, Streisand, Ross, Lee – heavily emphasizes romanticized loss, the dream that got away, the rootlessness of being alone. Not a few songs specifically advocate the lonely bar-stool and the whisky glass as the comfort in despair. The drinker's feelings are closer to the surface, his sense of loss and loneliness more available in that sad romantic haze than at any other time, when another voice is saying 'I am lonely: I need you'. Arnold – a wise clinician and himself a problem drinker for many years – utilizes this response to music in group work. He uses the first twenty minutes of two-hour discussion sessions simply listening to tapes of the 'saloon singers'. This situation provides a wealth of non-verbal and, later, verbal material which liberates and expresses feelings, which increases awareness of self-deception and romanticism and which is often used as a basis for making concrete plans of alternative ways of dealing with loneliness and failure.

One could cite numerous such examples of non-verbal means of both facilitating verbal communication about the shared problem and of confronting it. I will give one final reference of considerable current importance. With the apparent increase in sexual offences against and by children, including incestuous behaviour, we will be searching for a wide battery of preventive and treatment measures. An interesting example of activity-oriented group work in this area has been described by Ross and Bilson (1981). A group of eleven children had all been victims or offenders in sexual assaults, some of which were both sadistic and grotesque. Twelve structured sessions of activity and discussion were planned. There was contact with parents parallel with the sessions and they were present at a closing session. Members kept a journal and took photographs throughout, which were shown to parents and discussed. Many 'growth games' were used (see Brandes and Phillips, 1977) as well as other forms of creative play. These were chosen for their potential for increasing self-control, increasing ability to give and accept expressions of warmth, reducing anxiety about physical touching and increasing concentration span. Games were played such as 'waiting' and 'silence is fragile' (self-control), 'resent and appreciate' (expressing likes and dislikes verbally instead of violently), and 'computer' and 'passing the buck' (improving concentration and delay of impulse-gratification). Mime, video and drama written by the children themselves, were also used, and the children took increased responsibility from week to week for the conduct of the games and the group. A direct, yet supportive, attack on the effects of trauma was made possible by a diagnostically based choice of activities, which would have been quite unattainable by verbal means.

The worker is not restricted to existing games. Some colleagues have been particularly imaginative in designing new games whose aim is to facilitate communication about the particular problem common to group members. One example of this is Hawley and Brown's (1981) work with children of alcoholic parents. The stigmatizing effect of the parents' condition, and the anxiety, confusion and ignorance about alcoholism among this young vulnerable population indicated a group approach to the authors. Skits, puppet shows and drawing were used to facilitate verbalization and clarification of typical occurrences in alcoholic families and to allow both the discharge of strong feelings and experimentation with more adaptive ways of dealing with family stress. One card game was invented which brought the children into contact with words, concepts and statements about alcoholism, whilst another invited association to words like 'drunk, sad, embarrassed, lonely'.

AIDING SOCIAL LEARNING AND GROWTH

Much group work has the aim of furthering maturation and social learning. Some client groups have encountered obstacles to normal social growth, as in much youth work, delinquency services and some areas of child care. There is little point in just talking about this. Treatment is indicated which is experiential in nature, giving actual opportunities and a new and more benign setting for entering or continuing a maturational process. Experiences should be offered which provide the challenges, satisfactions, abrasions and chances for mutual adjustment necessary for social growth. Such groups provide, in a sense, a mini-society wherein social skills are necessary and have to be developed. Activities are therefore chosen which afford maximum opportunity to take decisions together, to practise bearing shared responsibility, to experience and solve conflicts of interest, and to achieve pleasure and satisfaction through successful co-operation. The worker thereby mobilizes constructively the immature client's self-interest, which one otherwise merely decries.

Such group work is experiential learning wherein group members are continually involved in self-presentation and contact with their peers. Responses are elicited not from wisely nodding therapists and not from control personnel with jingling key-rings but from the members' own immediate reference group, a much more potent source of influence to change. Responsibility, sharing, learning to wait, controlling impulses, and recognizing others' rights are fundamentals of social behaviour and they may only be learned experientially. The encouragement and gratitude or criticism and anger of other members of a peer group on which one is dependent are powerful forces in the development of these social skills. The principle comes to its logical conclusion in the wide use of democratic group activities in work with delinquents and other immature adults, in youth work in the community and in hostels for maladjusted and behaviourally disturbed youth, and so on. It is a version of group work which has an important organizational component in the sense that institutions, hostels, and clubs may be so organized that members experience the reality of responsibility, sharing, decision, etc. They experience also the reality both of their fellows' supportive responses to mature use of these freedoms and of their corrective responses to their misuse.

EXAMPLE 33

Some of my own group work experiences have been in leading groups of probation and aftercare clients in adventure, survival and climbing experiences of from one to two weeks' duration from camp bases in suitable mountain areas. Both the tangible necessities of camp living and the symbolic significance of the rope binding members together have provided experiences of intense mutual dependence, touching not only issues of comfort and convenience but also of physical safety. This mutual dependence has consistently compelled a concern for standards of behaviour which, viewed totally, has been more mature, responsible and mutually considerate than ever previously seen on the part of the clients concerned.

Such experiential learning as the above does not preclude the use of verbal means. On the contrary, the experiences, problems and – one hopes – the gains of such joint activity will usually bring up issues which strongly invite discussion; indeed, they often thrust important material into discussion whose fervour reflects the intensity and relevance of the experience. For example, avoiding a reasonable share of necessary work or acting irresponsibly during a climbing or survival exercise compels discussion of mutual responsibility at a level of engagement normally unattainable by the immature client. This is yet another example also of the constructive use of conflict. It is, further, most useful that such conflict also thrusts itself into the verbal sphere, since the gains of experiential learning may swiftly disappear if the experience is not expressed in words shortly afterwards.

Gold and Kolodny (1978) have reported just such an 'activity/ discussion approach' to a social group who are virtually inaccessible to any other kind of treatment. In describing group treatment of 'socially dispossessed youth' – vocational workshop clients aged from 17 to 22 who had been variously designated as 'retarded, schizoid, impulse-ridden, delinquent, explosive' – these authors remind us of the chaos and rage dominating such clients' personal lives and of the havoc which they wreak in therapeutic agencies who expect at least a minimum of motivation, predictability and self-structure as a condition for engagement in therapy. The group described employed food and eating as an early focus. This is often appropriate with immature groups, because of the reassuring experience of 'getting' and its symbolic reparation of early deprivation. The main action emphasis nevertheless, in their very well equipped facilities, was on the use of gymnastic equipment, the swimming pool and tough ball games. All of the pursuits chosen by the members – self-direction being a cardinal rule – gave both concrete gratifications and sublimation of their aggressive energy and restlessness. Their interpersonal difficulties, actualized by their competitive activities, were subsequently talked about in terms of their consequences for the group situation, which they gradually came to prize since it otherwise afforded them many satisfactions. Increased ability to express feelings and to talk about problems was an aim of the group and their activities actualized issues of violence, achievement, competition and sexuality among other important themes:

'Activity became the skeleton which allowed the flesh of discussion to develop. The workers' matter-of-fact, clearly stated comments which accompanies activities indicated to members the usefulness of verbalisation. The culture of the group was largely created by activity, but in the course of its development these severely deprived young people would find words to be less dangerous, dysfunctional, or just plain difficult' (Gold and Kolodny, 1978, p. 151).

We should not, however, think of activity in the service of social growth as being limited to the young, the immature and the delinquent. Social growth and learning should continue throughout life for us all. Group work with this aim is also relevant for social groups who have previously functioned well but who, because of such changed life situations as illness, sensory loss, or age, have lost roles which have provided a basis for social skills. The loss of these roles is also an assault on self-esteem. Group work with this aim of maintaining social skills often serves therefore the aim of raising or maintaining self-esteem, which we shall now consider.

INCREASING SELF-ESTEEM THROUGH ACHIEVEMENT AND LIFE ENRICHMENT

Many clients have physical, mental or social handicaps which reduce their level of functioning. In our competitive societies, such people readily experience both dependence and inferiority. It is all too likely that they equate their own deviance with failure and thus introject the rejecting and condemnatory attitudes which others display. Some have experienced years of disadvantage and have established a self-image of pervading ineptness, which is continually reinforced by further failures and errors of choice.

Such low self-esteem is self-nourishing, since it conditions the expectations and behaviour with which new situations are met and thereby maintains the likelihood of new failure. It also frequently inhibits clients from risking new encounters at all and causes their withdrawal into a protective but stultifying passivity. This problem is compounded by the strong tendency for many modern welfare services to be mediated in ways which are impersonal and manipulative, defining the helped person as an inferior and passive supplicant.

Where such situations obtain, group work may well be the method of choice. The resources of group support, generalization and collective power buttress threatened self-esteem. Particularly where group content includes the use of activity, appropriate experiences may in quite tangible ways compensate for the forces which undermine members' sense of worth and their mastery of important life skills. But what does 'appropriate' mean here? Choice of activities must be determined largely by consideration of what best meets the specific aim concerned. The activity needs to be relevant and meaningful to the members – self-esteem is reduced rather than enhanced by engagement in meaningless activity. It should also challenge the members in some area where their common problems effect their functioning, but where with group support they should be capable of success. Thus individual achievement in the group may be witnessed and applauded by others present. Joint achievement increases both cohesion and feelings of worth and mastery by the group as a whole.

For example, self-esteem is reinforced and social skills maintained when a group of severely handicapped young adults (those of example 28) successfully negotiate with resistant hotel and restaurant management who are reluctant to accept their custom. Self-esteem and social skills were increased in the group of teenage mothers (example 31b) who chose increasingly to share leisure time with each other, who arranged picnics, prepared food and drink for each other and experienced giving and being complimented and thanked. Similarly,

Wayne's (1979) account of group work in child-abuse prevention shows these isolated and failure-ridden people 'asking for and giving advice about parenting' to each other.

Perhaps in gerontological group work more than in any other sector we see activities used in the service of self-esteem and life enrichment. The trivialization of existence, the pacification, the dependence and the dearth of meaningful social roles in old age are providing social problems as retirement age sinks, the numbers of aged increase and the 'new class of the very old' emerges. Priority must be given to developing a battery of approaches to these problems. Activity-oriented group work is one tool in such a battery. There are already many variations of this. Services and social centres for the elderly in the community are increasingly involving the 'clients' in self-directive responsibility, both formally in elected bodies and informally in the recreational, social and creative daily life of such agencies. In Toronto, residents of an old people's home – some of whom are physically severely handicapped – provide a protracted individual special teaching service for immigrant children, themselves also meeting regularly in consultative groups (Sugar, 1982). In Oslo's youth clubs, some forty or fifty pensioners repair the furniture together with the teenagers, help in the canteen, supervise the doors and calmly help the drunks to find their way home and, in general, contribute actively to a cross-generational milieu. One psycho-geriatric facility activates a group of women patients, some of whom are far into dementia, in baking bread for the whole institution. One group in a community centre, having trained in photography and dark-room technique for a whole winter, made a thorough photographic record of their own old urban milieu. This was completed just before the bulldozers and the devotees of the high-rise moved in and was displayed in both the public library and the centre, as well as being reviewed in the press. This project conveyed gains in terms both of its intrinsic co-operative satisfactions and of the acclaim it was awarded. But in a very direct manner it also involved important work in the area of reminiscence and its connections with personal and cultural identity.

In the area of preventive work, the use of reminiscence in therapy is another group technique in increasing current use. Understanding reminiscence as an assertion of identity and in some cases as an attempt retrospectively to renew struggle with unresolved crises has been greatly furthered by the work of Butler (1963). This has given rise to reminiscence therapy, an activity/discussion technique where members in turn present souvenirs, pictures, music, books, newspaper cuttings, etc., which have connection with important features of their past. They are helped by the group's and the worker's further questioning to elaborate their reminiscences.[2] In this way, they arouse interest and regard for the teller's past, rather than the familiar bored withdrawal, and make possible a positive self-assertion and recognition.

CONTRIBUTING TO ENVIRONMENTAL CHANGE

Few experiences are more destructive of self-esteem and integrity than powerlessness in the face of imposed deprivation or humiliation. There is both logic and dignity therefore in the organization of disadvantaged groups to represent themselves through collective attack on external problems. This was mentioned as one possible aim of group work in Chapters 2 and 3. Almost by definition, it involves such combinations of action and discussion as we are dealing with here. We see such groups increasingly in modern practice, it being increasingly recognized that relatively little is gained by sitting in a circle and discussing a problem imposed by an external condition if the possibility exists of using collective pressure to change the condition itself. Of course there are limits to what may be achieved and clients are often in roles of such political poverty that their pressure does not have effect. But, in a period where media interest in social disadvantage is high, this way of working should always be considered, since many groups find themselves in stronger positions than anticipated.

However that may be, self-esteem increases by the mere act of manifesting oneself in a conflict whether or not the results are impressive. In this context, the dimensions of the problem to be attacked are not important. What is important is its subjective significance to the group. Thus, opposition to cuts in the municipal budget resulted, in example 27, in the reappointment of the keep-fit instructor to an old people's centre. This is a story of collective triumph. Example 26, which described young arthritic patients mobilizing against the great power of the hospital staff, was even more a description of social and emotional growth. In recent years we have seen homeless, unemployed hostel dwellers organizing, forming alliances and using the media to effect change in hostel conditions and other services. We have seen an old age pensioners' group demonstrate for many consecutive days against municipal housing planning which would result in their compulsory rehousing and in rent increases.

Using action to affect environmental conditions does not only involve protest and demands, however. Positive collective assertion too may both increase self-esteem and contribute to changes in the surrounding society, not least attitudinally. Examples of this include the joyous and highly visible participation of a group of young immigrant workers in the street celebrations of their host country's Constitution Day. They also include the production of film and videotape by a group of severely handicapped adults, institutionalized for life, which confronted both staff and the general public with the reality, inequity, dependence and richness – the humanity – of their situation.

In short, group effort may in many situations be constructively directed to attempts to influence some aspect of the environment which effects members' lives. Basic to group work is the notion of help to self-help. It is consistent with this important notion to consider at all times the possibility of the group's actively engaging in efforts to effect environmental change. Unless this possibility is consciously and continually kept open as a group option it becomes all too easy to approach the community on the group's behalf where they could very well do this themselves – or, worse, to accept unfavourable environmental conditions and defective services as unchangeable and thus to seek clients' adjustments to unreasonable situations rather than the reverse.

PREPARING FOR FUTURE CHANGE OR CRISIS

Much group work is concerned with helping members prepare themselves for a demanding or threatening future event or change. Such preparation includes making plans and decisions, gaining information about the realities of the approaching crisis and clarifying the feelings which it arouses.

Examples already given include group work with mastectomized women awaiting discharge, with prospective adoptive parents, with parents of terminally ill children, with pre-release prisoners and with psychiatric patients preparing for discharge. In the context of family life education, examples have been mentioned of group work with engaged couples, with couples expecting their first child and with families preparing for an elderly member's admission to a geriatric facility.

While many examples of this kind of group work draw their resources from the verbal exchanges and associated relationships between members, some groups in addition make use of activities which provide opportunities for actual rehearsal of the coming events.

Some of this anticipatory group work uses real-life situations, while some has more the quality of role play of the pending event. Anticipatory group work which uses reality as the arena of rehearsal may be illustrated by a pre-discharge group of psychiatric patients who, after lengthy hospitalization, experienced as highly threatening the transition to the unfamiliar choices, hustle and procedures of daily urban life. Members of the group therefore spent much of their time out in the city, travelling on the underground, managing the crowds and the supermarket, ordering and serving themselves in the crowded cafeteria, finding the service agencies, and so on – and talking and laughing about surviving it afterwards. Another group, to which I have referred elsewhere (Heap, 1979), was composed of psychiatric day-patients with chronic alcohol problems. The group used much time outside the hospital both to acquire new pleasures and interests and also to familiarize themselves with situations which aroused both anxiety and fear of failure. Members and the group worker went to the cinema and sports events together, wandered around the fishing harbour and yacht basin, visited one another's flats, went on bus trips, 'discovered' the public library, and frequently ate out. In intervening meetings, these events were discussed and members' feelings about them shared and considered. A very important feature of the group's evenings in eating-houses and inns was the repeated confrontation with the common need for the 'insurmountable' refusal – 'No thanks! I won't have a drink. I can't tolerate alcohol.'

The use of anticipatory role play may be a planned and agreed feature of group programme, but may equally well arise as a spontaneous and *ad hoc* approach to finding ways of dealing with a problem in a group which usually works quite differently. Thus, groups may role-play difficult homecomings, interviews for jobs, ways of 'breaking it to the family' (whatever 'it' might be), appearances in court or before the child care committee, – in short, they may experiment practically with alternative behaviours in many different anticipated crises. Such use of role play is becoming increasingly familiar in group work with families under stress, experiencing as do so many the repeated crises, readjustments and new upheavals characteristic of our time. One useful version of such role play consists of 'role reversal' ('you be me; I'll be you').

EXAMPLE 34

In a programme dealing with problems of chronic unemployment in the 1980s an open group was formed. Participation was invited from parents and teenagers in families where one or more members were in protracted unemployment. It had been observed that in families where a school-leaver had been unable to find work or training, his or her eventual resignation became misconstrued as laziness, irresponsibility, 'typical of youngsters today'. The teenagers concerned might in fact have struggled for months before becoming resigned. Conversely, when the youngsters had found a place and a parent lost a long-held job following closure or cuts (a frequent but neglected problem) the teenager's self-satisfaction and the parent's humiliation caused an equally wide gulf quickly to appear – ('Idle old bastard', 'Finished, aren't you?' 'Now you're sponging on me!', etc.)

This group worked by disseminating and discussing information and ideas, by raising consciousness of the causes and inevitability of the economic crisis and by trying to prevent a destructive degree of personalization of these global problems. Usually, the group used a quite conventional discussion format until on one occasion, when cross-generational accusation was particularly heated, the worker took the initiative of proposing a departure from discussion.

The worker suggested that they role-play a situation, simulating one which precipitated conflict and blaming at home. However, a father was to play a son, and vice versa. With variations according to sex and situation, this quickly became established as an accepted working method for the group, who at different times role-played 'getting the boy up at noon', 'trying to talk to Dad when he's lost in the telly', 'family budget' and 'how about drinking less beer, young man?' These role-reversal simulations and the ensuing discussions seemed to succeed in increasing members' understanding and acceptance of each other. It was reported in the group that the insights gained from the role plays were both referred to and used in resolving subsequent conflicts at home.

SUMMARY

In drawing attention to the use of action and activities as an alternative or supplement to discussion, I have proposed a differentiation between six possible aims for use of such activity. These were: stimulating contact and interaction; conveying and confronting the problem; aiding social learning and growth; contributing to environmental change; increasing self-esteem, and preparing for future change or crisis.

It is important that the group worker remains continually open to the option of using action, both on the basis of initial planning and as a spontaneous and opportunistic response to needs as expressed in the group process. There is a regeneration of interest in activity/discussion group work, reflecting awareness that many aims may more readily be attained by 'doing' rather than by 'talking'. Some perhaps may only be achieved by the experiential learning gained through action.

NOTES: CHAPTER 10

1 The interesting history of the ups and downs of the use of activity in group work
   has been documented and discussed by Middleman (1980, 1982).
2 The nursing literature on reminiscence therapy is to be recommended, Burnside
   (1981) and Ebersole (1976, 1978) being particularly informative.

Chapter 11

—————•—————

CO-LEADERSHIP

A striking feature in the recent development of group work in Europe is the emergence of co-leadership as the style of working with groups of clients or patients. It is significant that many case extracts in the present volume – most of which have been accumulated during the past five years – are from groups with two workers. Co-leadership (I find 'co-workership' an impossible word) is, of course, familiar from traditional activity group work in leisure-time and adventure settings. The sheer number of tasks involved in camping, sailing, climbing and so on necessitates there being several responsible people in leadership roles. But it has been much less familiar in group work aimed at the clarification, prevention or solution of such psycho-social problems as we meet in the social work and health fields.

WHY HAS CO-LEADERSHIP EMERGED?

Why is it happening that pairs of social workers, nurses, health visitors, doctors – or combinations of these – increasingly decide to share the tasks of group leadership? It is essential that we address ourselves to this question, since the practice is rapidly growing despite the lack of any theoretical foundation and, as yet, of any thorough evaluation. It is here to stay, I suspect, and it represents a major break with group work traditions. Development and refinement of co-leadership method and increased understanding of its possibilities and pitfalls are tasks to be awarded high priority in the next few years. This chapter is a contribution to such clarification.

Why is it happening? So far, I have observed in Scandinavian and British practice a number of contributing explanations for the growth of co-leadership. Briefly, they are as follows.

1 The lack of training facilities in group methods – particularly in field work – have caused co-leadership to develop as a training experience. Both students and colleagues without group work experience may be, as it were, inducted in the method by sharing leadership with an experienced colleague or supervisor. There is something to commend

this practice while field work placements are scarce and while some professional courses even lack theoretical input on group work method. It has the strengths and the weaknesses of any other system of learning by apprenticeship. Learning from someone by working with him or her is, rightly, time-honoured. But, in this context, it does raise some difficult issues about responsibility for and sharing the worker function, about the difficulties of working together on different bases of skill and professional authority and about the dangers and limitations of learning by imitation rather than by identification and integration.[1]

2 Colleagues who are beginning their professional life or who have experience in other traditions and are using group work for the first time inevitably feel anxious. There would be something seriously wrong if they did not. Sometimes, that anxiety is so overwhelming that it may not be overcome without support and many colleagues are finding just such support in co-leadership. The responsibility and the pressure are shared and there is hope of helpful intervention – 'rescue' might be a more accurate term – in otherwise unmanageable situations. To what extent it actually works out this way seems in the practice I have observed to vary greatly. But the belief that it will do so has enabled many colleagues to begin using groups who otherwise would probably never have cleared the hurdle of resistant anxiety.

There is another aspect of mutual support, however, which does seem to be realizable in practice and which provides quite a strong argument for the use of co-leadership. Co-leaders often 'monitor' each other, agreeing to observe each other's behaviour in the leader role and to give feedback in the 'post-mortem' following group sessions. The praise, criticism, acknowledgement of skill and questioning of interventions which characterize such evaluative discussions constitute both a good learning experience for the workers and a continuing safeguard on quality of service for the group.

3 Group work and the neighbouring fields of group psychotherapy, family therapy, and milieu therapy have long influenced each other. In some contexts it is no longer possible to draw valid boundaries between these methods. One aspect of their continuing influence is that they act as models in leadership style for group workers. Sometimes this is grotesquely inappropriate; at other times, a substantial enrichment. However that may be, much suggests that the common practice in these fields of leadership by co-therapists has contributed to both inspiring and legitimizing its use also in group work.

4 A strong argument for co-leadership is the opportunity which it

affords for interprofessional co-operation and contribution. Relevant knowledge is often fragmented between the various disciplines and some problems which become the focus of group work are so complex that few workers are qualified unaided to help members clarify them. This is particularly the case where problem-solving presupposes information about or orientation in relation to unfamiliar and threatening conditions. Thus, in example 7, a social worker and a physiotherapist jointly led a group of mastectomized women. In example 11, a pediatrician and a social worker led residential group work with families whose children suffered immobilizing diseases. In example 19, a psychiatric nurse and a social worker led a newly formed group of alcoholic in-patients. In examples 28 and 31a, young adults who suffered both sensory loss and severe disablement were led jointly by a social worker and a remedial teacher. And so on.

While group work is never merely a matter of giving information, such co-operation undeniably makes a greater fund of professional knowledge available. This may be used for mediation to the group if appropriate. In most cases the leaders will supplement each other in their observation and understanding, since we tend to register different aspects of behaviour and of the group process depending upon the emphases of our professional traditions.

5   Many contend that co-leadership increases the resources available to the group, irrespective of whether or not it is interprofessional. 'Two see more than one' is the argument and it is strongly held that quality of service increases with two workers. There is much to commend this argument. We bring different perspectives and experiences to the same group and we may complement each other, expanding the spectrum of possible responses to the group process. Not only may co-leaders complement each other's strengths in this way, they may also compensate for each other's weaknesses. We all have some. One of my own few experiences of co-leadership illustrates this.

EXAMPLE 35

In early work with foster care in Norwegian mountain districts (see Examples 15 and 18), I brought to the group my knowledge and experience of group work method and group dynamics as well as of child care and foster placement. I lacked entirely knowledge of the particular urban settings from which these latency-age children came, of traditions of the isolated smallholder families who provided foster care and of the ways in which the unavoidable culture conflicts had been manifested and coped with hitherto. At that time I was only superficially informed about Norwegian child-care legislation and practice.

I shared leadership with a colleague – also a social worker – who was profoundly knowledgeable about both the local culture and child care, but who up to that point had very little experience of group work practice. Either of us alone would have lacked at least one essential element for ensuring a defensible offer of service.

6 The unaccompanied group worker has an important function as model, already discussed. While this does not seem to be diminished by co-leadership, co-workers in addition represent a model of relationship. They have different personalities, backgrounds and emphases of interest. No matter how little the group members actually know about the workers, they at least know that they are different people and they sense some of the most salient areas of difference between them. It is therefore most valuable that these two people, despite their being different, are experienced at managing a complicated and responsible job of sharing and leading. Whatever other functions they may have, they give a visible demonstration of how two different people may work together in a field of considerable tension and challenge, may support each other, may respect and wait for each other, and may disagree.

This is a particularly useful resource in groups whose members are struggling with problems of relationships, since the workers' role, their authority and their comfort in their interaction invite identification with their ways of relating to one another. They become, inevitably, models of a relationship. Further, while each member may identify with the workers' shared interaction pattern, choice of individual model is enhanced by having two workers. This is particularly the case where the co-workers are of opposite sexes and where the group is mixed. For example, men and women in the group might be stimulated to develop new ways of relating to their marriage partners or of being 'male', 'female', or 'parent'. Shilkoff (1983) describes a particularly interesting example of male-female co-leadership, where the leaders' relationships and behaviour was a central concern in a group of adolescent girls. Similarly, in group treatment of incest victims, Gottlieb and Dean (1981) show how male – female co-leadership enriches the treatment situation, providing both a healthy model and a lasting situation which enable disengagement from the distortions and manipulation of the girls' own disturbed family relationships.

The foregoing represent some arguments for co-leadership and are the main explanations for its emergence. Co-leadership is, however, by no means free of problems. As a leadership style it is really quite complex and is currently the subject of disparate opinion. Out of this are emerging some conditions for the use of co-workers. I endorse these and will also supplement them with some of my own reservations in the remainder of this chapter.

CONDITIONS FOR THE USE OF CO-LEADERSHIP

1   No decisions about co-leadership may be made which set aside the primacy of the consideration of members' needs and feelings and of the group process. This particularly concerns proportionality between the number of members and the number of workers. Having two workers is itself the subject of legitimate contention, yet I have encountered situations where three − and even, on occasion, four − workers have led groups jointly, so that there have been nearly as many workers as members. This destroys group process. I have been unable to accept as valid the argument that the workers' regard for members' rights and autonomy compensates for the danger of their being overwhelmed by facing such a phalanx of expertise and professional authority This argument overlooks all we know about the development of relationships and about the anxiety of new group members who bring unsolved troubles and a history of inadequacy with them to the group, who look to experts for guidance and relief, and who in many cases are long since socialized to subservience. These obstacles to active and comfortable involvement in a group which is meant to be experienced as the members' 'own' will in most cases be unsurmountable.

I suspect that this curious distortion of group work method is a misapplication of a psychiatric tradition, where 'morning meetings' and large-group confrontive sessions in the allegedly therapeutic milieu often involve many staff and an only slightly larger number of patients. It is an inappropriate model for group work. All uses of co-leadership in group work must begin with the questions 'Does this facilitate group process or hinder it?' 'Are the backgrounds of these members such that two (or more) workers will increase members' feelings of helplessness and inferiority?', and 'Are there such proportions of members to workers (I would suggest 3:1 as an absolute minimum) that the group process may nevertheless dominate over the tendency to centralize expectations and attention on the workers' expertise?'

Finally, if a planning decision is nevertheless taken to have more than two workers, I would argue that the third worker should have no role in leadership. His or her role should be confined to passive functions such as observation or recording. (This is in my view a more suitable role for the field-work student than active co-leadership, for instance.)

2   Workers who decide to share leadership of a group must have

some reason for doing so which each is able to articulate, understand and accept. Such reasons might include their possessing complementary areas of knowledge and skill. They might include a clear mutual acknowledgement of their individual inadequacy as inexperienced solo workers, in which case preparation ('tuning in') would include specification of their respective perceived strengths and weaknesses. The choice of co-leadership might arise from an assessment of members' believed needs as including the possibility of diluting the relationship with the worker, specific advantages of alternative models or the need for male/female identification alternatives in leadership.

Whatever the reasons, they must be clear, in order that corresponding and appropriate ways of sharing the worker functions may be worked out.

3 Co-leadership must be carefully prepared. Members are confused by co-workers who use the group situation itself as the arena for discovering the ways in which they are to co-operate. It is both possible and necessary that workers clarify their respective roles, structuring them and defining the quality and form of their relationship as co-leaders, before embarking on the shared task of working with the group.

Such role-sharing has many variations. It also raises a number of problems.

Perhaps the most manageable situation is in interprofessional co-leadership or other co-leadership where the workers possess different areas of knowledge and skill which are clearly identifiable. For example, a social worker trained in group methods and a doctor working together with a group in an oncology ward could readily decide that requests for factual information about cancer, discussion of prognoses and treatment, and material about bodily sensations should be responded to mainly by the doctor. Information about social and economic provisions and functions concerning activating the group and clarifying or interpreting the group process might be agreed mainly to be the social worker's special province. The remaining areas of communication in the group and work with the social and emotional impact of the illness should be available for either worker to respond to as they are able to find appropriate responses. Similarly, in the foster parents' group referred to in example 35, one worker assumed the main responsibility for responding to culturally related issues and to questions and criticism of the regulations and remunerations governing fostering, while the other worker assumed responsibility for guiding, aiding and commenting on the group process. Again, an extensive and undefined area was available for response and intervention by either worker.

At least one author has suggested that co-leaders, irrespective of similarity or dissimilarity in their backgrounds, might effectively share roles by dividing between them emphasis on the task-oriented activity and the socio-emotional activity in the group (Yalom, 1975). I am in some doubt about this interesting idea. It introduces an extensive area of uncertainty about 'what is what', which I believe could in practice produce indecisiveness and hesitation by the workers. Further, good social functioning presupposes that these two aspects of group behaviour enrich and promote each other. The workers should not, therefore, be responsible for divorcing them.

This, of course, introduces the whole question of the worker's personal style of self-presentation and, thus, of leadership. While all competent and mature workers should be able to work as well in task as in socio-emotional roles, it is reasonable to suppose that many workers function better in the one than in the other area of inter-action. Galinsky and Schopler (1980) usefully review a number of sources in suggesting other considerations of personal style which might influence co-workers' decisions about how they should share leadership. Thus co-workers, according to style and personality, might in different degrees be active or passive, dominant or sub-missive, directive or non-directive, nurturing or confrontive, and so on. Again, I have some reservations about this. It is not only the echoes of Saturday-night TV with the stylized 'good' and 'bad' detec-tives alternating in the interrogation room with a view to maximizing both confusion and dependence. There is also a degree of artificiality in this version of role-sharing which bothers me. Neither worker is being authentic; both are withholding aspects of themselves which are important features of the kind of whole-person models which they wish to provide as leaders. I believe it to be more honest in relation to the group, more attainable in terms of practical co-operation in leadership and more in tune with the workers' own expectations of professional growth through co-leadership to take a different stance on this issue of style differentiation. Instead of saying 'I'll be confron-tive, I'm better at it. You be supportive, you're better at it', the workers should say something more like 'I will be more confrontive probably, since I tend to be, but I wish to extend my skills in suppor-tive responses. You will tend to be more supportive, because that's the way you are – but can't you try to engage me more actively in your supportive responses to the group? Pull me in, somehow, just as I shall try to pull you in so that we both come to represent models of both supportive and confrontive behaviour.'

4   Whatever other functions or styles may or may not be apportioned between co-workers, there are certain values and types of activity

which must in my view be demonstrated by both workers. These are the expression and acceptance of feelings, involvement in group control (in the sense of accepting some responsibility for keeping the group in the working position) and aiding the group in taking up both intragroup and intergroup conflict. All three of these functions are essential in a well functioning group and must be represented in leadership. All are, in addition, difficult. Therefore it is necessary that both workers, however different they may otherwise be, show that it is possible and necessary to express feeling, to take up conflict and to keep an eye on the ball during the work of the group whatever else is happening. This is vital to the development of purposive norms. If one worker is, as it were, 'excused' these vital and difficult role behaviours, a defensive model is offered and the total function of leadership is seriously weakened.

These essential and shared worker functions must be clarified, understood and agreed upon at the planning stage of co-leadership.

5　The effectiveness of co-leadership is dependent upon the workers concerned having a viable relationship. Planning must therefore include an open and honest appraisal of their relationship and should, further, be based on testing in earlier co-operative situations. It is not sufficient to be attracted to each other during the course of brief and benign acquaintanceship. I know of two colleagues with a short, positive acquaintance who enthusiastically entered co-leadership, then to discover a wall of unexplored difference and tension between them. The urbane mutual mayhem which followed might just possibly have entertained the group, but I doubt very much that it helped them.

The relationship must nevertheless be strong enough to tolerate disagreement.[2] While it is agreed that disagreement in early sessions tends to increase the insecurity of the exploratory phase, there is much experience to suggest that expression of disagreement between co-workers in later sessions is beneficial. It demonstrates open communication. It exemplifies the possibility of preventing accumulation of tension by examining dissimilar opinions instead of storing them until they generate aggressive pressure. This is a valuable version of the modelling function. It makes it easier for members to disagree with each other or with a worker and thus both develops functional norms in the group and contributes to better clarification of specific issues.

To be able to disagree in ways which are neither hostile nor anxious requires another quality of the co-workers' relationship. It must be non-competitive. In addition to being a good relationship model this is also necessary to prevent workers interrupting each other and leading away from lines of discussion which the other is pursuing.

Co-workers need to be very interested indeed in understanding where the other is trying to go and in supporting this. This implies respect, as does rational and friendly disagreement. But it also implies the need for co-workers to be familiar with each other's ways of thinking, formulating and approaching a problem, with each other's biases, enthusiasms and beliefs. This can only imply that co-workers should already have worked quite closely together in other contexts. They should have developed familiarity and respect and should have discovered compatibility. I use the term 'compatibility' rather than 'friendship'. A mutually positive relationship is necessary, but if it is too close members may experience the co-workers as a cohesive and powerful subgroup, so that leadership would inhibit rather than stimulate them. Co-workers who are friends seem also to be protective of one another, which tends both to close down communication and to further the image of leadership as a group within the group. A male-female co-leadership might also, if their relationship were too close, suggest a sexuality which would be disturbing and confusing to the group. Indeed, all the transference aspects of member–worker relationships are intensified with co-leadership and particularly so where workers clearly enjoy a relationship outside the group.

6   Compatibility does not of course assume equality, though compatible relationships tend to be more egalitarian than not. Equality is generally agreed to be a decisively important feature of the relationship of co-workers. Members have nothing to gain by observing one worker dominating the other and one accepting a subordinate role. Their use of the 'junior' leader is very limited where one worker is manifestly senior. Members should be able to relate with confidence to both workers and be able to identify with both their ways of relating and of approaching problems. They must therefore perceive them as of equal status, understanding and sensitivity, no matter in what other areas they are different. Again, this is an issue which workers are able to evaluate and consider together before deciding upon co-leadership. It must be dealt with honestly and confrontively. If workers decide to share leadership despite status differences – as in a training situation or in some hierarchical interprofessional agency – they must plan how to deal with this. Handling such a situation requires, minimally, that it is taken up with the group and that it is recognized as a possible source of difficulty and imbalance. In this way, norms of problem confrontation and open communication are served despite the lack of equality between workers. If the workers remain able to respect and support each other without respectively authoritative interruption or anxious subjugation, and if they are able to disagree rationally should disagreement arise, then the disadvantages

of inequality may be converted to strengths in a new version of the modelling function — all of which is very advanced group behaviour and demands a great deal of the workers.

SUMMARY

In this chapter, reasons for the increasing use of co-leadership in group work have been noted. These are:

the need for innovative training procedures;
mutual support for inexperienced group workers;
the influence of co-therapist leadership models from psychiatry and family therapy;
interprofessional co-operation and enrichment;
increase in total available resources;
the provision by the co-workers of a model of a relationship.

With concern for standards of service and in recognition of the difficulties of co-leadership, I have proposed a number of conditions for the guidance of workers considering sharing the leadership role. These are:

the proportion of workers to members must be evaluated;
reasons for the choice must be clarified and must be explicable and defensible in terms of members' interests;
co-leadership must include open, careful preparation involving clarification of workers' respective roles, both where roles are co-incident and where they are different;
both workers must represent common basic human values and notions about relationships and group processes, whatever other differences they may have;
workers must have an open, positive and compatible relationship, though close friendship is not advisable;
workers should have equal status.

NOTES: CHAPTER 11

1 Co-leadership in training for social work with groups is now so salient a feature of social work education in North America that a special issue of *Social Work with Groups* (vol. 3, no. 4, Winter 1980) dealt solely with experiences of it and views about it. Opinions ranged widely, but there runs through the issue clear signals of reservation and of the urgent need for guidelines and criteria. It should be closely studied by all who have a serious interest in the use of co-leadership as a training device.

2 Disagreement between co-leaders, a controversial issue, is further discussed in the literature by *inter alios* Heilfron (1969), Benjamin (1972), Yalom (1975) and Herzog (1980).

Chapter 12

THE FINAL PHASE – TERMINATION OF THE GROUP

THE MAIN CHARACTERISTICS OF TERMINATION

The group which has given its members so much (or so little) of what they have sought through their participation must, sooner or later, end.

Like all endings in life it may be more or less painful, depending upon how it is dealt with. It might more or less well help the members to go further to the next stage of their social life, both building upon the gains of the group experience and managing without its support. Despite its importance, termination has been rather neglected in the literature and has only relatively recently become the subject of general interest and clear formulation. (See, for example, Klein, 1972, Johnson, 1974, Shulman, 1979, Douglas, 1979, Garvin, 1981).

One fundamental notion common to these recent formulations and one which is evident in all well constructed practice is that termination is not to be regarded as an event, but as a process. It should not suddenly and without preparation face the members on a particular day – 'Well, this is our last meeting; thank you and goodbye.' It must be prepared for during an appropriate period, whose length varies from group to group, and its preparation should serve as a hopeful transition from the state of group membership to that of post-membership. One of the earliest writers on the subject, Levine (1967), emphasized that termination should serve as a 'bridge to self-dependence'. This statement is still not only valid, but is fundamental. Can it be realized in practice, and can the worker contribute to it?

TWO KEY CONCEPTS

During the termination process, just as with all the preceding work with the group, the worker's role and tasks are determined by the needs of the group and by the nature and emphases of the group process at that time. As the group approaches its close, two conditions tend most strongly to influence the group process. These are separation and ambivalence. Whether the group is terminating because aims have been attained, because an agreed time has elapsed, or even because of failure to establish a satisfactory working situation, ambivalent feelings about separation will be present and will usually in some way manifest themselves.

Ambivalence which is not recognized and separation anxiety which is not articulated and resolved hold people in positions of dependency and confusion. This is a general truth about human behaviour. Dealing with these conditions in a group work context is, then, a necessary condition for building a 'bridge into self-dependence' out of the termination process. The issues are sometimes mildly and indirectly expressed, requiring some skill to see that they are present at all. In other groups, they thrust themselves more compellingly forward. It is important, however, that termination issues are always taken seriously and that they are dealt with irrespective of how indirectly or how dramatically they evidence themselves.

What is the nature of this ambivalence about termination? What are the conflicting feelings?

First, some common positive reactions. Members about to dissolve a group or to leave an open group may feel relief from the pressures, demands and confrontations of group life. The work in the group may have been emotionally tiring and it may be pleasant to view a future free of such effort. Processes of change, no matter how strongly the change is wished, are disruptive and the termination of group life is a return to familiarity. There is hope and anticipation in consolidating the gains from the group and, above all, in exercising them in the reality of daily living. The experience of growth fathers the wish to individuate and experiment. There are often areas of privacy which have been threatened and there is relief in leaving the group with these areas unscathed. Few groups are entirely free of abrasive differences and some members may feel liberated from imposed intimacy with other members with whom they would never freely have chosen friendship. Where participation has not been successful, of course, some members will perceive termination as a safeguard of the secondary gains of a problem which has been maintained despite the group experience. (Examples of this are met in alcoholic and drug-treatment groups; also in unsuccessful treatment of family problems, where members gain spurious relief from responsibility or guilt by 'blaming' or 'labelling' a particular family member.) Finally, whether or not the group has been successful, termination means at a practical level that a commitment has ceased and that members are free of a time-consuming ritual.

This is rather a list of positives. What of the negative side of the ambivalence? This is predominantly an experience of loss. There is loss of a set of relationships which may have had quite special value, in that they have been formed during a period of growth and change. There is loss of a milieu which has had qualities usually lacking in everyday life: support, intimacy – and above all – a non-judgemental and informed understanding of the struggles and conflicts in which members are enmeshed. An experience of warmth and closeness, free of possessiveness and sexuality, is also about to be lost. There is loss of the encouragement, praise and hope with which members often imbue their relationships in groups of this kind. There may have been laughter in the group, for people who have become strangers to it. There may have been tears, giving to distressed people a freedom and release which is forbidden by the controlling norms of our denial-ridden culture. The group may have been an island of meaning and challenge in lives which lack these qualities. Indeed, for members who otherwise are socially impoverished, the group may for a time have been the only certain source of human contact and response. The regularity and predictability of the meetings – 'each Tuesday at 7 p.m.' – may itself have been a weekly milestone, something stable and good to anticipate, to know that that at least is there.

ON RESOLVING AMBIVALENCE

And so the feelings pull against each other – relief in one direction, loss in the other. Readers will no doubt be able to supplement yet further from their own group experiences the list of common conflicting feelings which I have made here. How is this ambivalence to be resolved? What indeed do we mean by 'resolving ambivalence' – a very common coin in the currency of professional jargon?

The aim is not to erase ambivalence, to arrive at a position where we seem to have no regrets about what we have lost. The aim is to have accepted the loss, to have ceased fantasizing about returning to the pre-loss state and to be sufficiently positive in one's attitude to the present condition to be able to use one's resources in adjusting to it and functioning in it rather than in looking regretfully backwards. It is an important point that we should not need to alienate ourselves from people or situations in order to accept having lost them. In separation or divorce, we do not need to hate our former spouse before we can get on with the business of living. In widowhood, we do not have to feel that the dead partner never existed before we may be free to form new relationships. In such situations, good memories are a part of the reality and richness of living through time and should be allowed a comfortable place in our minds, whilst nevertheless we are mainly occupied with the pleasures and concerns of our present living and with planning realistically for tomorrow.

This is also true of the loss involved in group termination. If feelings of closeness and caring – perhaps some kind of loving – have been present in our group experiences, why should we not keep and treasure them? They are an important part of the group's meaning and support, perhaps long after its actual termination. Memories of collective warmth are nourishing features of our mental and emotional lives and we wish to maintain some tendrils of contact with such good experiences. The resolution of ambivalence about group termination involves just such nourishment by past experience, while requiring that termination is accepted as a fact and that the balance of investment is now on the post-group experience – going further, building upon the gains won in the group-that-was.

DEALING WITH TERMINATION

The termination process should, then, aim at resolving ambivalence in this way. How may this be achieved? As already stated, we are helped here by the concept of 'worry work' which recognizes the gains of a certain kind of preparation for impending crisis. Such preparation is affective, in the sense of ventilating and confronting feelings about the approaching change. It is also cognitive, in the sense of anticipating and rationally considering the implications of the new situation. In worry work, the worker lends support, guidance and structure to the person in crisis.

These ideas are useful in helping us to deal with the termination phase of group work. They prescribe the conditions for dealing optimally well with it. There are three main conditions.

THE FIRST CONDITION

The first condition is that the transition is to be recognized and faced. At some time prior to the final meeting, if the members do not raise this issue themselves, the worker must take the initiative of reminding the group that termination is approaching. In groups with a very short sequence, for example a six-session parents' group in a family life education programme, it would be appropriate to do this in the fifth meeting. In a group which has had a protracted lifespan, where members have had many experiences both in their relationships and in their struggle with common problems, the subject must be raised a considerable number of sessions beforehand, spanning several weeks of work.

Another variable is whether the group has a contractually agreed duration or whether it is indeterminate. In either case the approach of termination is to be faced at some point. Indeterminate groups also close at some time. Members must never be seduced into believing that the group has the possibility of infinite life if this is not the case, and the reality of eventual termination must be introduced during both the offer of service and subsequent work on the group contract. The finite nature of the group should lie in the background of members' awareness during the work phase. When appropriate, consideration of whether and when to terminate may be introduced. This of course involves an additional task of evaluation. Is the group ready for termination? Have aims been attained?

An important factor here is the clarity with which aims were negotiated and clarified during the formative stage of the group. Particular attention should be paid to this early task in groups of indeterminate duration, otherwise criteria are lacking on which an invitation to consider group closure may later be based. If you don't know where you were going, you do not know whether you have arrived.

Another indicator of readiness for termination is the quality of interaction and relationships. In a group which has functioned well there seem often to be changes in the group process at this stage. The early processes of identification and solidarity, circumnavigating awareness of demographic differences, have enabled the group to cohere and thus to draw upon the reservoir of collective resources. Relationships have been egalitarian and, often, close. Interaction has been active, reflecting members' involvement in each other, and has been well distributed throughout the membership. But, when members begin to feel that they have gained something like the objectives which brought them to the group, a process of disengagement from the work of the group commences. Interaction becomes less task-centred and more social and superficial. Attendance may fall off. Involvement in one another seems, totally, to decrease although the more social quality of relationships sometimes produces a rebirth of subgrouping at this late stage. It is as if the decrease in mutual dependence permits a new awareness of areas of dissimilarity. Thus, relationships may be adjusted or re-formed, reflecting the criteria for friendships and alliances which we see in daily life — class, age, interests, etc. — rather than the purposive and inclusive criteria of problem-solving groups. With a decrease in need for each other, a degree of disengagement is often seen. This provides a clear signal of readiness for termination which is of particular use in groups of indeterminate life.

This aspect of group process could be illustrated diagrammatically, as in Figure 8.

While such indications of readiness to terminate are frequently seen, they do presuppose that needs have been met and problems solved up to some reasonable degree of expectation. Members must

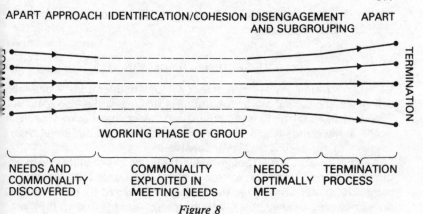

APART APPROACH IDENTIFICATION/COHESION DISENGAGEMENT   APART
AND SUBGROUPING

WORKING PHASE OF GROUP

| NEEDS AND COMMONALITY DISCOVERED | COMMONALITY EXPLOITED IN MEETING NEEDS | NEEDS OPTIMALLY MET | TERMINATION PROCESS |

Figure 8

also have been conscious of their aims for participation. They must, in addition, have had satisfactory opportunities for social contact and expression outside the group, so that they are not dependent upon it other than as a circumscribed problem-solving medium.

Where these conditions do not obtain, termination is resisted. It arouses anxiety and disorientation in such groups and these come to expression in a number of ways.

One common signal of resistance is the introduction of quite new problems. Whilst the worker thinks that the group's work is approaching completion, there is an unanticipated introduction of a quite new agenda or at least an entirely unexplored facet of the common problem, implying the need to begin a further process of protracted work. Similarly, there often occurs a kind of regression in groups which resist termination. This is partly a return to earlier and less mature ways of using the group and of relating to one another. Such regression is also, yet more typically, a return to earlier attitudes and approaches to the common problem, reintroducing some of the confusion, helplessness and ambivalence of earlier stages. The worker may also be surprised to find himself being rejected at this stage, encountering scepticism and hostility not previously experienced. This is, of course, the common and immature defence of rejecting in order to forestall being rejected – an indirect reflection of the loss and damage with which members' fantasies may imbue termination. A corollary of this is that some members may reject the group itself. This may represent a sharp reversal of individual members' attitudes to the group. An active and committed member may overtly reject the evaluations, activities and relationships which he has hitherto accepted or even sought. Thus, new and apparently inexplicable conflicts may be seen at this time, which also reflect members' unhappy struggle with the fact of termination.

THE SECOND CONDITION

Whether termination is approached without undue anxiety or with resistance, the second major condition for dealing with it also obtains. That is, in facing the fact of termination, recognition must be given to the ambivalence which it arouses and to both the nature and the strength of the feelings which it involves.

Again, this practice – though well established in the mainstream of group work tradition – is reinforced by lessons learned in crisis treatment. No matter how strong the feelings engendered by the threat of an unwelcome change, they become more manageable if they are recognized and named. No matter how great a loss one has actually suffered, it becomes a little easier to bear if others know, and show that they know, that one is suffering. Here of course we are somewhat in opposition to the traditions of Western culture, where feelings about problems tend to be regarded as troublesome irrelevancies, best ignored or avoided as far as possible. Ironically, it is the denial or repression of feelings that produces intransigence in problems, not the feelings themselves. Thus, if feelings about termination are ignored, denied or trivialized, they may never be worked through and will therefore prevent members from resolving their ambivalence in the direction of freedom from the group. If, on the other hand, they are recognized and articulated they may take their place as a natural and inevitable part of the termination process and may be dealt with as well as is possible according to the resources and limitations of different groups.

However, it is important not to dramatize feelings about termination. Some discussion of the termination process is a shade too colourful, inflating its dimensions by, for example, analogies with death. I would suggest that such dramatization makes it more rather than less difficult to deal with the process, adding to it the frightening burdens of other and perhaps irretrievable losses. We aim for the opposite effect. Recognizing the feelings, just as they are, makes them easier to accept, less alarming, and capable of being coped with.

There are three main avenues of entry into this part of preparation for termination. The first of these is outside the worker's control and is by far the most desirable. I am thinking here of the situation where feelings about termination arise in a spontaneous and appropriate way from the work of the group, a member or members taking the initiative to bring up the subject.

EXAMPLE 36

(a)   A child-care worker led a group of five parental pairs in a family
      life education programme. This was focused on the normal
      problems, conflicts and decisions arising in families with small
      children. There were to be eight meetings.

      Early in the seventh meeting, one father said 'We still have a
      lot of ground to cover and next week is our last meeting.' This
      was picked up by another member who said, 'Yes, we seem to
      have been meeting for so much longer than these few weeks. It
      will be strange not having the group to come to – but interesting
      to see what we can use of what we have learned together.'

(b)   A psychiatric nurse and a social worker led a group of aftercare
      patients through a loosely agreed period – 'finishing at the end
      of the winter'. All members lived alone and had long histories of
      dependence on alcohol and of periodic depressive episodes.
      Almost from the outset the group had worked well on a wide
      range of relevant themes. They had established highly purposive
      norms, which were both supportive and confrontive. The
      workers believed that much had been gained and consolidated
      and had begun to think about introducing the issue of
      termination.

      With the approach of spring, however, a member took the
      initiative of raising this question for the first time. He recalled the
      original agreement and said that 'finishing off the group' (*sic*)
      would no doubt be coming up soon. He wished to suggest that
      the idea be reconsidered. 'Why not just continue? We all get a
      lot out of coming. We will miss the group. It's been very good
      having somewhere to come and talk together like this. In any
      case, there are lots of important things we haven't started on yet.
      For instance ...'.

While these two episodes reflect very different degrees of readiness and
resistance, both provide positive conditions for the commencement of
the termination process. Members' own awareness of its approach
aroused feelings, some of which they were able to express in good time
to permit helpful work with this final, ambivalent issue.

The two remaining avenues of entry into this area depend upon
initiative from the worker, rather than from the group. Where the
worker believes that he hears or sees indirect (latent) expression of
feelings about termination, whatever they may be, he may choose to
indicate this with a view to facilitating more direct expression so that

it may be incorporated in the final work of the group. This is, of course, yet another example of the worker's function in furthering clear and open communication, which may well continue throughout the whole life of the group albeit with varying emphases and foci.

EXAMPLE 37

(a) In a prison: 'Discharge is coming very close for most of you. Now I seem to hear you describing as a problem the fact that we have helped each other to make decisions and to see difficulties more clearly. I wonder if this is a way of saying that you are worried about managing without the group? We should perhaps start to talk about this.'

(b) In a parents' group: 'These last few meetings we have heard quite a few negative remarks both about the group and the way I have led it. That, of course, is perfectly all right – but it is something quite new and I have not always been able to see that the criticism is justified. So I wonder whether this is partly a way of getting used to doing without the group – you know, "It was no good anyway." We can avoid a lot of sadness and disappointment that way.'

(c) In an alcoholics' group: 'Mr Hagen says that he is looking forward to the group finishing but feels impolite saying so. I doubt very much that he is alone in feeling some relief. After all, you have worked hard together with painful things here, you will be feeling all kinds of conflicting things, I imagine.'

These case extracts show workers' attempts to move the group from an indirect to a direct mode of expression of feelings about termination.

The worker may also take initiative in this area even when no indirect expression of feeling has occurred. The issue must be faced and it is the worker's responsibility to ensure that this happens. Of course, the very absence of comment about approaching termination might reflect anxiety and ambivalence about it, in the sense of representing denial defences. In this situation, which is very common, the worker finds generalization useful. Here, having introduced the fact or the suggestion that termination is approaching and having observed little or no response, the worker makes generalizations aimed at normalizing and accepting ambivalent feelings about termination and thereby at facilitating their expression. He might say: 'It probably isn't easy to talk about this; experience is that finishing such a group arouses many different feelings – often quite strong ones' or 'We seem to be avoiding saying anything about closing the group. But the time is getting nearer. We've had some strong experiences together since we started, so I would expect there to be very mixed feelings about getting near to the end', or 'Over the years I have usually seen a curious mixture of relief and loss when groups reach the stage where we are now. It is always useful to talk about it.'

Particularly when the worker senses resistance to termination, he might formulate his generalization so as to emphasize the frequency with which negative feelings such as loss, anxiety, anger and fear of being alone are experienced.

THE THIRD CONDITION

Hand in hand with working through feelings about termination are interdependent and equally important tasks of a more cognitive and tangible nature. The loss which arouses feelings is partly loss of relationships and a source of attachment. But it is also – often primarily – loss of a setting in which important work has been performed. Dealing with the approaching loss requires, therefore, that the actual work of the group be reviewed and evaluated.

In reviewing work done, it is intended that group members both perceive and assert their own achievements during the life of the group. Problems are seen to have been solved, decisions taken, satisfaction found, growth to have occurred. This serves a number of purposes: it increases self-esteem (some groups are astonished to discover how much they have achieved); it increases consciousness of improved capacity to relate to others and to deal with life problems; it increases freedom, both from the group itself and from the oppressiveness of the problems which brought members to the group in the first place.

It is unusual that members initiate such a review, since only rarely will members spontaneously perceive gain or find interest in such retrospection. It rests usually with the worker, therefore, to introduce it. This may be done with lesser or greater formality depending upon the norms and the contract for the group. Thus, in one group, the worker could say: 'You know, I have been thinking since we last met of how far we have come together. It surprised me when I realized how much ground we have covered. It might be useful to have a look at this together.' The worker in another group would be able to say: 'We should remind ourselves that we only have another four meetings. Now, when we started we worked hard on very clearly finding out what the aims of the group were to be. Experience is that it is very useful at about this point to have a look, quite systematically, at what has in fact been done of what the group set out to do. I'd like to suggest that we use this meeting for just such a review.'

One very important result of this review is that it identifies areas of uncompleted work. Such areas are untidy and half-concealed knots which must be untied before members may become free of the group. Thus in leading the discussion into this part of the termination process the worker must ask the group what they experience as unfinished work. He must also himself suggest areas of discussion or action which he believes relevant to agreed aims but not yet dealt with sufficiently or, indeed, at all.

EXAMPLE 38

A discussion group for old people living alone in the community was part of an extensive provision of gerontological group work in a Norwegian county.[1]

All agreed topics had been taken up at some level or other. These included the experience of living alone, adjustment to a non-productive lifestyle, the possibilities for new interests and activities, and available provisions and services.

When three meetings remained of an agreed ten-meeting programme, the worker took the initiative by saying: 'It occurs to me, since two-thirds of our time has already passed, that we ought to make sure that we in fact discuss all of the topics which we wished to take up. It would be a good idea if the group – during today's meeting – brought up either such new subjects as remain untouched or reminded us all of things we have touched earlier and could usefully come back to.'

Later in the meeting, one member recalled an early agreement to try to compare modern values with those of their own youth and to explore how social conditions affect what people regard as 'right behaviour'. The group supported her in her assertion that lack of clarity about this was an important source of old people's alienation. Another said that she wished to come back to the question of their relationship with their own children. 'Is it true', she asked, 'that we are so very understanding of how our children's busy lives prevent them keeping more contact with us – or are we really more disappointed and angry than we like to say? I'd like some more honest talk about that before we finish.' Similarly, the worker herself recalled a topic which had arisen very early and had been abandoned. This concerned members' varying attitudes toward forming relationships following their widowhood. She said that this had possibly been too difficult to discuss in the early days of the group, but that she believed it important to try to come back to it.

In this example we see how the worker's initiative ensured the inclusion in the group's work of a number of important issues. Security and cohesion gained during the working phase of the group often make it possible to return to themes which have earlier been too threatening to deal with adequately. Had these not been dealt with in the group quoted, members would have experienced some dissatisfaction with the group at closure and would probably have had diffuse difficulties in terminating. Most groups could provide some examples of this type of process. The completion of the work is a prerequisite for using the termination process as a 'bridge to self-dependence'.

Completing the work sometimes involves such tangible activity as taking decisions: 'On the basis of the clarification gained shall we or shall we not institutionalize our child? Move back to the valley? Fight the authorities?' 'Shall I or shall I not have the operation? Apply for aid? Move into a home?' And so on. By no means all group work is aimed at decision-taking, of course, and even when it is we must not necessarily expect the decision itself to be taken in the group, although the resultant increase in commitment may be a good argument for doing so. But it is desirable that members, during the termination process, consider the implications to them of their experiences in the group, both where these provide a basis for a particular circumscribed decision and where – as is most common – the gains of participation are more in terms of improved self-esteem or social functioning, changes in lifestyle, enhanced ability to solve problems, and increased skill in managing relationships.

Questions such as, 'What has the group meant to you?', 'Can you put into words what you have got out of it?', 'Will there be changes at home/work/in your community as a result of what we have done together here?' are among the questions which focus members' thoughts on the implications of the group experience for their future functioning in the post-group stage. This part of the termination process is a gathering and ordering of experiences into a manageable entity of perceptions, which may then be directed at consideration of the changes and challenges of the post-termination situation. Awareness of gains and reflecting on how to use them give an assurance of strength which makes possible the loosening of the ties to the group.

SOME SPECIAL CONSIDERATIONS

In practice, certain additional considerations regularly arise during termination which I wish finally to mention.

The first of these concerns variations in individual members' readiness. In a sense, terms such as 'group maturity', 'the group's ability' and 'group readiness' are fictions. No matter how cohesive the group becomes, it remains – and should remain – a collection of individual human beings. Among many other implications, this means that there must be variations in the extent to which members are ready for or resistant to termination. The worker's observation of the conditions for termination which I have specified – anticipation, dealing with feelings and completing the work – will always have some effect in reducing the distance between individual members' degrees of readiness. It may indeed be the decisive factor in enabling a common termination to take place at all. Nevertheless, it does occur from time to time that a member or members are so markedly less ready than the group as a whole that some special consideration has to be given. Such members may have had too great difficulty in engaging in the group, because of shyness, anxiety or inhibition. They may have discovered or disclosed during the working phase more extensive problems than were apparent at group formation. Or their dependence upon collective support remains too great to allow them to engage in separation.

Where this is the case, the worker may sometimes believe the group situation to be so supportive and generous that he feels able to risk a greater degree of individualizing of attention in the group without damaging the group bond. He may then attempt to focus the use of group resources on this member's particular needs in the hope of increasing his or her readiness up to something like the common level. The worker may also conclude that such a member's special needs are too extensive or too intransigent to be dealt with in this way. He will then consider the possibility of offering this member further service of some kind after the termination of the group as a whole. Such further service may consist of mediating contact with a caseworker or some other individually oriented source of help. It may also consist of offering membership of some subsequent group where this is possible. In such a case, the new group may be one which is intended to meet another range of needs than the original group. For example, time-limited group work aimed at the solution of specific psycho-social problems might so influence a given member that he both overcomes previous social inhibition and becomes painfully conscious of his own former isolation. He will then establish a high degree of dependence upon the group and will not enjoy the same readiness for termination as his fellow members. It would then be most helpful if the worker were able to mediate membership to another long-term group whose aims were those of countering isolation and promoting social growth. (For example, this particular solution is proving to be very common in a programme of gerontological group services with which the author is presently working.)

While the possibility of such differentiated or 'staggered' termination should be considered by the worker where necessary, I do not think it advisable to advertise its availability. A continuing theme of all group life is the conflict between integrating with the others and differentiating oneself out as a special individual. In group work contexts, the wish to be 'special' in the eyes of the worker is a common expression of this. Awareness from early on of the possibility of the worker giving such special attention at termination might therefore in some cases cause members to withhold themselves from engaging in and identifying with the work of the group as a whole.

The second concern is that in reviewing the experience and looking back at how the group has functioned and what work remains, groups may become aware of new common needs and of perceptions which give rise to a proposal for a 'new group' – a new contract. This must be distinguished from situations where resistance to termination leads to the construction of new problems in order to prevent separation from the group and the worker. In practice, it is not difficult to make this distinction. The worker perceives very different levels of both anxiety and rationality in these two situations.

Where the termination process produces the suggestion of a new contract, growth, clarification and discovery in the group has been so clearly perceived by members that they are free and able to go further in some new and constructive way. This may be with or without the present worker, or even with no worker at all. (The group's investment or lack of it in keeping the same worker is another indicator of the motives underlying the wish to continue.) Often, such transitions will involve quite new aims for the group and sometimes major changes in its organizational form.

EXAMPLE 39

(a) A group of parents was formed under the joint leadership of a health visitor and a social worker. The group was to give support in the post-crisis period following the birth of severely defective children. Aims were defined which emphasized helping members to cope both practically and emotionally with their traumatic experience and the subsequent chronic burden.

At the end of the agreed year, during which members had worked with courage, insight and great generosity towards one another, the wish was expressed to continue, though in an entirely new way.

The group had earlier discussed the need for some kind of easily accessible support facility and they now proposed forming a self-help organization. The group was to provide the nucleus of such an organization, which would offer an open and permanent source of support, information and counsel to other parents who came into their position. The workers were invited to support the group in a consultative capacity. They agreeed to do this as needed, acknowledging also that the group would in all senses be an autonomous organization.

(b) In a service centre for the elderly, discussion groups were regularly held on a wide range of topics. These related to the pensioner's life situation, its possibilities and problems, to the ageing process in general and to the facilities and resources available at the centre and elsewhere. While these groups were open to all interested, experience confirmed the assumption that on the whole new users of the centre would provide the bulk of membership.

One such group had been particularly engaged in the waste of the resources offered by old people – concerned about the atrophy of skills and the imposed dependence upon others. Towards the close of the discussion sequence, members raised the question of using the centre and their own group as a basis for developing a system of mutual aid for pensioners throughout the district.

Such a transition in fact took place. The worker moved into a new role by agreement, helping to organize funding and publicity and mediating contacts in the district with other elderly people who either needed or could offer services – sometimes both – so that a local system of exchange of skills and services developed.

The final consideration which I wish to raise concerns open groups – or 'rolling' groups, as they are currently being called in some English-speaking countries.

In this chapter I have so far assumed that the closure of the group is one event and that termination is a process involving all members collectively and occupying a given portion of the group's life towards the end of the working phase. In open groups, however, this cannot be the case. Termination is fragmented into an indefinite number of individual separations, just as formation is a number of individual attachments and inductions.

However, although termination in open groups is not a collective separation process, it may be understood and must be dealt with on the basis of the same principles. Termination must be recognized and faced as a recurrent theme in the life of open groups, feelings about it must be normalized and articulated, and the work of the group must be both reviewed and completed.

Whilst only one member leaves at a time (or contemplates doing so), it must not be assumed that the termination process concerns only that one person. As with all other transactions in the group, the factor of mutual identification is potent here. Much suggests that members remaining are very involved indeed with another member's departure and may be said to participate in it vicariously, sometimes with considerable intensity. How each individual termination proceeds therefore influences how each member regards and deals with his or her own later separation from the group.

It is common in open groups that each individual member's termination is contractually made a question for his or her personal evaluation and judgement. However, it is desirable, in order to facilitate the best possible separation, that the group also is involved in helping the member concerned. The group may aid him in evaluating his readiness, in expressing his feelings about leaving and in clarifying whatever may remain to clarify of his relationships in the group.

Thus, for example, in an open group of men and women with alcohol problems, contemplation of termination will be raised by the member or by the worker at a time when the member appears to have made gains from participating, when he is feeling a realistic degree of confidence in his self-control and when his life situation outside the group is as manageable as possible. Again, active anticipation is important and these questions should be taken up in time for the member concerned to consider them realistically in the group and for the group to accustom themselves to the idea of the loss of that particular member. Further, such collective anticipation – if appropriately timed – should result in the group adopting a supportive and encouraging stance. If the member feels both that the group experience him as ready to leave and that his presence will be missed, he carries with him two very strengthening experiences. In some groups – including groups with other than alcohol problems – there is an open invitation to return for a further period of participation. This may be advisable in most situations where recidivism is probable. In such cases, it is particularly important that the group's encouragement should not be facile and unrealistic. If it does not include recognition of the difficulties, coming back will not be possible.

Individual termination is not always determined by the member's own volition, however. In certain groups, profound life changes compel members' withdrawal from open groups. In particular, groups of members who suffer life-threatening illnesses may lose members through their death. In open groups in gerontological group work increased frailty, placement in nursing homes, or – again – death itself are common and inevitable causes of loss of members. While some such withdrawals may be discussed in the group with the member concerned, others by their very nature may not. They remain, however, compellingly important for the group to discuss since the future of all members involves one or other such departure. To avoid a topic, whether implicitly or explicitly, imbues it with anxiety, perhaps terror. To encourage its discussion makes it more manageable and removes the persecutory fantasies which so often result from silence and avoidance. The nursing home, instead of being a humiliating and frightening terminal station into which people disappear never more to be mentioned while living, may thus become normalized and perceived as a both acceptable and accessible part of a continuum of living. Even the forbidden area of one's own death seems to become permissible in an extension of the discussion of the death of a member or former member.

It has almost become a cliché to quote John Donne in such contexts. I will risk doing so yet again, since his lines written almost four hundred years ago, are particularly apposite here.

> 'No man is an island, entire of itself.
> Everyman is a piece of the continent, a part of the main.
> If a clod be washed away by the sea, Europe is the less
> As well as if a promontory were, as well as if a manor of
>   thy friends or of thine own were.
> Any man's death diminishes me, because I am involved in mankind,
> And therefore never send to know for whom the bell tolls,
>   – it tolls for thee!'

In dealing with such losses to open groups, it is often possible to take up this feeling of being 'diminished' and threatened and, by doing so, to relieve some of the anxiety. Whether or not such weighty associative material may be taken up, the experience of the loss itself must be expressed. That a member was respected and is missed, that his or her contribution was valued, and that he may still be remembered and mentioned are reassuring observations for members who may well be approaching similar life thresholds. Indeed, this is true of all open groups, including those to which members may return. Each single member's departure gives the group an opportunity to anticipate departure and, as it were, to rehearse the attitudes and ambivalence with which they will do so. A corollary of this is that the group's subsequent attitude to former members affects the present members' expectations of how they will themselves be regarded. They must be able to believe that after their departure they will be remembered with respect, interest and concern.

One final point. A pervasive problem with open groups is the frequency of change brought about by individual inductions and terminations. Since both of these events must always be dealt with in relation to both the group and the member concerned, there is the danger that doing so may dominate and block the task-focused work of the group. It is important to avoid this. With experience, the worker develops an eye for the regularities and the nuances of these processes in the type of group with which he works. He will establish procedures − flexible though they may be − which usually make possible the satisfactory handling of both the induction and termination processes. Thus, he will work economically with them and must be interested in doing so. Despite the potential gains of good induction and termination, the worker must have it in mind that only a limited proportion of the total time must be absorbed by them. The longer the average length of membership, the more time may be afforded and vice versa.

Perhaps nothing clearer may be said about this than that time spent on termination in open groups must reflect a sense of proportion, must utilize material presented by the group in the continued service of its goals and must be guided by the worker's best understanding of the group's needs − which might, come to think of it, also be said about termination in closed groups, and indeed about any other aspect of working with group processes in the social and health services.

SUMMARY

Termination is not an event. It is a process. The termination process is strongly characterized by ambivalence and by separation anxiety. It may involve crisis: crisis theory is useful in all termination processes.

The aim of the termination process is to resolve ambivalence and to help members free themselves from the group. It is a bridge to self-dependence. Three considerations are basic to a satisfactory termination process:

1 Termination must be actively anticipated (facing the fact of termination), during which degrees of readiness and resistance are observed.

2 Feelings about termination are taken up, either at the group's initiative; or through the worker's interpretation of indirect expression of feeling; or at the worker's initiative.

3 The work of the group has to be reviewed, completed, and its implications considered.

In *some* groups, additional considerations may arise. These are:

variations in individual readiness or resistance;
proposal of continuation under a new contract; and
dealing with sequential individual terminations in open groups.

NOTE: CHAPTER 12

1   Material from a currently uncompleted three-year demonstration project of group
     work in gerontological services (Heap and Østern, in press).

IN CONCLUSION

———◆———

This book having also arrived at the stage of termination, I would like to look back and share with the reader what the process of writing it has been about.

I have been fascinated by the uses of group methods in our field for many years and am profoundly convinced of their relevance and utility. I have felt compelled to write about them once more because their relevance and utility is about to increase.

It is my belief that group methods will move out of the position of an occasional and ancillary method into a position of more central relevance in the coming years. Economic, demographic and cultural changes are already occurring and they will continue throughout the foreseeable future. They will bring very large numbers of hitherto well functioning people into situations of crisis or chronic distress, so that a much more extensive coverage of social and mental health services will be necessary.

The qualitative aspects of service will also be subject to change. The emerging problems are interactional in nature: they involve alienation and failures in communication and in the functioning of vital collective social institutions, such as neighbourhood and family. For these reasons, both the remedial and the preventive measures which we employ must be interactional and collective in character. Thus, group methods are to make a greater contribution than ever before and we must engage now in updating, refinement, and renewed clarification of the principles of practice. Hence this book – one such contribution.

I hope that I have succeeded through my examples in both introducing ideas of innovative uses of groups and reasserting the relevance, complexity and interest of more traditional applications. We will need both in the years to come. But I hope, more than anything else, that I have succeeded in conveying the balance between the use of the group process and of the worker's interventions. That balance is at once the core and the major challenge of group work practice. Achieving it requires the ability to observe and understand what is happening in the group and the ability to judge when, if and how to contribute to what is happening. The understanding and empathy underlying such evaluations will not pose lesser challenges in the complex problems we will meet in the latter half of the 1980s and in the 1990s. I have tried to make these evaluations a little easier by constructing more readily available tools for use in practice. These are expressed in the series of overviews, summaries and models which appear in these chapters. I have attempted to make these as clear as possible, while expressing them at so general a level that colleagues may find them relevant whatever their field of practice.

Finally, I have enormously enjoyed writing this book. I hope very much indeed that you now reading it find it useful. If it also conveys some of the vibrance and fascination which I experience in working with groups I shall be delighted, though that perhaps requires another level of authorship than my own attempted precisions.

REFERENCES

Adelson, Gerald, and Peress, Elaine (1979), 'Single-couple and group sex therapy: a comparison', *Social Casework*, vol. 60, no. 8 (October), pp. 471–8.

Aguilera, Donna C., and Messick, Janice M. (1974), *Crisis Intervention: Theory and Methodology* (St. Louis, Mo.: C.V. Mosby Co.).

Aichhorn, August (1939), *Wayward Youth* (London: Imago).

Anderson, Joseph D. (1979), 'Social work with groups in the generic base of social work practice', *Social Work with Groups*, vol. 2, no. 4 (winter), pp. 281–93.

Arnold, Robert J. (1980), ' "They're playing our song" – the use of popular music in confronting the loneliness of the alcoholic', *Social Work with Groups*, vol. 3, no. 2 (summer), pp. 53–63.

Axelson, Barbo Lenéer, and Thylefors, Ingela (1976), *Samtalsgrupper – teori och praktik* (Stockholm: Wahlström och Widstrand).

Bales, Robert F. (1970), *Personality and Interpersonal Behaviour* (New York: Holt, Rinehart & Winston).

Ball, G., and Bailey, J. (1971), 'A group of experienced foster parents', in R. Tod (ed.), *Social Work in Foster Care* (London: Longman).

Bandura, H. (1971), 'Psychotherapy based on modelling principles', in A. E. Bergin and S. L. Garfield (eds), *Handbook of Psychotherapy and Behavior Change* (New York: Wiley).

Beaulieu, Elsie M., and Karpinski, Judith A. (1981), 'Group treatment of elderly with ill spouses', *Social Casework*, vol. 62, no. 9 (November), pp. 551–7.

Bednar, Richard L., Weet, Connie, Evensen, Paul, Larnier, David, and Melnick, Joseph (1974), 'Empirical guidelines for group therapy: pretraining cohesion and modelling', *Journal of Applied Behavioural Science*, vol. 10, no. 2, pp. 149–66.

Benjamin, S., Jr. (1972), 'Co-therapy: a growth experience for therapists', *International Journal of Group Psychotherapy*, vol. 22, pp. 199–209.

Bennett, Linda (1979), 'Group service for COPD out-patients: surmounting the obstacles', *Social Work with Groups*, vol. 2, no. 2 (spring), pp. 145–60.

Bergofsky, Rebecca E., Forgash, Carol S., and Glassel, Arline F. (1979), 'Establishing therapeutic groups with the families of spina bifida children in a hospital setting', *Social Work with Groups*, vol. 2, no. 7 (spring), pp. 45–54.

Bernstein, Saul (1967), 'Conflict and group work', in S. Bernstein (ed.), *Explorations in Group Work* (Boston, Mass.: Boston University), pp. 54–80.

Bertcher, Harvey J., and Maple, Frank F. (1977), *Creating Groups* (Beverly Hills, Calif., and London: Sage).

Bertcher, Harvey J. (1978), *Group Participation: Techniques for Leaders and Members* (Beverly Hills, Calif.: Sage).

Bice, H. V. (1955), 'Parent counselling and parent education', in W. M. Cruickshank and G. M. Raus (eds), *Cerebral Palsy – its Individual and Community Problems* (Syracuse, NY.: Syracuse University Press), pp. 411–28.

Borgelin, Marianne (1972), 'En gruppuppgift inom barnavårdsnämndens fritidsverksamhet', *Socialt grupparbete*, (Stockholm: Sveriges socionom-förbunds småskrifter), pp. 11–16 and 19.

Bornstein, Susan Botvinik (1980), *Parents of Newborns* (workshop manual), (New York: Family Service Association of America).

Brammer, Lawrence M. (1973), *The Helping Relationship – Process and Skills* (Englewood Cliffs, NJ: Prentice-Hall).

Brandes, D., and Phillips, H. (1977), *The Gamester's Handbook* (London: Hutchinson).

Bratt, Nancy (1963), *Samtaleteknikk og klientbehandling* (Copenhagen: Nyt Nordisk Forlag Arnold Busck).

Breslin, Alice, and Sturton, Sheila (1978), 'Group work in a hotel for the mentally handicapped', in Nano McCaughan (ed.), *Group Work: Learning and Practice* (London: Allen & Unwin), pp 146–56.

Breton, Margot (1979), 'Nurturing abused and abusive mothers – the hair-dressing group', *Social Work with Groups*, vol. 2, no. 2 (summer), pp. 161–74.

Brown, Allan (1979), *Groupwork* (London: Heinemann).

Brown, Allan, Caddick, Brian, Gardiner, Mike, and Sleeman, Sylvia (1982), 'Towards a British model of groupwork', *British Journal of Social Work*, vol. 12, no. 6 (December), pp. 587–605.

Brown, P. A. (1971), 'Group meetings for adopters', *Social Service News*, vol. 1, no. 5, pp. 7–10.

Burch, Genevieve, and Mohr, Vicki (1980), 'Evaluating a child abuse intervention program', *'Social Casework*, vol. 61, no. 2 (February), pp. 90–9.

Burnside, Irene M. (1971), 'Long-term group work with hospitalised aged', *The Gerontologist*, vol. 11, no. 3 (autumn), pp. 213–21.

Burnside, Irene M. (1978), *Working with the Elderly: Group Processes and Techniques* (North Scituate, Mass.: Duxbury Press).

Burnside, Irene M. (1981), 'Reminiscing as therapy: an overview', in I. M. Burnside (ed), *Nursing and the Aged* (New York: McGraw-Hill), pp. 98–113.

Butler, Robert N. (1963), 'The life review: an interpretation of reminiscence in the aged', *Psychiatry, Journal for the Study of Interpersonal Processes*, vol. 26, no. 1, pp. 65–76.

Caplan, Gerald, (1961), *A Community Approach to Mental Health* (London: Tavistock).

Caple, Richard B. (1978), 'The sequential stages of group development', *Small Group Behaviour*, vol. 9, no. 4 (November), pp. 470–6.

Carter, W. (1971). 'Group counselling for adolescent foster children', in R. Tod (ed.), *Social Work in Foster Care* (London: Longman).

Chapman, S. (1982), 'Post-natal groups for mothers with serious mothering problems', *Health Visitor*, vol. 55, no. 9 (September), pp. 461–6.

Christie, Nils (1977), 'Conflicts as property', *British Journal of Criminology*, no. 7, pp. 1–15, and *Tidsskrift for rettsvitenskap* (Oslo: University of Oslo Press) no. 90, pp. 113–32.

Coplon, Jennifer, and Apgar, Kathryn J. (1982), 'Debunking myths about structured educational groups', *Proceedings of the 4th Symposium on the Advancement of Social Work with Groups* (Toronto: University of Toronto).

Coser, Lewis (1956), *The Functions of Social Conflict* (Glencoe, Ill.: Free Press).

Cowger, Charles G. (1979), 'Conflict and conflict management in working with groups', *Social Work with Groups*, vol. 2, no. 4 (winter), pp. 309–20.

Craft, Martha, *et al.* (1982), 'Nursing care in childhood cancer-coping', *American Journal of Nursing*, vol. 82, no. 3 (March), pp. 440–2.

D'Affliti, J. G., and Swanson, D. (1975), 'Group sessions for wives of home hemodialysis patients', *American Journal of Nursing*, vol. 75, no. 4 (April), pp. 633–8.

Douglas, Tom (1978), *Basic Groupwork* (London: Tavistock).

Douglas, Tom (1979), *Groupwork Practice* (London: Tavistock).

Drum, David L., and Knott, Eugene J. (1977), *Structured Groups for Facilitating Development: Acquiring Life Skills, Resolving Life Themes and Making Transitions*, New Vistas in Counselling Series (New York: Human Sciences Press).

Ebersole, Priscilla P. (1976) 'Problems of group reminiscing with the institutionalised aged', *Journal of Gerontological Nursing*, vol. 2, no. 6 (November/December), pp. 23–7.

Ebersole, Priscilla P. (1978), 'A theoretical approach to the use of reminiscence', in I. M. Burnside, *Working with the Elderly: Group Processes and Techniques* (North Scituate, Mass.: Duxbury Press), pp. 139–54.

Eisenstein, Fanny (1959), 'Life enrichment of the seriously handicapped through the group work process', *Social Work with Groups* (New York: National Association for Social Work).

Ericsson, Kjersti, and Johanssen, Monica (1980), *På parti med ungdomsgruppa* (Oslo: Universitetsforlaget).

Euster, Sona (1979), 'Rehabilitation after mastectomy: the group process', *Social Work in Health Care*, vol. 4, no. 3 (spring), pp. 251–63.

Ezriel, H. (1950), 'A psychoanalytic approach to group treatment', *British Journal of Medical Psychology*, no. 23, pp. 59–74.

Falck, Hans S. (1978), 'Crisis theory and social group work', *Social Work with Groups*, vol. 7, no. 3 (spring), pp. 75–84.

Feinberg, Norma (1980), 'A study of group stages in a self-help setting', *Social Work with Groups*, vol. 3, no. 1 (spring), pp. 41-9.

Feldman, Robert A. (1967), 'Determinants and objectives of social group work intervention', *Social Work Practice*, (Columbia, NY: National Association of Social Workers), pp. 34–55.

Feldman, Robert A. (1969), 'Group integration, intense interpersonal dislike, and social group work intervention', *Social Work*, vol. 14, no. 3, pp. 30–9.

Fengler, Alfred P., and Goodrich, Nancy (1979), 'Wives of disabled men: the hidden patients', *The Gerontologist*, vol. 19, no. 2 (April), pp. 175–83.

Ferard, Margaret C., and Hunnybun, Noël K. (1962), *The Caseworker's Use of Relationship* (London: Tavistock).

Foren, Robert, and Bailey, Royston (1968), *Authority in Social Casework* (Oxford: Pergamon).

Forman, Mark (1967), 'Conflict, controversy and confrontation in group work with older adults', *Social Work*, vol. 12, no. 1 (January), pp. 80–5.

Forthun, Gerald J., and Nuehring, Ronald E. (1971), 'Group work in a maximum security prison', in W. Schwartz and S. Zalba (eds), *The Practice of Group Work* (Columbia, NY: Columbia University Press), pp. 199–220.

Freese, Amarilla L. (1972), 'Group therapy with exhibitionists and voyeurs', *Social Work*, vol. 17, no. 2 (March), pp. 44–52.

Friis, Jorunn, and Müller, Turid (1979), 'Samtalegrupper på sykehjem', *Fysioterapeuten* (Oslo), vol. 46 (September), pp. 360–1.

Fritz, Anna (1982), 'Parent group education: a preventive approach', *Proceedings of the 4th Symposium on the Advancement of Social Work with Groups* (Toronto: University of Toronto).

Frønes, Ivar (1979), *Et sted å være, et sted å lære* (Oslo: Tiden).

Galinsky, Maeda J., and Schopler, Janice H. (1980), 'Structuring co-leadership in social work training', *Social Work with Groups*, vol. 3, no. 4 (winter), pp. 51–63.

Garvin, Charles (1981), *Contemporary Groupwork* (Englewood Cliffs, NJ; Prentice-Hall).

Gitterman, Naomi P. (1979), 'Group services for learning-disabled children and their parents', *Social Casework*, vol. 60, no. 4 (April), pp. 217–26.

Glass, Lora and Hickerson, Martha D. (1976), 'Dialysis and transplantation: a mother's group', *Social Work in Health Care*, vol. 1, no. 3 (spring), pp. 287–96.

Goetschius, George W., and Tash, Joan (1967), *Working with Unattached Youth* (London: Routledge & Kegan Paul).

Goetschius, George W. (1969), *Working with Community Groups* (London: Routledge & Kegan Paul).

Goffman, Erving (1961), *Encounters* (New York: Bobbs Merrill).

Golan, Naomi, (1969), 'When is a client in crisis?', *Social Casework*, vol. 50, no. 4 (July), pp. 389–94.

Golan, Naomi, (1978), *Treatment in Crisis Situations* (Glencoe, Ill: The Free Press).

Gold, Jeffrey A., and Kolodny, Ralph L. (1978), 'Group treatment of socially dispossessed youth', *Social Work with Groups*, vol. 1, no. 2 (summer), pp. 145–59.

Goldner, R., and Kyle, E. H. (1979), 'A group approach to the cardiac patient', *Social Casework*, vol. 41, no. 7 (July), pp. 346–53.

Gordy, Patricia L. (1983), 'Group work that supports adult victims of childhood incest', *Social Casework*, vol. 64, no. 5 (May), pp. 300–7.

Gottlieb, Bruce, and Dean, Janet (1981), 'The co-therapy relationship in group treatment of sexually-mistreated adolescent girls', in P. B. Mrazek and C. Henry Kempe (eds), *Sexually Abused Children and their Families* (Oxford: Pergamon).

Gross, E. (1956), 'Symbiosis and consensus as integrative factors in small groups', *American Sociological Review*, vol. 21, no. 3, pp. 174–9.

Grossbard, Hyram, (1954), 'Methodology for developing self-awareness', *Social Casework*, vol. 35, no. 9 (November), pp. 380–6.

Habermann, Ulla, m.fl. (1977), *Informasjonsbutikk Østerbro–efterårsrapport* (Copenhagen: Den Sociale højskolen).

Hackett, Thomas P. (1972), 'Group therapy in cardiac rehabilitation', review paper submitted to 1st International Congress on Cardiac Rehabilitation and Cardiology (May).

Halmos, Paul (1965), *The Faith of the Counsellors, a Study in the Theory and Practice of Social Casework and Therapy* (London: Constable).

Hamilton, Gordon (1940), *Theory and Practice of Social Casework* (New York: Columbia University Press).

Harris, Phyllis, B. (1979), 'Being old: a confrontation group with nursing home residents', *Health and Social Work*, vol. 4, no. 1 (February), pp. 152–66.

Hartford, Margaret E. (1971), *Groups in Social Work. Application of Small-Group Theory and Research to Social Work Practice* (New York: Columbia University Press).

Harmann, Lauriane L. (1979), 'Therapeutic group activities in a nursing home', *Health and Social Work*, vol. 4, no. 7 (May), pp. 135–41.

Hawley, Nancy P., and Brown, Elizabeth (1981), 'Children of alcoholics: the use of group treatment', *Social Casework*, vol. 62, no. 1 (January), pp. 40–6.

Heap, Ken (1966), 'The scapegoat role in youth groups', *Case Conference*, vol. 12, no. 7 (January), pp. 215–21. In Norwegian as pamphlet 'Rollen som syndebukk i ungdomsgrupper', (Oslo: Sosionomen, 1969).

Heap, Ken, (1968), 'The group worker as "central person" ' *Social Work, British Quarterly Journal*, vol. 25, no. 1, pp. 20–9.

Heap, Ken (1977a), *Noen målsettinger for Ikke-Verbale Aktiviteter i Sosialt Gruppearbeide*, Sosialt Arbeid og Sosialpolitikk No. 1 (Oslo: Diakonhjemmets Sosialhøgskole).

Heap, Ken (1977b), *Group Theory for Social Workers – an Introduction* (Oxford: Pergamon).

Heap, Ken (1979), *Process and Action in Work with Groups – the preconditions for treatment and growth* (Oxford: Pergamon).

Heap, Ken (1982), 'Purposes in social work with groups: their interrelatedness with values and methods. A historical and prospective view', *Proceedings of the 4th Symposium on the Advancement of Social Work with Groups*, (Toronto: University of Toronto).

Heap, Ken, and Tvedt, Astrid M. (1971), 'Et notat om gruppearbeid for fosterfordeldre', *Norsk Tidsskrift for miljøterapi*, no. 3, pp. 4–10.

Heap, Ken, and Østern, Oddny Helland (in press), *Bruk av gruppemetoder i eldreomsorgen-et metodeutviklingsprosjekt* (Oslo: Det kgl. Sosialdepartement).

Heilfron, M. (1969), 'Co-therapy; the relationship between therapists', *International Journal of Psychotherapy*, vol. 19, no. 30, pp. 366–81.

Herzog, Jyll (1980), 'Communication between co-leaders: fact or myth. A student's perspective', *Social Work with Groups*, vol. 3, no. 4 (winter), pp. 19–29.

Hill, William F. (1978), *Learning thru' Discussion* (Palo Alto: Sage Publications), 3rd edition.

Hilson, J. K., and Heaton, D. (1971), 'Common concerns and cookies: a foster parents' group in Ontario', *Social Work Today*, vol. 3, no. 1 pp. 27–8.

Hollis, Florence (1972), *Casework: A Psycho-Social Therapy* (New York: Random House).

Hollon, T. H. (1972), 'Modified group therapy in treatment of patients on chronic hemodialysis', *American Journal of Psychotherapy* (October), pp. 501–10.

Hybertsen, Nils (1982), 'Samtalegrupper med psykiatriske langtidspasienter', *Nordisk Sosialt Arbeid*, vol. 2, no. 4, pp. 38–49.

Irvine, Elizabeth E. (1964), 'What kind of loving?', *New Society* 29 August, London.

Irvine, Elizabeth E. (1979), *Social Work and Human Problems* (Oxford: Pergamon).

Johnson, Carole (1974), 'Planning for termination of the group', in R. Vinter, R. Sarri and P. Glasser (eds), *Individual Change Through Small Groups* (New York: The Free Press), pp. 258–65.

Jones, Herbert (1959), *Reluctant Rebels* (London: Tavistock).

Joseph, Sister M. Vincentia, and Conrad, Sister Ann Patrick (1980), 'A parish neighbourhood model for social work practice', *Social Casework*, vol. 61, no. 7 (September), pp. 423–32.

Kahn, Jack, and Earle, Elspeth (1982), *The Cry for Help and the Professional Response* (Oxford: Pergamon).

Kalisch, Beatrice (1971), 'Strategies for developing nurse empathy', *Nursing Outlook*, vol. 19, no. 11 (November), pp. 714–18.

Kaplan, D. M., Smith, A., Grobstein, R., and Fischman, S. E. (1973), 'Family mediation of stress', *Social Work*, vol. 18, no. 4 (July) pp. 60–9.

Kartha, M., and Ertel, E. J. (1976), 'Short-term group therapy for mothers of leukemia children', *American Clinical Pediatrics*, vol. 15, no. 9 (September), pp. 803–6.

Kartman, Lauraine L. (1979), 'Therapeutic group activities in a nursing home', *Health and Social Work*, vol. 4, no. 2 (May), pp. 135–41.

Keefe, Thomas (1976), 'Empathy, the critical skill', *Social Work*, vol. 21, no. 1 (January), pp. 10–14.

Keefe, Thomas (1978), 'The economic context of empathy', *Social Work*, vol. 23, no. 6 (November), pp. 460–5.

Keefe, Thomas (1980), 'Empathy skill and critical consciousness', *Social Casework*, vol. 61, no. 7 (September), pp. 387–93.

Keith-Lucas, Allan (1974), *Giving and Taking Help* (Chapel Hill: University of N. Carolina Press).

Killèn-Heap, Kari (1979), *Veiledningsmetodikk i sosionomutdanningen* (Oslo: Universitetsforlaget). Also in Swedish as *Handledning i Socialt arbete* (Stockholm: Wahlström och Widstrand).

Killèn-Heap, Kari (1981), *Forsømte Familier, Tanum-Norli* (Oslo: Universitetsforlaget).

Klein, Alan F. (1970), *Social Work through Group Process* (Albany: University of New York).

Klein, Alan F. (1972), *Effective Groupwork – an Introduction to Principle and Method* (New York: Association Press).

Knapp, V. S., and Hansen, H. (1973)., 'Helping the parents of children with leukemia', *Social Work*, vol. 18, no. 4 (July), pp. 70–5.

Kolodny, Ralph, and Reilly, Willow V. (1972), 'Group work with today's unmarried mother', *Social Casework*, vol. 53, no. 10 (December), pp. 613–22.

Kolodny, Ralph (1976), *Peer-oriented Group Work for the Physically Handicapped Child* (Boston: Charles River Books).

Kolodny, Ralph, Jones, Hubert, and Garland, James A. (1965), 'A model for stages of development in social work groups', in *Explorations in Group Work* (Boston: University of Boston), pp. 12–53.

Konopka, Gisela (1963), *Social Group Work: a Helping Process* (Englewood Cliffs, NJ: Prentice Hall).

Konopka, Gisela (1970), 'Our outcast youth', *Social Work*, vol. 15, no. 4 (October), pp. 76–86.

Kruger, Lois, Moore, Dori, Schmidt, Patricia, and Wiens, Ronna (1979), 'Group work with abusive parents', *Social Work*, vol. 24, no. 4 (July), pp. 337–8.

Lang, Norma C. (1978), 'The selection of small group for service delivery – an exploration of the literature on group use in social work', *Social Work with Groups*, vol. 1, no. 3 (fall), pp. 247–64.

Larsen, Jo A., and Mitchell, Craig T. (1980), 'Task-centred, strength-oriented group work with delinquents', *Social Casework*, vol. 61., no. 3 (March), pp. 154–63.

Laterza, Phyllis (1979), 'An eclectic approach to group work with the mentally retarded', *Social Work with Groups*, vol. 2, no. 3 (fall), pp. 235–46.

La Vorgna, D. (1979), 'Group treatment for wives of patients with Alzheimer's disease', *Social Work in Health Care*, vol. 5, no. 2 (winter), pp. 219–21.

Lee, Judith A. (1978), 'Group work with mentally retarded foster adolescents', *Social Casework*, vol. 58, no. 3 (March), pp. 164–73.

Levine, Baruch (1967), *Fundamentals of Group Treatment* (Chicago: Whitehall).

Levinson, Valerie R. (1979), 'The decision group, beginning treatment in an alcoholism clinic', *Health and Social Work*, vol. 4, no. 4 (November), pp 199–221.

Lewis, Benjamin F. (1977), 'Group silences', *Small Group Behaviour*, vol. 8, no. 1 (February), pp. 109–21.

Lie, Gro (1981), *Gatelangs – om oppsøkende ungdoms arbeid* (Oslo: Universitetsforlaget).

Lopiccolo, J., and Miller, V. (1975), 'A program for enhancing the sexual relationship for normal couples', *Counselling Psychologist'*, no. 5, pp. 41–6.

Ludlow, B., and Epstein, N. (1972), 'Groups for foster children', *Social Work*, vol. 17, no. 5 (September), pp. 10–12.

Mandelbaum, Arthur (1970), 'The group process in helping parents of retarded children', in R. W. Klenk and R. M. Ryan (eds), *The Practice of Social Work* (Belmont, Calif.: Wadsworth), pp. 193–203.

Marchant, Harold, and Smith, Herbert M. (1977), *Adolescent Girls at Risk* (Oxford: Pergamon).

Marchant, Harold, Smith, Cyril S., and Farrant, M. R. (1972), *The Wincroft Youth Project: a social work programme in a Slum Area* (London: Tavistock).

Mayfield, Judy, and Neil, Jennifer F. (1983), 'Group treatment for children in substitute care', *Social Casework*, vol. 64, no. 10 (December), pp. 579–84.

McCaughan, Nano (1978), *Group Work: Learning and Practice*, National Institute Social Services Library, No. 33 (London: Allen & Unwin).

McNeil, John S., and McBride, Mary L. (1979), 'Group therapy and abusive parents', *Social Casework*, vol. 60, no. 1 (January), pp. 36–42.

McWhinnie, Alice M. (1968), 'Group counselling with 78 adoptive families', *Case Conference*, vol. 14, no. 11/12 (March and April), pp. 407–12.

Middleman, Ruth R. (1980), 'The use of program: review and update', *Social Work with Groups*, vol. 3, no. 3 (fall), pp. 5-24.

Middleman, Ruth R. (1982), 'Interaction and experience in groups: doing as life-learning', Invitational presentation at symposium, 'Clinical Social Work: Practice Excellence for the 80's', National Association for Social Work, New York.

Miller, Dereck (1964), *Growth to Freedom* (London: Tavistock).

Miller, Sherod (ed). (1975), 'Marriages and families: enrichment through communication', *Small Group Behaviour*, vol. 6, no. 1 (February).

Morse, Joan (1965), 'Making hospitalisation a growth experience for arthritic children', *Social Casework*, vol. 46, no. 9 (November), pp. 550–6.

Mott, S., and Taylor, P. (1975), 'A group therapy approach with hemodialysis patients and their families', *Journal of the American Association of Nephrology Nurses and Technicians*, 2, pp. 105–8.

Munk, Dora (1975), 'Gruppearbejde i Mødrehjaelpens adopsjonsarbejde' *Socialrådgiveren*, Copenhagen, vol. 37, no. 1 (January), pp. 10–12.

Murphy, Ann, Pueschel, Siegfried M., and Schneider, Jane (1973), 'Group work with parents of children with Down's syndrome', *Social Casework*, vol. 54, no. 2 (February), pp. 114–19.

Northern, Helen (1970), *Social Work with Groups* (New York: Columbia University Press).

Nyman, J., and Nyman, M. (1971), 'Foster parents and CCOs – an experiment in group work', *Social Work Today*, vol. 2, no. 1 pp. 25–9.

Ochetti, Armand E., and Ochetti, Dianne B. (1981), 'Group therapy with married couples', *Social Casework*, vol. 62, no. 2 (February) pp. 74–9.

Ogren, Evelyn H., Crum, Houston L., and Swain, David (1979), 'Typology of group work with "drunk and proud" alcoholics', *Social Work with Groups*, vol. 2, no. 1 (spring), pp. 19–34.

Olshansky, Simon (1962), 'Chronic sorrow; a response to having a mentally defective child', *Social Casework*, vol. 43, no. 4 (April), pp. 190–3.

Oradei, D., and Waite, N. (1974), 'Group psychotherapy with stroke patients during the immediate recovery phase', *American Journal of Orthopsychiatry*, 44, pp. 386–95.

Parad, Howard J. (ed.) (1970), *Crisis Invervention – Selected Readings* (New York: Family Service Association of America).

Parry, Joan K. (1980), 'Group services for the chronically ill and disabled', *Social Work with Groups*, vol. 3, no. 1 (spring), pp. 59–67.

Paulsen, Maurice; Savino, Anne; Chaleff, Anne; Sanders, R. Wyman; Frisch, Florence; and Dunn, Richard, (1974), 'Parents of the battered child: a multidisciplinary group therapy approach to life-threatening behaviour', *Life-threatening Behaviour*, 4 (spring), pp. 18–31.

Payne, Chris (1978), 'Working with groups in the residential setting', in Nano McCaughan (ed.), *Group Work: Learning and Practice* (London: Allen & Unwin), pp. 58–69.

Pernell, Ruby B. (1962), 'Identifying and teaching the skill components of social group work', in *Educational Developments in Social Group Work* (New York: Council on Social Work Education), pp. 18–36.

Philipp, Connie (1981), 'A support group for adults with severe physical disabilities', *Social Casework*, vol. 62, no. 7 (September), pp. 434–8.

Phillips, Helen U. (1957), *The Essentials of Social Group Work Skill*, (New York: Association Press).

Rapoport, Lydia (1970), 'Crisis intervention as a mode of brief treatment', in R. W. Roberts and R. H. Nee (eds), *Theories of Social Casework* (Chicago: University of Chicago Press).

Redl, Fritz (1953), 'The art of group composition', in Susanne Schulze (ed.), *Creative Group Living in a Children's Institution* (New York: Association Press).

Reynolds, Bertha C. (1942), *Learning and Teaching in the Practice of Social Work* (New York; Russell & Russell).

Richmond, Mary (1917), *Social Diagnosis* (New York: Russel Sage Foundation).

Robinovitch, Arlene E., and Ransohoff, Marta E. (1981), 'Group work in general hospitals: crisis intervention and politics', *Social Work with Groups*, vol. 4, nos. 3/4 (fall/winter), pp. 59–66.

Robinson, N. M., and Robinson, H. B. (1976), *The Mentally Retarded Child: a psychological approach*, 2nd edition (New York: McGraw-Hill).

Ross, Judith W. (1979), 'Coping with childhood cancer: group intervention as an aid to parents in crisis', *Social Work in Health Care*, vol. 4, no. 4 (summer), pp. 381–91.

Ross, Sue, and Bilson, Andy (1980), 'Playing the game', *Community Care*, 31 July, pp. 15–17.

Ross, Sue, and Bilson, Andy (1981), 'The Sunshine Group: an example of social work intervention through the use of a group', *Social Work with Groups*, vol. 4, nos. 1/2 (spring), pp. 15–28.

Roy, Carrol, Flynn, Eileen and Atcherson, Esther (1982), 'Group sessions for home hemodialysis patients', *Health and Social Work*, vol. 7, no. 1 (February), pp. 65–71.

Røren, Owe (1976), *Gruppesamtaler med utviklingshemmede* (Oslo: Universitetsforlaget).

Saloshin, Henrietta E. (1954), 'Development of an instrument for analysis of social group work in therapeutic settings', PhD thesis, University of Minnesota.

Salzberger-Wittenberg, Isca (1970), *Psychoanalytic Insight and Relationships: A Kleinian Approach* (London: Routledge & Kegan Paul).

Samit, Carol, Nash, Kathleen, and Meyers, Janeen (1980), 'The parents' group: a therapeutic tool', *Social Casework*, vol. 61, no. 4 (April), pp. 215–22.

Sandgrund, G. (1971), 'Group counselling with adoptive families after legal adoption', in R. Tod (ed.), *Social Work in Adoption* (London: Longman).

Sarri, Rosemary, and Galinsky, Maeda (1975), 'A conceptual framework for group development', in P. Glasser, R. Sarri and R. Vinter (eds), *Individual Change through Small Groups* (New York: Free Press), pp. 71–80.

Saul, Shura (ed.) (1982), 'Groupwork with frail elderly', *Social Work with Groups*, Special issue (New York: Haworth Press).

Schrøeder, Max, and Pegg, Mike (1978), *Idébog for familiebehandlere* (Copenhagen: Munksgaards Socialpædagogiske Bibliotek).

Schwartz, William (1961), 'The social worker in the group', in *New Perspectives on Services to Groups: Theory, Organisation and Practice* (New York, National Association for Social Work), pp. 7–34.

Schwartz, William (1971), 'On the use of groups in social work practice', in William Schwartz and Serafio Zalba (eds), *The Practice of Group Work* (New York: Columbia University Press), pp. 3–24.

Schwartz, William (1977), 'Between client and system: the mediating function', in Robert W. Roberts and Helen Northern (eds), *Theories of Social Work with Groups* (New York: Columbia University Press), pp. 171–97.

Shalinsky, William (1969), 'Group composition as an element of group work practice', *Social Service Review*, vol. 43, no. 1 (March), pp. 42–9.

Sheridan, Mary S. (1975), 'Talk-time with hospitalised children', *Social Work*, vol. 20, no. 1 (January), pp. 40–4.

Sherif, Mustafa, and Sherif, C. W. (1964), *Reference Groups* (New York: Harper & Row), p. 166.

Shilkoff, Deborah (1983), 'The use of male–female co-leadership in an early-adolescent girls' activity group', *Social Work with Groups*, vol. 6, no. 2 (summer), pp. 67–80.

Showalter, David, and Jones, Charlotte W. (1980), 'Marital and family counselling in prisons', *Social Work*, vol. 25, no. 3 (May), pp. 224–8.

Shulman, Lawrence (1971), *Socialt arbete med grupper* (Lund: Studentlitteratur).

Shulman, Lawrence (1979), *The Skills of Helping Individuals and Groups* (Itasca, Ill.: Peacock Publishers).

Sigrell, Bo (1972), *Gruppebehandling – teori og praksis* (Copenhagen: Munksgaard).

Slavson, Samuel R. (1966), 'The phenomenology and dynamics of silence in psychotherapy groups', *International Journal of Group Psychotherapy* vol. 16, (October), pp. 395–8.

Spergel, I. (1966), *Street Gang Work, Theory and Practice* (Boston, Mass.: Addison-Wesley).

Stein, Terry S. (1983), 'An overview of men's groups', *Social Work with Groups*, vol. 6, nos. 3/4 (fall/winter) (special 'gender' issue), pp. 149–61.

Sterne, M. W., and Pittman, D. J. (1965), 'The concept of motivation – a source of blockage in the treatment of alcoholics', *Quarterly Journal of Studies on Alcohol*, vol. 26, no. 1 (March), pp. 40–57.

Stephenson, Stephen J., and Boler, Michael F. (1981), 'Group treatment for divorcing persons', *Social Work with Groups*, vol. 4, no. 3/4 (fall/winter), pp. 67–78.

Strickler, Martin, and Allgeyer, Jean (1967), 'The crisis group: a new application of crisis theory', *Social Work*, vol. 12, no. 3 (July), pp. 28–32.

Sugar, Jo-Ellen (1982), 'A social-action group of elderly residents in a home for the aged', unpublished paper, *Proceedings of the 4th Symposium on the Advancement of Social Work with Groups* (Toronto: University of Toronto).

Taylor, John W. (1980), 'Using short-term structured groups with divorce clients', *Social Casework*, vol. 51, no. 7 (September), pp. 433–7.

Thibault, J. W., and Kelley, H. H. (1959), *The Social Psychology of Groups* (New York: Wiley).

Thomas, David (1978), 'Journey into the acting community: experiences of learning and change in community groups', in Nano McCaughan (ed.), *Group Work: Learning and Practice* (London: Allen & Unwin), pp. 167–81.

Toth, André, and Toth, Susan (1980), 'Group work with widows', *Social Work*, vol. 25, no. 1 (January), pp. 63–5. (See also Letters, *Social Work*, vol. 25, no. 4 (July), pp. 334–5)

Truax, Charles B., Rogers, Guidlin and Kiesler (1967), *The Therapeutic Relationship and its Impact* (Madison: University of Wisconsin Press). (See also digest of Truax's work in Birgin and Garfield (eds) *Handbook of Psychotherapy and Behavioural Change*, (New York: Wiley, 1972).

Vinter, Robert D., and Sarri, Rosemary C. (1962), 'Learning objectives, teaching methods and performance patterns in group work education', in *Educational Developments in Social Group Work* (New York: Council on Social Work Education).

Vinter, Robert D. (1974), 'The essential components of social group work practice', in R. D. Vinter, R. C. Sarri and P. Glasser (eds), *Individual Change through Small Groups* (New York: The Free Press), pp. 9–33.

Walker, Lorna (1978), 'Work with a parents' group: individual and social learning through peer group experience', in Nano McCaughan (ed.), *Group Work: Learning and Practice* (London: Allen & Unwin), pp. 129–45.

Wayne, Julianne L., and Avery, Nancy C. (1980), *Child Abuse: Prevention and Treatment through Social Group Work* (Boston; Charles River Books)

Wayne, Julianne L. (1979), 'A group work model to reach isolated mothers: preventing child abuse', *Social Work with Groups*, vol. 2, no. 1 (spring), pp. 7–18.

Weisman, Irving (1978), 'A natural group as vehicle for change', *Social Work with Groups*, vol. 1, no. 4 (winter), pp. 355–640.

Welch, Gary J., and Stevens, Kathleen (1979), 'Group work intervention with a multiple sclerosis population', *Social Work with Groups*, vol. 2, no. 2 (fall), pp. 221–34.

West, Margaret, McIlvaine, Robin, and Sells, Clifford J. (1979), 'An inter-disciplinary health care setting's experience with groups for parents of children having specific disabilities', *Social Work in Health Care*, vol. 4, no. 3 (spring), pp. 287–98.

Whitaker, D. Stock, and Lieberman, Morton A. (1965), *Psychotherapy through the Group Process* (London: Tavistock).

Wicks, Leone K. (1977), 'Trans-sexualism: a social work approach', *Health and Social Work*, vol. 2, no. 3 (August), pp. 181–93.

Wickström-Stormats, Anne (1972), 'Socialt grupparbete med adoptiv-föráldrar', *Socionomförbundet Tidsskrift* (Stockholm: Socionomför-bundet), nos 4/5, pp. 25–9.

Wilson, Gertrude, and Ryland, Gladys (1949), *Social Group Work Practice* (New York: Houghton-Mifflin), p. 68.

Winnicott, Clare (1959), *The Development of Insight*, Sociological Review Monograph No. 2 (Keele: University of North Staffordshire), pp. 25–36.

Witkin, Lynne (1979), 'Groups help widowed parents deal with children's grief', *Practice Digest*, no. 2 (September), pp. 27–8.

Yalom, I. D. (1975), *The Theory and Practice of Group Psychotherapy*, 2nd edition (New York: Basic Books).

Ziller, Robert C. (1965), 'Towards a theory of open and closed groups', *Psychological Bulletin*, vol. 64, no. 3, pp. 164–82.

INDEX